CURRICULUM IMPROVEMENT:

Decision-Making and Process

CURRICULUM IMPROVEMENT:

Decision-Making and Process

RONALD C. DOLL

Professor of Education
Hunter College of the City
University of New York

ALLYN AND
BACON, INC.
BOSTON
1964

To Ruth

Printed in the United States of America.

Library of Congress Catalog Card Number:
64–13896

⚜ ⚜ ⚜ ⚜ ⚜ ⚜ ⚜ ⚜ ⚜ ⚜ ⚜ ⚜ ⚜ ⚜ ⚜ ⚜

Preface

GIVE US A BOOK THAT IS BRIEF, pointed, practical, interesting, and soundly based in the best that is known about curriculum improvement," said an experienced classroom teacher who was preparing for instructional leadership.

The teacher's request seemed to represent the wishes of instructional leaders who were already in service as curriculum coordinators, supervisors, and principals, and whom I had asked what professional problems concerned them most. Accordingly, I have tried to make the character of this book fit the requirements of brevity, pointedness, practicality, interest, and scholarliness which both pre-service and in-service leaders appear to demand.

Curriculum Improvement: Decision-Making and Process may be used in courses relating to the curriculum of elementary and/or secondary schools, as well as in courses, seminars, and workshops in supervision, curriculum improvement, and administration. It should also prove a valuable reference source for practitioners in the field. The book is divided into three parts, the first part dealing with bases for decision-making about what the curriculum shall be; the second part, with process in improving the curriculum; and the third part (a final chapter), with evaluation of curriculum improvement programs. Ten of the twelve chapters contain, at intervals, practical situations which call for analysis by the reader. I have made few of these situations out of the whole cloth of my imagination. The great majority of them have originated in suggestions and anecdotes submitted by experienced practitioners who have been either colleagues in instructional leadership or students in my classes. A few situations have, of course, come directly from my own experience during pleasant and satisfying years of service as principal, guidance director, curriculum coordinator, central office administrator, and consultant. Most of the situations, while adding spice to classroom discussions, should provide opportunities for simulation in solving problems which occur

v

commonly in the process of improving curriculum. Situations in the form of anecdotes yield to classic methods of case analysis. Their treatment may, if the instructor wishes, proceed with the following questions:

> What are the issues or problems in this situation?
> What don't we know about the situation as it is reported here?
> What solutions or ameliorations for the situation can you suggest?
> What related issues or problems are involved in putting these solutions or ameliorations into effect?

Students need to be taught that, in educational decision-making, the facts are never complete, else no issue or problem might exist.

The situations in the text are sometimes varied with student activities which call for thinking, observing, reading, and writing. I have included these activities because they appear to be valuable learning exercises with reference to particular items of subject-matter.

I have already mentioned my action in polling the concerns of 160 instructional leaders. When I asked these persons what problems or concerns had proved most troublesome to them during their years of curriculum leadership, they named communication within schools or school systems as the most pressing and pervasive one. Their other major problems included finding appropriate bases on which to make curriculum decisions, identifying procedures which might be most helpful in effecting change, determining ways of getting started toward improvement, understanding and interpreting process of change, organizing personnel to perform curriculum improvement tasks, and supplying leadership that frees people to do their best work. Several chapters have resulted directly from these suggestions. Justification for the presence of other chapters lies in the apparent necessity for curriculum leaders to understand the content of these chapters so that they may do their work with maximal effectiveness.

I have obtained more specific information about the problems and concerns which practitioners experience by conferring with curriculum leaders at length, preparing a master checklist of problems derived from my conferences, and asking the 160 persons in my jury to find items in the checklist which seem especially important. A report of the jury's reactions is in the Appendix. Most of the problems which practitioners have highlighted are treated in the book. However, some of the problems are so specialized, *e.g.*, "working with people in groups . . . ," that they deserve consideration in less general sources.

Curriculum Improvement: Decision-Making and Process is meant to be a first or introductory book in curriculum improvement. Obviously, personnel who make a career of curriculum improvement need understandings which this book does not provide. All who aspire to insightful curriculum leadership should expect to extend their study and practice beyond the level at which the present text is written.

I owe a significant debt of gratitude to Paul M. Halverson, Professor of Education at Syracuse University, who was for some time my co-author until his heavy responsibilities in other assignments caused him to relinquish his part of the task. The conversations I had with him as we prepared the outline helped materially in establishing the design of the book and in identifying suitable content for it.

I am indebted, as always, to my wife, Ruth E. Doll, who has provided stimulation and encouragement, and who has urged upon me a balanced judiciousness in ways of expressing myself when my prejudices might have induced me to be rash or unfair.

Ronald C. Doll

Contents

CURRICULUM IMPROVEMENT:

Decision-Making and Process

part one

Decision-Making in Curriculum Improvement

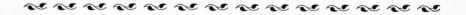

chapter one

In EDUCATION AS IN OTHER AFFAIRS, man's purpose is to move forward and upward. Sometimes he moves slowly and painfully; occasionally he thrusts onward with amazing speed. Inevitably he demonstrates that change is an unalterable fact of human existence, and that, while he has no control of some of the influences that create change, he has direct control of other influences. What man does with the influences he can control makes a real difference in the quality of his living.

In that limited area of human life and progress called curriculum improvement in elementary and secondary schools, change is created consciously by persons both inside and outside the schools. Each generation of teachers, pupils, and adult laymen has the responsibility to improve schooling for the current generation of learners and to establish models of good schooling for generations to come.

The history of curriculum change in the United States reveals the presence of issues which have been peculiar to the times and places in which they developed. Other issues have appeared and then have recurred at intervals throughout the history of American education. Still other issues seem to have remained continuously on the American scene since colonial days. Some

Historical
Foundations
of Curriculum
Decision-Making

of the more pervasive issues concerning the curriculum of elementary and secondary schools have been these:

1. Who shall be educated? Is education really meant for nearly *all* the children of *all* the people?

2. What types of educational experiences should be provided to given groups of learners? Of what tasks and responsibilities does the business of the schools really consist? Is it possible for schools to go too far in providing educational experiences for learners? Have the schools gone far enough in offering varied experiences?

3. How much can Americans afford to spend for education? To what extent should people sacrifice to educate their own and others' children?

4. Are the schools as good as they used to be? What are the major virtues and defects we find in schools today?

5. What shall be the organizing center of the curriculum? Subject-matter? Learners? What?

6. To what extent shall the curriculum be made uniform within the school district, county, state, and nation? Are there identifiable minimum essentials to be mastered by all learners at given stages of their development?

7. How can the needs of individual learners be met? Are there feasible ways of organizing or grouping pupils to achieve individualization in teaching and learning?

8. Is improving the curriculum worth the effort? Is not a stable, tried, and tested curriculum to be desired and to be utilized in educating each new generation?

For many persons within the teaching profession, some of these issues may have been satisfactorily resolved on the basis of their own knowledge of learners, learning, social forces, and subject-matter. Nevertheless, segments of the profession and of the public at large obviously consider the issues to be entirely unresolved, and therefore worth raising for re-examination many times each century.

Let us consider three vignettes which are intended to present current issues concerning the curriculum of American schools. State the issues which the vignettes seem to present. Might these issues have appeared in other periods of American history? If so, with what degree of regularity or continuity?

VIGNETTE 1: A CONTROVERSY OCCASIONED BY ADMIRAL RICKOVER'S VIEWS

Women's clubs are places at which all sorts of interesting discussions occur. Sometimes the most stimulating ones develop informally.

The menu at the Savoy Club was neither appetizing nor varied today, but the conversation had a lot of variety. Beginning with women's fashions and proceeding to home decoration and thence to husbands and children, it finally settled, at Table Seven, upon a key issue or two in public education. One of the women at the table had been reading books, speeches, and articles by Hyman G. Rickover. When she expressed reservations about some of Rickover's statements, her opinions ran squarely in opposition to those of Mrs. Baylor-Smythe, whose husband had been bringing her copies of Rickover's speeches.

"Admiral Rickover is right," declared Mrs. Baylor-Smythe, "when he says the top percentage of our children are not being sought out and properly educated by the schools. I agree with him that the Dutch and Swiss systems of education are better than ours. My own opinion is that the schools are trying to educate children who shouldn't be there in the first place."

"Where would you put them?" asked Mrs. Conley.

"Why, they belong in apprenticeships so that they can learn trades and work with their hands; then education in the best sense could be for the bright and privileged children who are going to be our leaders," Mrs. Baylor-Smythe replied.

"I don't agree with you at all," Mrs. Carradine chimed in. "You would destroy the very principles our club and, in fact, our whole democracy stand for if you tried to deny millions of children the opportunity to rise in America by having a good education. What you have just said isn't American!"

And so a controversy developed. It was a major controversy which could obviously not have been settled before the president's gavel banged to signal the formal part of today's meeting.

VIGNETTE 2: THE SUPERINTENDENT WHO TRIED TO FIND RELAXATION

Superintendent Schooley had nearly completed a difficult week—the week the school system's budget had been "put to bed" after final hearings before the Board of School Estimate. Now Dr. Schooley looked forward to a restful hour-and-a-half at the Friday noon meeting of his service club. As he left the driveway of the administration building, the superintendent thought, "Today I have no responsibilities at the Club. I should have a pleasant lunch."

Dr. Schooley's mistake was that, when he arrived at the Club's meeting place, he sat at a table with four other members, two of whom were noted for their argumentativeness. Recently, the newspapers had been filled with news of the school budget, which had risen enough this year to necessitate the addition of 26 points of property tax-load, and the conversation soon shifted to a familiar topic.

Steven Carruthers, a real estate dealer with 30 years of business experience in the community, opened the discussion with a blast at the expensiveness of schools today compared with the moderate cost of schooling a quarter-century ago. His arguments about the need for economy by the school administration and the board of education were countered with equally vehement remarks by Abel Mathers, a contractor who had been deprived of a high-school education and who wanted for his two children the best education that public money could buy. As the argument waxed hotter, the superintendent had all he could do to correct errors of fact. Eventually, the two docile members of the group began to speak, one on the side of "keeping the exorbitant taxes down," and the other on the side of "getting an education for our children that we ourselves couldn't have."

Dr. Schooley wished that, after weeks of hearing and participating in discussions of the same issue or issues, he had taken a quiet automobile ride instead of attending the meeting of the Club that day.

VIGNETTE 3: DOES THE EDUCATIONAL APPLECART NEED UPSETTING?

Lillie Steadwell, one of the two fourth-grade teachers in Walnut Street School, dropped into a chair in the teachers' room. It was the end of a hot and humid day in September. A new school term had been under way for two weeks, and the old pressures were already on.

"Who wants to attend a curriculum meeting on a day like this?" Lillie asked rhetorically.

"Who wants to attend curriculum meetings on *any* day of the year?" Clara Dowling asked directly, as she removed her shoes. "In the old days, school was not like this. You took the kids in at 8:30, and you went home with them at 3:15, except for an occasional faculty meeting where old Mr. Big did all the talking. The curriculum stayed as it was because we didn't bother with it. Now they pay people to think up changes—and trouble—for us."

"How do you think all that's happened in education has come about if people weren't working on the curriculum?" one of the teachers new to the school inquired innocently.

"You'll find out," said Clara. "It's the new superintendent who wants the applecart upset, and our principal is falling right in line with him. Our former school administration had the idea: 'Don't get things stirred up,' we used to hear. I'm not in favor of hunting around for better ways of doing things when you're not sure they'll be better anyway. We should let well enough alone!"

Several fundamental curriculum issues have pervaded much of the history of American education. When these issues reappear during the 1960's, or during any other decade, they are considered by some people to be completely new ones, despite their age-old significance. Note the following history of a set of related issues, illuminated by comments made from our vantage point in the 1960's.

A HISTORY OF CERTAIN RELATED ISSUES

During the Nineteenth Century, a group of related issues arose concerning the center about which learners' school experiences should be organized. Should the curriculum be adult-centered or child-centered? Should it consist of logically-organized subject-matter or, in the language of our own day, of psychologically-organized subject matter? Should emphasis be placed on subject-matter "set out to be learned," or on subject-matter that relates closely to the interests and needs of growing learners?

These related issues are still alive today.

Prior to the Nineteenth Century, the assumption had generally been made that subject-matter should be organized logically and "dispensed" to children and youth under close control and supervision by adults. Ancient and early-modern science had aided this view by holding that objective reality had a logical structure which could readily be described; accordingly, the curriculum could be fixed in advance. Inasmuch as the curriculum could be fixed and learners are by nature pliable, learners must "stretch" to fit the standard curriculum.

Many authors of current books and magazine articles seem to share these views.

During the Eighteenth Century, these concepts had, of course, been challenged by Jean Jacques Rousseau (1712–1778), who placed the nature of the child superior to the nature of the curriculum. Rousseau was succeeded in his views by Friederich Froebel (1782–1852), who developed a curriculum centering in the nature of the child, establishing as his chief educational goal the child's "self-realization." According to Froebel, the curriculum must originate within the learner, not outside him, though the learner must draw upon the culture for the substance of his learning.

Does this remind you of core programs based on pupils' interests, concerns, and evident needs?

Somewhat later, William James (1842–1910) and Edward L. Thorndike (1874–1949) formulated a psychology of education which was used by others to support the child-centered curriculum. Soon the studies of child growth and development were under way, and John Dewey was developing a curriculum that emphasized the life-activities of children. Outspoken advocates of the child-centered curriculum now ran into serious conflict with advocates of the adult-organized curriculum. Opponents of child-centeredness accused Dewey and his supporters of providing "soft pedagogy" for pampered children. The accusation gained strength as a consequence of certain excesses committed by teachers who came to be considered extreme progressives. Dewey himself, writing in *The Child and the Curriculum*, deprecated both the common underestimates of children's maturity and the rising sentimentality about children. But the battle between the Progressives and the Essentialists had now been joined, and, though the Progressive Education Association is officially dead, the battle continues today. Much of the recent criticism of schools has centered about the issue, "Shall the curriculum be set for learners by specialists in education?" and a movement has recently developed to have the curriculum determined by specialists in the individual subject-matter fields.

Does this accusation sound familiar to you today?

Can you identify the relative positions of proponents of various curriculum plans, as these positions relate to the issues mentioned in the first paragraph of this brief history?

A PANORAMA OF CURRICULUM CHANGE IN EARLY AMERICA[1]

In the early days of American history, curriculum change occurred slowly, but it frequently proved to be deep-moving and enduring. The basic historical impact on the curriculum was made by English-speaking peoples who settled along the Atlantic seaboard. When the British established colonies in America between 1607 and 1733, they transplanted three major types of education from Europe: the *church-state type*, exemplified in New England; the *parochial school type*, established in Catholic Maryland and Protestant Pennsylvania; and both *private and charity education*, commonplace in certain southern colonies, notably in Virginia. Religion dominated all three

---

[1] The sweep of curriculum change in much or all of American history can be seen in books like those by Cremin, Cubberley, and Reisner, listed in the bibliography at the end of this chapter; also in Hollis L. Caswell, *Curriculum Improvement in Public School Systems*. New York: Bureau of Publications, Teachers College, 1950.

types, but in quite different ways. In New England, church and state served a common purpose: to prepare a ministry capable of propagating the true faith, and to educate laymen in reading and interpreting the Bible, the sure foundation of the faith. In the middle colonies, the prevailing branches of Christianity, whether Protestant or Catholic, founded their own schools to educate children in religion and the fundamentals of literacy. In the South, those who, like the Washingtons, had sufficient means sent their children to private schools oriented to the classics and religion, and those who lacked means shared some prospect of placing their children in charity schools to be trained for apprenticeships. Education everywhere in the colonies was designed chiefly for boys, and the chief method of learning was memorization. The curriculum for children of the privileged was heavy in intellectual studies. Practical and artistic subjects, which were said to "educate the senses," were considered suitable for training the servant class and entertaining young ladies, who because of their sex could not realistically aspire to leadership roles. For boys of the upper classes, *dame schools,* or schools of reading and writing, provided basic education, which was succeeded by secondary education in the *Latin grammar school,* a New England institution which had its counterpart in the other colonies. Here, Latin, Greek, the Catechism, Bible, and arithmetic were the chief subjects.

During the mid-Eighteenth Century, political, economic, and social changes were occurring rapidly enough to assure at least minor transformation of the curriculum. Though commerce and trade were increasing, students had not been prepared to engage in them. People were moving away from their original settlements, pioneer life on the frontier was beginning, urban growth was flourishing, and religion was becoming a less powerful force in society. The educational system responded by establishing district schools instead of town schools, by combining reading and writing schools into a new unit called "the school of the three R's," and by establishing *English grammar schools* and academies to replace the inflexible Latin grammar school. Meanwhile, private tutors were teaching vocational subjects like navigation, surveying, and bookkeeping. *Franklin's Academy,* in developing a new concept of schooling, extended the traditional list of subjects to include modern foreign languages and natural science, the content of which was deemed useful in educating enlightened men of affairs.

The post-Revolutionary period brought several developments which influenced anew the curricula of American schools. The *Ordinance of 1785* set aside land for schools in each township in the new West, and as people moved into the territories, they brought with them a dominant pattern of schooling, chiefly that of the New England district school, which provided the basis for eventual establishment of the free public school. The 1820's and the 1830's were a time of political consciousness, when American statesmen became convinced that children should be educated to love their country and to perpetuate its ideals. If enough children were to be educated to have a favorable effect on national welfare, there must be education of the masses. Finally, though many statesmen were saying it without comprehending its full meaning, the people of a democracy were seen as having a right to education, that they might prepare themselves to their own personal advantage.

These startling ideas, so foreign to the European heritage of education for the privileged only, eventually caused curriculum reform. Horace Mann, Henry Barnard, and others spearheaded the drive toward establishment of common, tax-supported schools in which the curriculum would theoretically accommodate the abilities and interests of all learners. By 1860, arithmetic, algebra, geometry, ancient history, geography, and English grammar were being accepted by the colleges as subjects which partially fulfilled entrance requirements. The curriculum for girls, who were now being admitted much more freely to schooling, was being differentiated to include music, painting, and dancing. *Academies* were preparing, in practical subjects, those pupils who were not going to college; then these academies began to give way to *public high schools.*

By mid-century, at least some Americans had an educational ladder on which they could climb from primary education to the university. By 1860, New England had *public elementary schools* which taught, at primary grade-level, reading, spelling, writing, and arithmetic; at intermediate grade-level, reading, arithmetic, geography, spelling, writing, and elementary grammar; and in the "grammar school," advanced reading, advanced arithmetic, elementary algebra, spelling, word analysis, penmanship, grammar, composition, declamation, geography, United States history, and general history. The high-school program in New England in 1860 included these subjects: United States history, ancient history, natural philosophy (elements of chemistry and botany), Latin, advanced algebra, geometry, bookkeeping, and surveying. Curriculum development, as it represented changes in American society, and as it was reflected in the addition of school subjects, was now well under way.

A CATALOG OF EVENTS FROM 1860 TO THE PRESENT

A steady progression of incidents has occurred during the century from the 1860's to the 1960's to affect the curriculum of American elementary and secondary schools. This progression can be seen in the following catalog of events:

Period or Date	Event
1860 to 1890	A continued struggle for establishment of free public schools was in process.
1860 to 1890	Technical and commercial high schools were organized separately from academic high schools.
1860 to 1890	Arrival of immigrants and doubling of population created demands for new and broadened types of schooling.
1860 to 1890	Manual training, which had originated in the Scandinavian countries, was introduced widely in both elementary and secondary schools.
1860 to 1890	The oral instruction and object-teaching proposed by *Pestalozzi* took root in the United States. Oral language, mental arithmetic, and teaching by demonstration resulted.
1860 to 1890	The elementary-school curriculum broadened and became somewhat less dedicated to rote memorization.
1860 to 1890	The content of high-school subjects broadened to admit the arithmetic of business, the English of business, American literature, general science, and family care.
1860 to 1890	Educational experiments included those of *Francis Parker* in breaking down the barriers among subjects; of *Batavia, New York*, in providing remedial instruction; and of *Santa Barbara, California*, in preparing parallel courses of study.
The 1860's	Newly-established normal schools assumed from the academies responsibility for preparing teachers, and continued to transform schoolkeeping into schoolteaching.
1862 and 1890	The first and second *Morrill Acts* arranged for development of and aid to land-grant colleges, which accepted, in admitting their students, high-school subjects which had previously been considered inferior to respected academic subjects.
1873	The first public-school kindergarten was opened in St. Louis.
1874	The famous *Kalamazoo Case* legalized establishment of high schools at public expense.
1880	The first manual training high school was opened (St. Louis).
1886	The first cooking and sewing high school was established (Toledo).
1890 to 1920	*Herbart's* view of "apperception," formulated into his famous *five steps* (preparation, presentation, comparison and abstraction, generalization, and application), encouraged correlation of subject-matter, especially in the elementary schools.
1890 to 1920	*Edward L. Thorndike* and *Charles Judd* began studying the curriculum quantitatively and scientifically as they opened an era of mental measurement.

1893	The *Committee of Ten on Secondary School Studies* asserted that all subjects taught equally well for equal periods of time had equal educational value, and that four programs of study might well be developed in high schools: the Classical, the Scientific, the Modern Language, and the English.
1895	The *Committee of Fifteen on Elementary Education* urged concentration and correlation of subjects taught in the elementary schools.
1896	*John Dewey* founded his *Laboratory School* at the University of Chicago, a school which had special concern for the interests and purposes of learners.
1899	The *Committee on College Entrance Requirements* approved "restricted election" of subjects by high-school pupils, early completion of the high-school program by gifted pupils, acceptance of a year's work in any subject as counting toward college entrance, and extension of the high-school program to six years. The report of this Committee marked the beginning of the "unit system" which has dominated secondary education.
1900 to 1920	The *junior-high school* was invented; vocational education received Federal aid; and a psychology of individual differences began to develop. Also, the *Progressive Movement* was given its initial impetus; faculty psychology was seriously attacked; and the *Gestaltist viewpoint* grew up beside connectionism.
1911	The *Committee on the Economy of Time in Education* advocated child-centeredness in learning. Partly as a consequence of the work of this committee, art, music, handicrafts, and health education became recognized subjects in the elementary and secondary schools.
1918	The *Committee on the Reorganization of Secondary Education* enunciated the famous *Seven Cardinal Principles of Secondary Education*, thereby stating objectives that received wide, though nominal, acceptance.
1920 to the present	The past four decades—the 1920's, 1930's, 1940's, and 1950's—have brought an interesting array of developments, the origin of which can be found in an interplay of forces which have crowded the educational scene. A desire to learn more about learners launched the great testing and measurement movement in the 1920's, a movement which some educators have now deprecated. There developed during the first two or three decades of this period several plans designed to make teaching easier and more effective: the *project method*, the *Dalton plan*, the *Winnetka plan*, the *unit method*, *ability grouping*, and the *activity program*, to mention a few. Most of these plans have withered away, to be replaced recently by organizational schemes like the *Trump plan* and the *ungraded elementary school unit*. In some school systems, subjects have been correlated with other subjects. Core programs, once much discussed, have yielded place to limited numbers of similar programs bearing the

names "general education" and "block of time." Work experience consumes a portion of each school day for a minority of high-school pupils. Textbooks and other teaching materials have improved, and facilities are the best ever. The curriculum of the elementary school is broad enough to drive many a teacher to distraction, and the elective system in secondary schools has come to full bloom. Individualized instruction in reading and other subjects, together with individualized help with psychological, speech, hearing, and other problems, is being given pupils in many school systems.

During the 1950's and the early 1960's, schools have been attacked for expensiveness, failure to teach "fundamental subjects" adequately, and allegiance to John Dewey and Progressivism. The curriculum has been developed, in part, by specialists in subject-fields, who have begun to rival curriculum generalists and educational psychologists as resource personnel in curriculum improvement.

A DIGEST OF TRENDS IN THE EVOLUTION OF THE CURRICULUM

Running through the whole panorama of American education from colonial times to the present, there appear several trends in the evolution of the curriculum:

1. In the past, ideas have often been developed in private schools, and public schools have then adopted them.

2. Schools and school systems everywhere have frankly copied plans, procedures, and curriculum content from other schools and school systems.

3. New institutions, such as the early academy and the more recent junior-high school, have been established to satisfy unmet needs.

4. Educational principles, such as that of schooling for everyone, have been adopted in substance and modified in detail whenever they have struck a popular chord.

5. Experimentation has occurred, but it has usually been informal and its results have remained largely untested.

6. National committees have determined general objectives, policies, and programs.

7. Psychological and social theories and revelations have turned the efforts of curriculum planners in new directions.

8. American educators have been susceptible to using plans, some of them delusive, for making the difficult processes of teaching and learning easier.

9. Even those educational ideas which have been based on the soundest evidence have been adopted very slowly by practitioners.

10. The schools, as an instrument of American society, have been subjected to numerous public pressures.

THE EVOLVING PROCESS OF CURRICULUM IMPROVEMENT

In the preceding sections of the chapter, we have noted some of the events which have affected the curriculum during more than three centuries of American history. The present section deals with history of the *process* of curriculum improvement, a history which covers a much shorter period of time. Though curriculum improvement had obviously been occurring for generations, conscious efforts to make the process more effective have been expended only during the past half-century.

The history of curriculum planning can scarcely be written in sequential order. For one thing, it has too little content to form a valid sequence. Furthermore, many of the older procedures considered largely unprofitable in sophisticated circles today are still being utilized in numerous schools of the nation. Contrariwise, the abler curriculum planners were using, during the 1920's, some of the procedures now considered by curriculum specialists to be completely acceptable. Thus, in the process of curriculum improvement, a very recent field of inquiry, there can be no clean break in order of time between the antiquated and the novel, the formerly fashionable and the presently fashionable.

The process of curriculum improvement was made manifest only when it was first reported in the literature. Prior to 1920, practically nothing about this process was written in professional journals. A curriculum was considered by many persons to be the courses of study and other written materials which a given school system or individual school produced. Customarily, the superintendent of schools assembled several persons whom he believed to be competent "to write the curriculum." In the larger school systems during the 1920's, committees of representative teachers met with one or more assistant superintendents and directors of subjects to prepare courses of study, which were then submitted to the system's board of superintendents for approval and subsequently to the board of education for authority to print as school documents.[2] Participating teachers were selected on the basis of teaching ability, interest in curriculum work, college preparation, and ability to write.[3]

The actual authority for curriculum planning centered strongly in superintendents and their immediate staffs, with teachers, parents, and pupils taking minor parts. Courses of study contained what, in the teachers' view, was precise "ground to be covered," and supervisors urged teachers to cover this ground in quantity and sequence. Most administrators in the cities reported that their programs of improvement were continuous, though the programs centered upon only a few recurrent problems in "revising subject-matter."[4] One, two, or three subject-matter areas were revised at a given time, and revision was "completed" within a few months, to be resumed by rearranging the same subject-matter a few years later.

Generally, teachers were not asked what instructional problems needed attention. Decisions of this sort were made by top administrators, who tended to think of curriculum improvement as being a rewriting of courses of study and addition or elimination of subjects and course offerings. Curriculum decisions were made on the basis of individual opinion and consensus of groups, inasmuch as experimentation, research, and evaluation were relatively unknown.[5]

Forty years have brought into being several discernible trends in the process of curriculum improvement. The commonly-accepted definition of the curriculum has changed from *content of courses of study and lists of subjects and courses* to *all the experiences which are offered to learners under the auspices or direction of the school*. The change to a broader definition has magnified the task of curriculum improvement because *all* the experiences of learners over which the school has control may now be eligible for improvement. These experiences may occur in school buses, cafeterias, and corridors, as well as in classrooms and auditoriums. If, in line with Gestaltist thinking, the *whole* child is said to come to school, teachers must have concern for his attitudes and appreciations as well as for his cognate learning.

Furthermore, if pupils' experiences are to improve, teachers must likewise have new and improved experiences, since it is axiomatic that the blind cannot be expected to lead the blind. Curriculum improvement is, according to the broadened view, more than alteration or rearrangement of pupil ex-

[2] National Society for the Study of Education, *The Foundations and Techniques of Curriculum Construction*. Bloomington, Ill.: Public School Publishing Company, 1926.

[3] C. C. Trillingham, *The Organization and Administration of Curriculum Programs*. Los Angeles: University of Southern California Press, 1934.

[4] Edwin S. Lide, *Procedures in Curriculum Making*, Bulletin No. 17, National Survey of Secondary Education. Washington, D.C.: Government Printing Office, 1933.

[5] W. W. Charters, *Curriculum Construction*. New York: The Macmillan Co., 1923.

periences according to a simple, preconceived plan; it involves the re-education of teachers through individualized in-service education and constructive supervision. Finally, the newer conception of curriculum improvement requires that teachers *of* teachers—supervisors and administrators—be re-educated, so that they may learn to identify teachers' needs and desirable ways of satisfying those needs.

An enlarged definition of curriculum improvement, application of newer findings in psychology and sociology to the process of improvement, and increased experience in attempting to improve school programs have opened the whole educational enterprise to these trends:

> Changes are being planned both in the environments within which people operate and in the individuals who occupy these environments. Changing an environment requires setting or re-setting the stage for learning, and helping individuals change themselves requires deep understanding of the dynamics of human behavior. Both also demand a thorough knowledge of the best practice in education.
>
> Curriculum planning is being regarded as a necessary, continuing activity. There can be only incidental improvement unless we plan for it. Moreover, if teachers are not active in planning their own teaching-learning programs, ill-informed persons may soon do the planning for them.
>
> Today we see more and more variation in the kinds of activities which curriculum planning encompasses. These activities range from the planning of experimental projects to selection of teaching materials, to development of teaching units, to formation of study groups, to plotting of guidelines to action, and so on.
>
> Many activities now occur at the same time, a far cry from the one, two, or three concurrent activities of the 1920's. The number of activities, which include the large projects and the small, may be determined chiefly by the energies and talents of school staffs.
>
> Improvement is now commonly considered to occur on a broken front. This means that "modifications in practice have small beginnings, with a few teachers taking the lead in the difficult process of testing new ideas. As new practices are demonstrated to be feasible, more teachers take over their use. Thus, change in the actual curriculum is represented by a jagged line of emerging practice in response to new ideas and needs."[6]
>
> Curriculum planners are now demonstrating need for renewed concern about the objectives of education. Many curriculum ideas, new and old, need to be assessed in light of their contribution to achievement of accepted objectives of the school.
>
> Teachers are being involved in curriculum study in various ways. Some teachers contribute helpfully to group discussion; others organize programs successfully; still others write and edit materials well; and still others succeed in experimentation, tryout, and evaluation. As formerly, all teachers make decisions about the curriculum within their classrooms.

[6] Caswell, *op. cit.*, p. 51.

But the present expectation of curriculum leaders is usually that teachers
will work additionally in group planning, and that they will involve themselves at differing levels and to differing degrees in the improvement tasks
the school undertakes.

Whereas pupils were once involved very little in curriculum planning, they
are now consulted at least informally in classrooms and school activities,
as well as in certain minor matters of curriculum design. The learner,
though he is neither expert nor professional, sometimes provides significant cues about actions to be taken.

Involvement of laymen has passed through stages which began with mini-
mal involvement and which continued toward random, unplanned uses of
the talents of community members. Laymen who have been utilized beyond
their depth have sometimes revolted or have created disturbances by constituting themselves rivals to boards of education and professional staffs.
Consequently, curriculum leaders have come to realize that the purposes
of education and certain broad, general policy matters are suitable subjects for public discussion, and that laymen can sometimes be helpful in
other direct ways, but that clear distinctions must be made between matters of lay concern and matters of professional concern.

Curriculum planning is not thought of as constituting a series of discrete
and fixed steps. No single pattern, beginning, for instance, with stating
objectives, will suffice in solving all curriculum problems. The dynamics
of given school situations and the resources provided by interdisciplinary
study and practical experience in curriculum planning determine the
ways in which problems should be attacked.

Curriculum materials, which formed a major starting-point of activity in
the 1920's, are still widely produced and used. However, the course of
study has given way to the less prescriptive course guide. Helps for
teachers include manuals accompanying textbooks, resource units, and
audio-visual lists. The focus today is increasingly on helpfulness to competent professional persons rather than on further limitation of teachers'
opportunity to make decisions.

SUMMARY

**Much has happened to the curriculum and to the process of
curriculum improvement from the beginnings of our nation to the
present time. From the private system of education which existed
during colonial times and the early days of the republic, schooling
has been transferred to a fifty-state system of public education and
indigenous developments in private education. Some of the informal
experimentation with the curriculum which has occurred during the
past three centuries has resulted in marked changes in curriculum
practices. On several major occasions, national groups and the federal government have initiated change.**

One of the significant evolutions concerns the meanings of the terms *curriculum* and *curriculum improvement* as they affect action for improvement. The curriculum is now generally considered to be all the experiences that learners have under the auspices or direction of the school. Curriculum improvement refers not only to improving the structure and the documents of the curriculum but also to stimulating growth, learning, and alteration of perceptions and values on the part of all the persons who are concerned with the curriculum.

In subsequent chapters, the significance of psychological, social, and subject-matter influences on decision-making about the curriculum will be discussed. The relevance of these forces can be seen most clearly against the overview of historical events which this chapter has presented.

SELECTED BIBLIOGRAPHY

Brubacher, John S., *A History of the Problems of Education* (New York: McGraw-Hill Book Co., Inc., 1947).

Butts, R. Freeman, and Lawrence A. Cremin, *A History of Education in American Culture* (New York: Holt, Rinehart & Winston, Inc., 1953).

Charters, W. W., *Curriculum Construction* (New York: The Macmillan Co., 1923).

Cremin, Lawrence A., *The American Common School: An Historical Conception* (New York: Bureau of Publications, Teachers College, 1961).

Cubberley, Elwood P., *Public Education in the United States*, Revised Edition (Boston: Houghton-Mifflin Co., 1956).

Drake, W. E., *The American School in Transition* (Englewood Cliffs, N.J.: Prentice-Hall, Inc., 1955).

Good, H. G., *A History of American Education* (New York: The Macmillan Co., 1956).

Meyer, A. E., *An Educational History of the American People* (New York: McGraw-Hill Book Co., Inc., 1957).

Reisner, Edward, *The Evolution of the Common School* (New York: The Macmillan Co., 1930).

chapter two

Ⓗ OW DO LEARNERS GROW AND DEVELOP? What are some of
the ways in which they learn? What does psychology say specifically to the
curriculum improver?

Today, psychological factors are at the root of many curriculum decisions, for psychology is one of the mother disciplines in which education
finds its rationale. The present chapter treats of psychological bases for curriculum decisions according to four emphases: some applications of psychology to curriculum improvement, current understandings of the learner,
understandings of the learning process, and representative frontiers in the
study of learning.

SOME APPLICATIONS OF PSYCHOLOGY TO
CURRICULUM IMPROVEMENT

One needs to apply psychology at many major steps in the curriculum
improvement process. To this end, he needs grounding in educational psy-

Psychological Bases for Curriculum Decisions

chology, an understanding of the growth and development of children and adolescents, grasp of a learning theory to which he can subscribe, and knowledge of social psychology as it relates to the behavior of both adults and children. All these accretions of knowledge must be based, of course, upon fundamental study of general psychology. Applications of psychology to curriculum improvement pervade the whole second part of this book, which deals with the process of improvement. Basically, however, psychology bears upon four facets of curriculum improvement: the objectives we establish for and with learners, the means we use in gauging the attainment of these objectives, the kinds of experiences we utilize to achieve the objectives, and the ways in which we organize educational experiences. Brief attention to psychology's relationship to each of these facets is now in order.

1. SELECTING OBJECTIVES

Several psychological considerations affect the objectives which curriculum workers may legitimately identify for and with learners. These considerations are suggested by the following key questions:

Is the objective attainable by the school?——Some objectives cannot be attained through schooling. Schools may, for instance, educate children in principles of safe living, but they cannot do anything through group instruction to harness the inner compulsion of a boy who insists on sitting dangerously on the window ledge of a second-floor classroom. Schools may teach children the fundamentals of arithmetic, but they may fail in dealing with the child whose disturbance will not permit him to learn arithmetic. Evidently, personal maladjustments are the business of psychologists and psychiatrists much more than of teachers. Psychology, then, has a major role in helping curriculum personnel distinguish between objectives which are readily attainable by the school and those which are not.

How long will it take to attain a given objective?——The answer to this question varies in part with the nature of the subject-matter to be learned. Psychology tells us that certain skills in physical training can be developed quickly, but that significant changes in attitudes usually occur only over long periods of time. Much is still unknown about the periods of time needed for the attainment of particular objectives, but we are gradually learning to be more realistic about the duration of school experiences.

At approximately what age should striving for the achievement of given objectives be initiated?——A commendable desire to assure economy of time and also to avoid frustrating children has led curriculum workers to delay certain experiences until learners were "ready" for them. Recently, however, psychological research and experimentation have suggested that certain experiences can be initiated earlier in pupils' lives. For instance, we may be able to increase language content for preschool children, and we may find it possible to introduce reading earlier in the primary grades. Still other experiences, such as some of those in arithmetic, may be delayed until concept-formation and understanding occur more easily. Curriculum workers should keep abreast of studies of readiness, and should encourage experimentation in moving the introduction of subject-matter up and down the age scale.

In what sequence should the more specific objectives be placed?—— Certain gross problems of sequence which were once considered solved have become unsolved. One of these affects the teaching of second-year algebra, or of plane geometry, immediately after first-year algebra. Furthermore, within high-school courses in mathematics and other subjects the proper sequence of subject-matter content is often unclear. Marked progress has been made, however, in relating objectives of abstract learning to objectives of use. Thus it is now realized that abstract information about health habits will probably be retained best if it is immediately utilized in everyday living. In mathematics, the learning of given skills leads directly to the development of additional, related skills. In language study, understanding of structure leads promptly to further understanding of structure. Sequence is less obvious and often less important in certain other subjects, as in the social studies.

To what extent should objectives be repeated in subsequent years of schooling?——Continuity of objectives, and therefore of the same order or type of educational experiences, has its basis in the psychology of learning. The importance of continuity can be seen in subjects like foreign languages. Once a child begins to learn a language, he should generally continue to learn it without any long-term interruption. Thus, the curriculum worker who advocates the teaching of French in the third and fourth grades should make sure that experience with French is not lost between grade four and grade nine, when the pupil customarily begins college-preparatory French in high school. In some subject-matter, continuous mastery is not so necessary. Thus, exploratory subject-matter in the junior high school may be discontinued at the end of a year or a half-year, inasmuch as the original objective of the learning was exploration.

In what ways are objectives multiple in their effects?——The teacher who thinks he is driving straight to a single goal, like helping children memorize their number facts, is probably deluding himself. While the children are memorizing and repeating the facts, they are almost certainly developing attitudes toward arithmetic and the teacher. They may also be learning the multiples of eight better than they are learning the multiples of seven because the teacher always had difficulty with the eights, and she now drills the eights with rigor. In addition, children develop their own learning styles, some of which are efficient and others of which are inefficient. Children's perceptions of a given learning situation differ, and these perceptions are carried along from one learning situation to another. In their daily conversations, children who are classmates report identical experiences in quite different ways. Truly, objectives follow devious and multiple routes in achieving effects which are also multiple.[1]

2. EVALUATING THE ACHIEVEMENT OF OBJECTIVES

As soon as objectives have been accepted, means of evaluating their achievement should be sought. Many unfortunate time gaps develop between formulation of objectives and their evaluation because the evaluation process is characteristically short-circuited by moving directly to the experiences through which objectives may be achieved. As soon as the objectives are clear,

[1] For a discussion of the determination of objectives by application of psychological principles, see Ralph W. Tyler, *Basic Principles of Curriculum and Instruction* (Syllabus for Education 360). Chicago: University of Chicago Press, 1950, pp. 24–28.

then, the means of their evaluation should be considered, and these means will in turn suggest learning experiences. Placing the steps in this order tends to prevent teachers from becoming lost in a forest of experiences and activities, the purposes and the means of evaluation of which may have been forgotten. In developing course guides and preparing units of instruction, the order or sequence suggested above should usually be followed.

Evaluation procedures should be designed to measure the achievement of every desired behavior the objectives express. Thus, if one of the objectives is development of appreciation, evaluation questions or other evaluation devices should be prepared to show the extent to which appreciation has been developed. Modern teachers often subscribe to several objectives at a time, but the tests they prepare continue to show their success with only one or two objectives, such as garnering of knowledge and attainment of understanding. Changes in attitudes, appreciations, and interests are difficult to evaluate. Pencil-and-paper tests frequently will not fulfill the need; therefore more ingenious instruments must be prepared. Some of these may be both informal and semi-projective: *e.g.*, thought questions to which the pupil gives oral answers, "playing out" a situation through sociodrama, or serving as an interview subject.

Psychology reveals that evaluation can become a powerful force for either good or evil. On the one hand, it stimulates learners to better achievement; on the other, it creates anxieties that inhibit worthwhile learning. According to Symonds, "all of the anxiety inherent in the examination situation comes from the reactions of other individuals—parents and teachers—to examination results. Teachers have the power to make an examination a challenge, or an ordeal to be dreaded and avoided if possible, by the attitude they take toward it and toward the results that individual children achieve."[2] Desirably, tests are used as media of learning, and not merely to effect traumatic checkup. They are used by alert teachers to help pupils learn to take tests; they are sometimes given a second time so that the factor of novelty does not affect the result; and they may sometimes even be given for fun rather than "for keeps."

3. SELECTING EXPERIENCES IN LINE WITH OBJECTIVES

Findings in educational psychology suggest certain criteria which may be used in selecting educational experiences that lead to certain objectives:

[2] Percival M. Symonds, *What Education Has to Learn from Psychology*. New York: Bureau of Publications, Teachers College, Columbia University, 1958, p. 72.

a. Learning experiences should be designed to allow practice of the behaviors which the objective suggests. Practice must give satisfaction to the pupil in learning what the objective specifies. If the opportunity for practice does not seem to the pupil to be relevant to his view of the objective, he will tend to reject it.

b. Learning experiences should express what the learner believes he is expected to know. The learner's background and present environment suggest to him that some experiences are worthwhile and that other experiences are fruitless. The perceived worthwhileness of the experiences makes a significant contribution to learning.

c. Learning experiences should sometimes be of the self-activating type. Pupils need opportunities to proceed at their own rate through subject-matter which suits them. Thus individual learning, with or without teaching machines, is justified and necessary. Obviously, keeping pupils in group situations in both elementary and secondary schools too consistently can lessen learning effectiveness. Invention and creativeness are often aided by the silences during which individual activity occurs.

d. Learning experiences should be fostered, whenever possible, in intimate face-to-face relationships within small groups. Desirable interaction and learning can apparently be achieved more readily in groups of five to eight members than in groups of 30 to 40. Teachers and other curriculum workers should pay more attention to this finding.

e. Learning experiences should be as varied as the objectives they represent. There has been too great a tendency to utilize a few kinds of experiences to achieve several objectives. Ingenuity is needed in devising experiences that achieve given objectives.

Selecting educational experiences which are clearly in line with specific objectives is one of the matters to which we have given too little attention. Nevertheless, it is a fundamental of curriculum improvement which deserves consideration in every school system.

4. ORGANIZING EXPERIENCES TO ACHIEVE OBJECTIVES

The ways in which learning experiences are put together greatly affect achievement of objectives. Helpful organization of experiences provides for sequence where sequence is needed, and for continuity where continuity is needed. It also provides for balance, so that there is not an overemphasis on one kind of experience at the expense of other kinds. At the same time, it affords enough scope of experiences to guarantee that a broad range will supply all that is needful in total educational development. Finally, organization assists with correlation of subject-matter that is closely related, *e.g.*, the history of the Westward Movement in the United States in clear relationship with the literature of the Westward Movement.[3] The educational dimensions known as sequence, balance, scope, continuity, and correlation demand consideration by master planners of the curriculum.

At a different level of operation, the classroom, there are characteristics of effective organization of learning experiences as seen by classroom teachers:

> *The good organizing center for learning encompasses ability floors and ceilings of the group.* . . . Some kinds of content, such as mathematics and science, require the development of rigorous concepts. Solving mathematical problems demands high-level insight into concepts of quantity. Learning to read involves acquiring skill in word attack. There are very definite limits to the range of concept or skill development that can be challenged by a single organizing center for learning. When these limits are narrower than the range in group abilities in the particular skill or concept sought, the teacher must plan to make the two more comparable by dividing the class into smaller groups. The development of certain social skills, on the other hand, demands the interaction of individuals varying widely in interests, abilities and backgrounds. The best organizing center for such learning may be one that plans for inclusion of the entire class. . . .
>
> *The good organizing center for learning is comprehensive in that it permits inclusion of several ideas and several catch-hold points for differing student interests.* An organizing center of limited complexity is soon exhausted of its appeal and must be replaced by another. . . . But a truly comprehensive center invites exploration at several points and poses a variety of student appeals. . . .
>
> *The good organizing center for learning has capacity for movement—intellectual, social, geographic, or chronological.* The class must be able to move somewhere with it. Such a capacity is almost always present in certain favorite units of study. . . .[4]

There are, then, two levels of operation in organizing learning experiences. The first of these involves seeing the curriculum whole and letting general curriculum objectives, reflected against a background supplied especially by psychology, determine the sequence, scope, continuity, balance, and correlation which programs of teaching and learning should have. The second involves decision-making by teachers in classrooms about how to organize both their pupils and the blocks of subject-matter they study so that the

---

[3] Problems of sequence, scope, continuity, balance, and correlation are discussed in general and specific references on the curriculum and curriculum planning such as those by Anderson and by Saylor and Alexander, which are listed in the bibliography at the end of this chapter. In Chapter 5 of the present book, these problems are dealt with in connection with finding a locus of the forces which make for curriculum improvement.

[4] Association for Supervision and Curriculum Development, *Learning and the Teacher* (1959 Yearbook). Washington, D.C.: The Association, 1959, pp. 56–58.

maximum achievement of objectives can be attained. Curriculum leaders are much concerned with the first level, which requires master-planning of large segments of the school program. They should be concerned also with the second level, which consists of helping teachers to do better that which they have already learned to do in part. On neither level are the tasks simple, for the locus of them is a complex human being, the learner. We must, therefore, continue to study the learner's reactions to sequences, unit plans, ways of grouping him with others, and other strategies of organization.

With respect to applications of psychology to a wide range of tasks in curriculum improvement, much more knowledge will some day be available. Funds are currently being spent in several major projects in human development, mental health, the education of the culturally disadvantaged, and other specialties. Curriculum workers should watch for the appearance of reports, monographs, and articles which will provide them with many additional cues for decision-making.

SITUATION 2-1—IDENTIFYING NEEDS FOR CURRICULUM IMPROVEMENT WITH WHICH PSYCHOLOGY CAN HELP

A curriculum leader surveyed some of the literature of psychology which he thought might be applied to curriculum improvement activities in his school system. Among the generalizations he noted were these:

Learning by wholes usually works better than learning by parts.

Mild emotion supplies an important incentive to learning, but emotion that is intense may interfere with learning.

"Education produces learning not essentially by what a teacher says, thinks, or does, but by what a pupil can be encouraged to say, think, do, and feel."[5]

If you were the curriculum leader, what meaning might each of these statements have for you in seeking practical improvements in teaching and learning in the classrooms with which you are now acquainted?

Applications of psychology to curriculum improvement relate directly to the nature of the learner. Accordingly, the next section of this chapter deals with learners as "consumers of education."

[5] Symonds, op. cit., p. 48.

CURRENT UNDERSTANDINGS OF THE LEARNER

In this country and abroad, many investigations of the nature of learners have been conducted during the past half-century. Much has been discovered about children's sequence in growth and development, about factors that affect growth and development, about the mental equipment which learners bring to their tasks, about the importance of individual personality and personal experiences, and about the effect of the social order on individual learners. Following is a digest of some of the findings which have special meaning for persons who want to improve the curriculum.

PATTERNS AND BASIC CONSIDERATIONS IN GROWTH
AND DEVELOPMENT

Learners as individual children and youth have been studied from several points of view. Arnold Gesell and his followers have used a "cross-sectional" approach, which involves studying thousands of children at specified ages and then generalizing about their physical, mental, and behavioral characteristics at these ages. Willard C. Olson has used a longitudinal method, by which children are observed and examined at intervals during their development from childhood to adolescence, and their individual patterns of growth and development are plotted. Psychoanalysts have discussed undesirable feelings and experiences which, when present during childhood, cause young people to grow into disordered adults. The sociologist Robert Havighurst has outlined developmental tasks which range from infancy through later life. These four approaches, being quite different in nature, often yield different findings about growth and development of learners. But they do tend toward a view of the learner as a whole being rather than as a parcel of unrelated skills, understandings, and attitudes. Because the findings from these and other approaches generally reinforce each other, the interrelatedness of growth factors becomes increasingly clear. In the physical area, researchers view *growth* as involving increase in the size of individuals, and *development* as involving increase in their physical complexity. However, in matters of mentality and emotionality, with which curriculum workers are chiefly concerned, the same and other researchers regard *growth* and *development* as having interchangeable meanings.

After a long look at the varied literature on child and youth development, a committee of teachers in one school system adapted Daniel Prescott's child study methodology to a study of children in their own schools.[6] They observed children against a background of study in general developmental patterns, and then stated in a course guide the characteristics and needs of the children they knew best. These children occupied age and grade brackets which classified them as follows: kindergarten and grade one, grades two and three, grades four and five, and grades six and seven. Because they lacked the time necessary to do so, the teachers were unable to proceed further into a study of the adolescent period. But they made the following categorizations for children in kindergarten and the first seven grades:

KINDERGARTEN AND GRADE ONE

Characteristics:
1. Children begin to lose baby teeth, causing lisping, etc.
2. Right- or left-handedness is established. No change should be made without expert advice.
3. Bone structure growth is slower than in previous years.
4. Heart growth is rapid. The child should not be overtaxed physically.
5. Eyes are increasing in size. Watch reading and writing habits.
6. Feeling of tension may be evident in thumb-sucking, nailbiting, and mistakes in toilet habits.
7. Motor skills begin to develop; coordination may be awkward and uneven.
8. Large muscles are much more developed than smaller ones.
9. The child responds to rhythms—skips, beats time, etc.
10. The average child of these ages is full of vitality. He has good facial color, and he stands and sits erect.
11. Children are interested in an activity rather than its outcome.
12. Self-dependence and a desire to help others are developing.
13. Children prefer activity—climbing, jumping, running—but they tire easily.

Needs:
1. Short periods of activity.
2. Twelve hours of sleep.
3. Vigorous and noisy games so essential to growth.
4. Many opportunities to do things for oneself.
5. Frequent participation in organized groups—games, dramatics, rhythms.
6. Chances for the shy child to join in the routine and be important.

GRADES TWO AND THREE

Characteristics:
1. Small muscles continue to develop, with coordination improving.
2. Increased attention span and a greater number of interests are evident.

---

[6] See D. A. Prescott, *The Child in the Educative Process.* New York: McGraw-Hill Book Co., Inc., 1957.

3. Rhythmic sense is increasing.
4. Overabundance of energy is present, with frequent accidents resulting from being in a hurry.
5. Physical growth is slow but steady.
6. The heart is not growing as fast as the rest of the body; one must watch overtaxing.
7. Posture demands attention.
8. Sex differences may lead to a questioning attitude.
9. The child takes personal satisfaction in assuming responsibility.
10. The children are becoming more cooperative, as indicated in group activities.
11. Adult authority is generally accepted.
12. Children show little self-consciousness.
13. Children are interested in being like grown-ups.

Needs:
1. Competition with others of his own size and strength.
2. Continued rhythmic activities as well as dramatic expression.
3. Increased length of activities in terms of longer interest span.
4. Equipment for exercise—jungle gym, corral, walking beam, etc.
5. Guidance to be a good follower as well as a good leader.
6. Games which call for entire body action—running, throwing, jumping, etc.
7. Help in finding a place in a group to satisfy growing gang instincts.
8. Greater degree of freedom with careful guidance.
9. Love of parents and friendship of teachers for emotional security.

GRADES FOUR AND FIVE

Characteristics:
1. Small muscles continue to develop increasing manipulative skills.
2. Coordination is improving, especially hand-eye.
3. This is the period of pre-pubescence at which time physical growth slows down. Beginning of pubescence may appear in a very few boys and girls.
4. Overtaxing of heart needs watching.
5. Posture needs watching.
6. Eyes need to be considered. Attention now may prevent more serious trouble later.
7. This is a period of untidiness, overabundance of energy, frequent accidents.
8. Children show increased interest span in a wide range of activities.
9. This is the gang age, the age of secret clubs.
10. Children are critical of their families.
11. Relationship to group and approval of peers are important.
12. It is the age of collecting—cards, stamps, etc.

Needs:
1. Opportunities to develop independence.
2. At least ten hours of sleep.
3. Physical equipment (desks, chairs, etc.) carefully adjusted to each individual.
4. Uniformity and fairness in rules and punishment.
5. Real need of regularity, as opposed to schedule changes.
6. Whole body activities.
7. Sympathy and understanding of adults.
8. Help in finding a place in the group.
9. Opportunity to learn to be a good follower as well as a good leader.

GRADES SIX AND SEVEN

Characteristics:
1. Increased muscle development and body growth in this period of pubescence may show in awkwardness and lack of control.
2. Girls develop faster than boys and tire more easily.
3. Overfatigue should be watched—a great deal of rest is needed.
4. Both boys and girls may become embarrassed about physical development during this period when pubescence is in progress.
5. Children have huge appetites.
6. These are days of hero worship and loyalty to an individual.
7. The approval of the group is more important than that of adults.
8. Interest in the opposite sex may be evident in showing off, boasting, teasing, etc.—also in a desire to improve one's personal appearance.
9. Loyalty to the gang is a common characteristic.

Needs:
1. Outdoor physical activities, within limits of physical growth.
2. At least ten hours of sleep.
3. Increased opportunity to participate in social activities.
4. Team games—different for boys and girls.
5. Rhythmic games now replaced by group and social dancing; help needed by the shy or self-conscious child.
6. Slow learner's need of help in finding satisfaction and approval of others in fields other than the academic—art, sports, handwork.
7. Development of skills for participation in group activities.
8. Security in associations with adults.[7]

The committee which prepared these lists of characteristics and needs recognized that they were directed heavily toward physical development, with overtones of the intellectual and the emotional. The lists needed, therefore, to be supplemented with data from other findings in human growth and de-

[7] From *Language Arts Guide, Kindergarten and Grades One Through Seven.* Montclair, N.J.: The Public Schools of Montclair, 1956.

velopment, with special reference to the observations made by teachers concerning the learners in their own school system. In studies of this kind, specific, crucial observations should be related to the ways particular learners master particular subject-matter. Thus the committee which made the lists mentioned several applications of given characteristics and needs to the teaching of the language arts, and requested other teachers to watch for and report additional applications on blank pages which were included with the course guide.

An example of the applications is a proposed list of activities for development of listening skills in kindergarten and the first grade: 1) Hear stories of pets, news about each other, descriptions of objects. 2) Recognize sounds made by animals, insects, machines; rhythm changes in music. 3) Be alert to directions for dismissal, fire drills, rest periods, care of supplies and clothing.

The characteristics and needs of adolescents who occupy grades seven through twelve, inclusive, of American school systems have often been stated broadly, *i.e.*, without reference to the adolescents of any one community. Learners who are in grades seven and eight, as well as a few of those in grade nine, are said to share the physical development, characteristic reactions, and special needs of preadolescents and early adolescents, which may be stated in brief form as follows:

Physical Development:
1. Wide variations in rate of development become strikingly obvious.
2. The beginning of puberty is marked by a period of rapid but uneven growth, following a plateau period in both height and weight.
3. The "pubescent spurt" usually starts between nine and thirteen.
4. Girls are usually taller and heavier than boys during this period. They are in many respects two years ahead of boys in development.
5. Reproductive organs are maturing, and secondary sex characteristics are developing.
6. Energy is at a high level among those not yet maturing. There is sometimes fatigue among those who are maturing.
7. The heart is not developing as rapidly as the remainder of the body, and bone growth is not always matched by corresponding muscular development.
8. Unevenness of growth causes features, hands, feet, and legs to be out of proportion for a time.
9. Awkwardness, poor control, and poor posture often result from uneven growth.
10. Appetite may be enormous but uncertain.
11. The child who is coming into adolescence needs eight to nine hours of sleep.

Characteristic Reactions:
1. Seeks acceptance by age-mates.
2. Gangs continue, though loyalty to the gang is stronger among boys than among girls.
3. Sometimes much teasing and seeming antagonism between boy and girl groups.
4. Those who are maturing beginning to show interest in the opposite sex.
5. Interested in team games, outdoor activities, pets, hobbies, collections, radio, television, comics, motion pictures, and ways of earning money. Interests of boys and girls diverging.
6. May become moody, overcritical, changeable, rebellious, uncooperative.
7. Opinion of own group frequently valued more highly than that of adults.
8. Can work cooperatively on teams and in groups. Strong emphasis on fairness and on rules.
9. Self-conscious about body changes.

Special Needs:
1. Varied programs to meet different maturity levels.
2. Organized clubs and group activities based on boys' and girls' needs and interests.
3. Help in understanding physical and emotional changes which are beginning to take place.
4. Warm affection and sense of humor in adults; no nagging, scolding, or talking down.
5. Sense of belonging in the peer group.
6. Opportunities for boys and girls to do things together in group situations.
7. Opportunities for greater independence and for carrying more responsibility without pressure.
8. Special help for those who are maturing much faster or much more slowly than their companions.
9. Personal acceptance of the irregularities of both physical and emotional growth.
10. Acceptance of continued need for some dependence on adults.
11. Help in developing skills which make it possible to take part successfully in group activities.
12. Recognition of individual capacities and abilities, with planning of special programs to meet needs and avoid discouragements.

Learners in senior high schools are generally believed to share the following characteristics and needs:

Physical Development:
1. Most children have matured by age fifteen, with accompanying physical and emotional changes.
2. In many respects, girls are about two years ahead of boys until the end of the adolescent period.
3. The awkward period of uneven growth is passing.

4. Adult appearance is developing. By the end of the adolescent period, bone growth has been completed, and adult height has been reached.
5. The heart is still increasing greatly in size at the beginning of the adolescent period.
6. Acne often presents a problem.
7. The energy level is unstable.
8. Appetites—especially boys' appetites—are large.
9. Adolescents usually need at least eight hours of sleep.

Characteristic Reactions:
1. Mood swings—sometimes defiant and rebellious, sometimes cooperative and responsible.
2. Often searching for ideals and standards; anxious about the future, trying to "find himself."
3. Preoccupied with acceptance by one social group, particularly by members of the opposite sex.
4. Afraid of not being popular, of ridicule, of not being like other adolescents; oversensitive to the opinions of others.
5. Concerned about his own bodily appearance.
6. Desirous of asserting independence from his family, but willing to return to adults for moral support.
7. Sometimes responds better to teachers than to parents. Tends to identify with an admired adult.
8. Wants responsibility, but is often unstable in judgment.
9. Wants the independence of earning his own money.
10. Sometimes acts as if he "knew it all," but is insecure within himself.
11. Responds well to group responsibility and group participation.
12. Shows intense loyalty to his own group.

Special Needs:
1. Acceptance by his age-mates.
2. Adequate knowledge and understanding of sexual relationships and attitudes.
3. Help in accepting his permanent physical appearance.
4. Opportunities to carry responsibility and make decisions.
5. Opportunities to earn and save money.
6. Provision for recreation with members of the opposite sex.
7. Assistance in learning about and choosing a vocation.
8. Organized group activities, based on group planning and participation.
9. Help in establishing more mature relationships with other members of the family.
10. Guidance which is kindly, unobtrusive, and free of threat to one's freedom.
11. Warm, understanding, supportive acceptance by parents.
12. Guidance in physical activities to prevent overdoing.
13. Opportunities to develop his own interests and skills.
14. Help in keeping a balance between group needs and individual needs and interests.

15. Guidance in developing special skills and talents.
16. Help in accepting and understanding those outside one's own group.
17. Help in understanding why people feel and behave as they do.

Lists of this kind have been produced and reproduced widely during the past two decades. Those who have created them have usually warned that they are not to be regarded as models or norms but only as general descriptions or "age profiles." They result from observation of numbers of children and youth, and they are useful in viewing broadly the expectations which may be held for groups of pupils in the schools.

Havighurst has provided a somewhat different dimension, which he calls "developmental tasks," *i.e.*, tasks which arise at or about a certain period in an individual's life. The tasks emerge from a combination of factors: maturation, the culture in which children are reared, and the nature of the individual child himself. The concept of developmental tasks is therefore an interdisciplinary one, originating in individual psychology, human growth and development, and sociology.

For children between ages six and twelve, Havighurst's list of tasks includes: learning physical skills necessary for ordinary games; building wholesome attitudes toward oneself as a growing organism; learning to get along with age-mates; learning an appropriate masculine or feminine social role; developing fundamental skills in reading, writing, and calculating; developing concepts necessary for everyday living; developing conscience, morality, and a scale of values; achieving personal independence; and developing attitudes toward social groups and institutions.

For youth between ages twelve and eighteen, the list includes: achieving new and more mature relations with age-mates of both sexes; achieving a masculine or feminine social role; accepting one's physique and using the body effectively; achieving emotional independence of parents and other adults; achieving assurance of economic independence; selecting and preparing for an occupation; preparing for marriage and family life; developing intellectual skills and concepts necessary for civic competence; desiring and achieving socially responsible behavior; and acquiring a set of values and an ethical system as a guide to behavior.

Translating characteristics, needs, and tasks into meaningful concepts to be used in curriculum improvement is a special and difficult task for the curriculum worker. He must realize, first, that characteristics, needs, and tasks overlap among the age groups, with the greatest overlap occurring when age groups are finely distinguished in groupings of two ages (six and seven, eight and nine, etc.) or three ages, rather than in broader groupings (six to twelve). Then he must give careful thought to what a particular characteristic, need, or task means for school programs. Some inferences can be drawn immediately, *e.g.*, about physical capabilities as they relate to learning experiences. Other inferences are harder to draw, and the school experiences which seem to fit require tryout to confirm their appropriateness. On the assumption that a characteristic, need, or task has been validly identified, it must be thought about in relationship to other factors. The question here is, "What relative weight should be given to this particular characteristic, need, or task?" Finally, evidence about the growth and development of learners should be checked against the objectives to which teachers and pupils subscribe.

SITUATION 2-2—JUDGING WHAT USE TO MAKE OF CERTAIN CHARACTERISTICS AND NEEDS

A committee of teachers of fourth- and fifth-grade children concerned itself with art experiences for children of these grades. Both the learning activities of the children and the facilities the children were to use came within the purview of the committee, which was charged with developing program and facilities for a new elementary school. The committee's attention was drawn particularly to the following characteristics and needs of fourth- and fifth-grade children:

Characteristics——Small muscles are developing more and more manipulative power; children are often untidy and energetic, and they have frequent accidents; children are interested in collecting items which they and other people produce.

Needs——Independent creative ability should be developed; children need a wide range of activities in which to expend their energies.

Assuming that the characteristics and needs of children of these age groups, as listed above, are valid, what are some of the inferences concerning program and facilities in art which you can make?

Study of the growth and development of large numbers of learners yields some useful guidelines. However, exceptions to general findings about children and youth are both numerous and interesting. The challenge to education in a democracy appears much more prominently in the differences among children and youth than in their similarities. School practices unrealistically tend toward treating learners as though they were substantially alike, whereas they actually vary beyond teachers' wildest imaginings. Following are some statements about individual differences in growth and development which are commonly believed today:

> Many of the obvious differences among learners can be seen in five minutes in any classroom. Other, less obvious differences can be revealed only by careful study.

> Learners differ in their ability to perform tasks. Thus a child may be good in arithmetic, poor in spelling, and fair in reading according to an arbitrary standard of quality. To complicate matters, the same child displays differing abilities in performing specific tasks within each of these school subjects.

> Growth and development apparently occur in spurts, sometimes referred to as the "thrustration" involved in pushing forward, with a subsequent period of quiescence and reinforcement following each push.

> If individual differences are really taken into account, the school cannot hope to maintain a single or minimum standard for a given group of children, comfortable though this standard might be for teachers. Education should cultivate differences rather than restrict them. If this were done, the range of differences would be even more obvious. Though high schools often tend to teach adolescents as though they were all alike, maturation brings out more apparent differences in learners than were present or obvious when the same learners were young children.

> Differences in rates of growth, with other factors, cause some children to be "early bloomers" and other children to be "late bloomers."

> Given desirable educational conditions, children of whom we have expected little can often give much. Teachers have shown an unfortunate tendency to write off as hopeless those children who have not succeeded well at first.

> Since factors of growth are interrelated, the causes of learning difficulty at a given time may be found in some factor which we are not presently considering. For instance, an excellent biology student's sudden block to learning more biology may originate in a hidden emotional upset or physical illness.

Lists like this one give curriculum workers pause as they begin to consider factors of growth and development which teachers fail to take into account. Interestingly, every learner brings with him *individualized conditioners* of learning. These include his personality, his personal experiences, his mental ability, and the effects of the social order. The nature of the learner himself and of his background has a marked effect on what he learns and on his style of learning. Furthermore, the personality of the learner becomes evident in his emotional organization, which affects his sensitivity to social and other phenomena, his ties with adults, his desire or lack of desire to master his environment, and the extent of his preoccupation with personal problems which may prevent learning. It appears, of course, in the quality of his relationships with people of all sorts. The learner's insecurities may cause him to "show off" his abilities by achieving to the maximum, or they may cause him so to undervalue his powers that he suffers from emotional paralysis. He is affected further by his sex status, which partly determines what he may appropriately learn, and by physical characteristics such as muscular coordination and visual and auditory acuity.

One's past experience conditions learning in many ways. Interests developed early in life often carry into subsequent years. Sometimes they coincide with the curriculum of the school, but too often they are unknown to teachers, or they seem to have no relevance to anything people do in schools. Socially and in other ways, modern children have more opportunities for wide experience than children had a generation or two ago, and wide experience shows itself in the sophistication, whether real or artificial, which modern children often manifest.[8]

Learners bring to their tasks widely varied mental equipment, which is usually discussed under the heading of *intelligence*. Intelligence may be defined as that cluster of aptitudes and abilities which permits one to acquire new learnings. Man has not yet succeeded in measuring intelligence directly, only in inferring intelligence from the results of certain tests which search out elements of common background in learners, the elements being drawn mainly from the world of words and other symbols. Modern intelligence tests yield a series of scores, including scores in reasoning ability, manual dexterity, spatial perception, and memory. Thus, intelligence is believed to come in varied dimensions rather than merely in the vague form of "general intelligence." However, the school customarily tests, and so educates, along only a few of the possible dimensions. Without question, the human potential which is going to waste in our society, and thus in our schools, is appallingly large; so a key function of the schools of the future must be to educate intelligence along additional dimensions. Recently, the tendency of culturally deprived children to attain higher scores on intelligence tests when they have been exposed to an improved environment for even a few weeks has been explored. When children have better concepts of themselves, their scores on intelligence tests are likely to improve. A significant finding for education is that, while the learner's basic intelligence remains quite constant, we can achieve variations

[8] Association for Supervision and Curriculum Development, *op. cit.*, pp. 29–32.

in his performance by altering certain important conditions in his environment. What, one wonders, might conceivably be done to develop human potential by manipulating environment to free intelligence?

The broad effects of society on the curriculum are discussed in Chapter 3. In the present discussion, it is important to see how the social order affects the individual learner. First, it affects him within the dynamic of his social status. For instance, the worth of study and learning is keenly felt by middle- and upper-class people, but it is not always appreciated by the lower classes. Accordingly, middle- and upper-class children are often considered "good" students and conformers, while learners from the lower classes resist school tasks which they consider impractical. Second, the social order affects the learner with reference to the ethnic or national background from which he comes. His ethnic or national group has developed certain expectations of schooling, and of the status in society which a person of his background may hope to reach. Soon the learner himself comes to share these expectations. A third source of effect from the social order is the family in which one has been reared. The interest of family members, their cultural advantages, and the extensiveness of their travel are but a few of the direct influences of family life. Other sources of effect are one's neighborhood, the occupations of the people he knows, and the cultural level and aspirations of his associates. "Every child learns what he lives and he is motivated only to learn more about those things which he knows or imagines."[9]

SITUATION 2-3—HOMEWORK FOR AN EIGHTH-GRADE CLASS

Mr. Simpson's work as assistant principal of a junior high school took him into a number of classrooms. In most of them, he noticed homework assignments being given in the following manner: "For tomorrow, read pages 145 to 153, and be ready to talk about what you have read." To Mr. Simpson, this way of assigning homework seemed oversimplified and insensitive. He found a sympathetic spirit in an eighth-grade science teacher, Miss Carey, to whom it seemed that assigning homework had become a special problem of which she was poignantly aware. On the day she assigned to all her pupils ten pages of textbook reading on the age of the earth, she came to Mr. Simpson for help.

"A single assignment for all these dozens of children whom I

[9] *Ibid.*, p. 33.

meet daily doesn't make sense," said Miss Carey. "But earth science is so remote from them! How can I vary my assignment to reach children of differing abilities and interests?"

If you were Mr. Simpson, what facts of human growth and development would you wish to take into account in working with Miss Carey in improving her assignment-making? What assignments other than her routine one would you recommend that Miss Carey make?

ACTIVITY 2-1—DIAGNOSING THE LEARNING POTENTIAL OF AN INDIVIDUAL

To see the advantages and disadvantages which individual learners possess, one should study individuals carefully. Each learner operates amid a cluster or complex of forces. Some of these forces have been noted above.

Choose an individual learner for study, or encourage a teacher whom you supervise to do so. Through interview, analysis of cumulative records, home visitation, and/or any other means at your disposal, find out all you can about this learner—the pattern of his development; his personal characteristics, talents, strengths, and weaknesses; and the social forces that impinge upon him. Describe your expectations concerning him and the extent to which these expectations are being realized. Tell what you think could be done concretely by his school to develop his potential.

PRESENT UNDERSTANDINGS OF THE LEARNING PROCESS

Much that has been said in the preceding pages has implied the importance of having a point of view about how learning proceeds. Schools of psychological thought are so numerous and so varied in their viewpoints about learning that a real service has been rendered by scholars who have tried to reconcile the differing viewpoints. Two of these scholars are Ernest R. Hilgard and Goodwin Watson. On the following pages, quotations and paraphrases of some of Hilgard's and Watson's statements are presented. The statements chosen have special interest for teachers and other curriculum workers. They are, of course, subject to change as more is learned about psychology and about concrete psychological bases for curriculum decisions.

A motivated learner acquires what he learns more readily than one who is not motivated. The relevant motives include both general and specific ones; for example, desire to learn, need for achievement (general), desire for a reward or for avoidance of a threatened punishment (specific).

Motivation that is too intense (especially pain, fear, and anxiety) may be accompanied by distracting emotional states, so that excessive motivation may be less effective than moderate motivation for learning some kinds of tasks, particularly those involving difficult discriminations.

Learning under the control of reward is usually preferable to learning under the control of punishment. Correspondingly, learning motivated by success is preferable to learning motivated by failure. Even though the theoretical issue is still unresolved, the practical outcome must take into account the social by-products, which tend to be more favorable under reward than under punishment.

Learning under intrinsic motivation is preferable to learning under extrinsic motivation.

Tolerance of failure is best taught through providing a backlog of success.

Individuals need practice in setting goals for themselves: goals which are neither so low and limited as to elicit little effort nor so high and difficult as to foreordain failure. Realistic goal-setting leads to more satisfactory improvement than does unrealistic goal-setting.

The personal history of the individual—for example, his record of reaction to authority—may hamper or enhance his ability to learn from a given teacher.

Active participation by learners is preferable to passive reception of the content to be learned.

Meaningful materials are learned more readily than nonsense materials; meaningful tasks, more readily than tasks not understood by the learner.

There is no substitute for repetitive practice in the overlearning of skills or in the memorization of unrelated facts which must be automatized.

Information about the nature of a good performance, knowledge of one's own mistakes, and knowledge of successful results assist the learner.

Transfer to new tasks will occur more smoothly if, in learning, the learner can discover relationships for himself, and if he has experience in applying principles of relationship within a variety of tasks.

Spaced or distributed recalls are advantageous in fixing material that is to be retained a long time.[10]

"Learners progress in any area of learning only as far as they need to in order to achieve their purposes. Often they do only well enough to 'get by'; with increased motivation they improve."[11]

---

[10] Ernest R. Hilgard, *Theories of Learning* (Second Edition). New York: Appleton-Century-Crofts, Inc., 1956.
[11] Goodwin Watson, "What Psychology Can We Feel Sure About?" *Teachers College Record*, Vol. 61, No. 5, February, 1960.

"The most effective effort is put forth by children when they attempt tasks which fall in the 'range of challenge'—not too easy and not too hard—where success seems quite possible but not certain."[12]

Learners engage in an activity most willingly if they have helped select and plan the activity.

When learners are grouped by ability according to any one criterion, such as age, I.Q., or reading ability, they vary over a range of several grades according to other criteria.

Learners think when they encounter obstacles or challenges to action that interest them. In thinking, they design and test plausible ways of overcoming the obstacles or challenges.

When pupils learn concepts, they need to have the concepts presented in varied and specific situations. Then they should try the concepts in situations different from those in which they were originally learned.

Pupils learn a great deal from each other. When they have been together a long time, they learn from each other more rapidly than they do from peers who are strange to them.

The problem of "isolates" appears in every school. Isolates are those children who are generally not chosen by their classmates, and who are also likely to be unpopular with teachers.

No school subject is strikingly superior to any other subject for strengthening one's mental powers.

Pupils remember new subject-matter that conforms with their previous attitudes better than they remember new subject-matter that opposes their previous attitudes.

Learning is aided by formulating and asking questions that stimulate thinking and imagination.[13]

Additional principles of learning about which there is general agreement could, of course, be enunciated. However, the ones listed above are applied too seldom in the classrooms of American schools; therefore, curriculum leaders can find much to do in helping teachers apply even the most obvious principles. A series of questions expresses several of the needs for help which classroom teachers exhibit: How can the children in these classrooms be motivated most readily and effectively? Specifically, how can intrinsic motivation be caused to proceed? How can our pupils be assisted in setting goals in common, and also individually? In our situation, what can and should activity in learning mean? How can we cause true meaning to emerge through the learning experiences we provide? What principles and practices in teacher-pupil planning seem to function best?

Similar challenge can be found in many other questions which show the

[12] *Ibid.*
[13] *Ibid.*

relevance of psychology to the classroom teacher's work. For the curriculum leader himself, another order of psychologically-based questions arises. They include the following: Where can teachers find motivation for self-improvement? How can curriculum planners discover learning experiences which are suited to the attainment of specific goals? How can teachers best involve themselves in the planning of curriculum improvement activities? What do we really believe about mental discipline and transfer of training as revealed by our practices in selecting curriculum content?

SITUATION 2-4—PUTTING SELECTED LEARNING PRINCIPLES TO WORK

A central office supervisor and a building principal visited every classroom in the principal's building. As they did so, they spent most of their time observing pupils rather than teachers. They tried to ask themselves, "What are these pupils learning? What difficulties are they encountering? What principles of learning could we help teachers apply to improve the learning situation in this school?" They decided that the chief difficulties were these:

1. Too many items of content were being learned in isolation and without interrelationship.
2. Most of the reading material used in the school was too far above the comprehension level of the pupils, but most of the classroom discussion, if it could be called that, was simple and repetitive.
3. Pupils were learning under threat of punishment more often than they were learning because the content seemed to them to be worthwhile.

What important principle of learning does each of the difficulties suggest?

What could teachers do concretely to apply each of the principles?

REPRESENTATIVE FRONTIERS IN THE STUDY OF LEARNING

The preceding section of this chapter has dealt with some of our current knowledge of learning. Much remains to be done in studying the learning process and the conditions surrounding learning. Attention is now being given, if only on a fragmentary and limited basis, to several facets of process and environment.

Learning styles and patterns of thinking are now under consideration. Few definitive answers about learning styles have been given to date, but psychologists are sure that pupils do learn the same content in individual and different ways. Questions about ways of learning which need answering include these: To what extent is there a common methodology in learning? How can we help children analyze how they learn? How can we individualize the teaching of various kinds of content? How can we help learners formulate and evaluate their own special goals?[14] Thinking, as an important function of learning, needs to be understood more clearly. Raths has categorized the thinking problems that learners face as being those connected with impulsiveness, overdependence, rigidity, the tendency to miss meanings, dogmatism and overassertiveness, underconfidence, inadequate concentration, and unwillingness to think.[15] He and others have made a small start in helping upper elementary-school children remove some of their problems within these categories. The school has had much to do with approving certain ways of learning and discouraging other ways. The person who "thinks at right angles" to his group may be considered an eccentric or a deviate, whereas he might be described more accurately as being a creative person.[16] While learners need to generalize and conceptualize in common, they also need opportunities to experiment with *divergent thinking*.

Another problem, that of seeing what the learner sees, becomes especially prominent when the teacher tries to help him develop concepts. Close observation of pupils in schools has led to a conclusion, which needs further testing, that children can develop certain concepts at an earlier age than has heretofore been thought possible. With the numerous opportunities for learning which are now available, there is need to deepen important understandings, and we are not at all certain how to do this. Children are probably developing misconceptions rapidly, partly because the experiences they are having do not help them toward accuracy in concept development.[17] A be-

[14] Association for Supervision and Curriculum Development, *Learning More About Learning*. Washington, D.C.: The Association, 1959, p. 79.

[15] Louis Raths, in James B. Macdonald, ed., *Research Frontiers in the Study of Children's Learning*. Milwaukee: School of Education, University of Wisconsin, 1960, pp. 39–42.

[16] Association for Supervision and Curriculum Development, *Human Variability and Learning*. Washington, D.C.: The Association, 1961, pp. 82 and 83.

[17] Association for Supervision and Curriculum Development, *Learning More About Learning*, pp. 76–79.

ginning point would seem to be finding out what concepts learners presently hold. Little effort has been expended so far in doing even this.

Previously in this chapter, reference was made to the few dimensions along which we are measuring learners' abilities and, accordingly, the inadequacy of the education we provide. "To find what is behind each face" was the schoolmaster's goal in the film *Passion for Life*. We still know little about what's behind the faces, especially about what potential resides there: potential, for instance, for special leadership, for creating ideas, for working with media, for organizing and adapting, for performing in the arts. We know less about ways of developing what we find. Related to the need to discover potential is the well-recognized need to help underachieving, able learners make better uses of their known capacities.

We are sure, as has been said earlier, that the kind of person the learner *is* makes a genuine difference in what he looks for and gets in formal instruction. Motivation, we say, really comes from within the learner. Behind the motivation is the structure of his personality. His view of himself, commonly called his self-concept, requires analysis, especially with respect to its nature, dimensions, and means of development. Already there has been some investigation to answer a basic question: How much of what self-concept? We desperately need an understanding of children's views of themselves as learners so that we may help them alter these views, whenever necessary, in more positive directions.[18]

Emphasis on learners' values has recently come to the fore. In our complex and often troubled society, the values of many young people are conflicted and confused. Raths has identified eight manifestations of difficulty in valuing: 1) apathy, listlessness, or dullness; 2) flightiness; 3) over-conformity; 4) nagging dissent; 5) extreme hesitancy, doubt, or uncertainty; 6) persistent, continuing underachievement; 7) the playing of roles, posing, or pretending; and 8) extreme inconsistency. He estimates that about 30 per cent of upper elementary-school children have difficulties with their values.[19] Through skillful questioning and provision of clarifying experiences, learners in a few places and situations have been helped to clarify their values. They have come to know why they believe what they believe, and have subsequently helped themselves alter values which were detrimental to themselves and others. In this, as in other areas of the learning process, much remains to be done.

Again, the general effects of favorable and unfavorable environment

---

[18] Ira J. Gordon, *Children's Views of Themselves*. Washington, D.C.: Association for Childhood Education International, 1959.

[19] Raths, *op. cit.*, pp. 25–28.

have long been recognized. However, there is now considerable experimentation in enriching the environments of young children and of older, culturally deprived persons. The *Higher Horizons Program* of the New York City Public Schools is an example of this enrichment. While environments external to the school have a significant effect on learners, the teacher obviously does much to condition the day-to-day environment in which pupils work. For instance, teachers build or reduce anxiety about tests and examinations. They organize groups which increase or inhibit learning. Thelen, Lippitt, and others are discovering interesting things about grouping and the social-emotional climate which classroom groups help to create. Experimentation is needed to determine whether permissive classroom situations increase motivation to the extent to which many persons have believed them to do. Investigation is also needed to determine the extent to which learning as searching, as opposed to learning as telling, is to be prized, and the extent to which learning can be made the responsibility of individual children, as under systems of programmed instruction.

A special aspect of environment is the effect of sub-cultures and social class. Sub-cultures form according to age, race, occupation, language, and geography. Parents' concepts of schools and schooling vary according to the sub-cultures, often multiple in nature, to which they belong. These concepts, in revised form, become the property of their children. From the days of the initial work of Allison Davis and other social scientists, differences in social class have been noted but little reckoned with. A significant frontier exists in diagnosing the learnings children accept from teachers and learning materials which differ in social class origin from the children themselves. Sub-cultures and social class status apparently condition children's desire to learn, and cause them to accept some learnings more readily than they can or will accept others.

Complicating the whole teaching-learning scene are both gross and refined differences in the giftedness of children. Though recent years have seen much experimentation with the teaching of atypical children, especially those who are intellectually gifted and those who are mentally retarded, the literature concerning the teaching of the atypical reveals marked disagreements about many fundamental matters.

These, then, are some of the frontiers of inquiry. Curriculum workers should test the discoveries of psychologists in practical school situations. At times they should develop their own hypotheses and make discoveries of their own without undue fear of being "out of their field." The inevitable closeness of psychology and education requires that educators help psychologists just as psychologists need to help educators. Each group requires in-service education in the lore of the other. For their part, curriculum workers can be certain that many, if not most, of the problems with which they deal will involve the nature of learners and of the learning process.

SITUATION 2-5—EXPLORING A FRONTIER IN LEARNING

A group of teachers sought to design an investigation of differences among their pupils according to sub-culture and social class. To do so, they took the following steps:

1. They inspected pupil records and interviewed pupils concerning their homelife and general background.
2. They asked the pupils to react in small groups to experiences which the school provided through formal instruction and through informal programs.
3. They asked specific questions about photographs and ideas appearing in textbooks and other teaching materials, as these photographs and ideas reflected sub-cultural levels and social class.
4. They asked the pupils to respond freely to words and expressions which might evoke particular memories and reactions: Negro, Knights of Columbus, Fundamentalist, The Labor Union News, etc.

What is your reaction to these methods of finding out about sub-cultures and social classes which the pupils represent? Would you use methods in addition to or instead of the four listed above? What useful information would you expect to get by employing these four methods and/or your own?

SUMMARY

This chapter has reported some of the influences which individual psychology and social psychology, as applied to decision-making about the curriculum, inevitably have upon the endeavors of learners, teachers, and curriculum leaders. The impact of psychology on decision-making has been discussed in four contexts: applications to be made in improving the curriculum, the relevance of data about learners, the importance of understanding the learning process, and the promise that appears on new frontiers of learning theory and research. We turn now from psychology to sociology and cultural anthropology, whose contributions are to be referred to in a chapter on social forces that help mold the curriculum.

SELECTED BIBLIOGRAPHY

Almy, Millie, *Child Development* (New York: Holt, Rinehart & Winston, Inc., 1955).

Anderson, Vernon E., *Principles and Procedures of Curriculum Improvement* (New York: The Ronald Press Company, 1956).

Association for Supervision and Curriculum Development, *Freeing Capacity to Learn* (Washington, D.C.: The Association, 1960).

————, *Human Variability and Learning* (Washington, D.C.: The Association, 1961).

————, *Learning and the Teacher*, 1959 Yearbook (Washington, D.C.: The Association, 1959).

————, *Learning More About Learning* (Washington, D.C.: The Association, 1959).

————, *New Insights and the Curriculum*, 1963 Yearbook (Washington, D.C.: The Association, 1963).

Breckenridge, Marian E., and E. Lee Vincent, *Child Development* (Philadelphia: W. B. Saunders Co., 1960).

Havighurst, Robert J., *Human Development and Education* (New York: Longmans, Green & Co., Inc., 1953).

Hilgard, Ernest R., *Theories of Learning*, Second Edition (New York: Appleton-Century-Crofts, Inc., 1956).

Jersild, Arthur T., *In Search of Self* (New York: Bureau of Publication, Teachers College, Columbia University, 1952).

Macdonald, James B., ed., *Research Frontiers in the Study of Children's Learning* (Milwaukee: School of Education, University of Wisconsin, 1960).

Prescott, D. A., *The Child in the Educative Process* (New York: McGraw-Hill Book Co., Inc., 1957).

Saylor, J. Galen, and William M. Alexander, *Curriculum Planning for Better Teaching and Learning* (New York: Holt, Rinehart & Winston, Inc., 1954).

Symonds, Percival M., *What Education Has to Learn from Psychology* (New York: Bureau of Publications, Teachers College, Columbia University, 1958).

Watson, Goodwin, "What Psychology Can We Feel Sure About?" *Teachers College Record*, Vol. 61, No. 5 (February, 1960).

chapter three

SOCIETY, THE CULTURE, and our American system of values have a marked effect on efforts to improve the curriculum. Their impact develops at two levels: the remote but significant level of society's influence, and the immediate and practical level of the community's contact with the schools.

The first portion of this chapter deals with influences from society at large. The second portion discusses community influences for and against curriculum improvement, and the final portion suggests several strategies which curriculum personnel can use in dealing with social influences on the schools.

INFLUENCES FROM SOCIETY AT LARGE

The society at large affects curriculum improvement in four major ways: by inhibiting change through the power of *tradition*; by speeding *change* which stems in turn from broader social and cultural changes; by creating problems which result from *value conflicts* within our society, and by apply-

~~~~~~~~~~~~~~~~~~~~~~~~~~~~~~~~

Social Forces
Affecting
Curriculum
Decisions

ing *pressures* that originate in major segments of American society and culture. Each of these influences will be discussed in order.

1. THE BOON AND THE WEIGHT OF TRADITION

Tradition has sometimes been referred to as a "dead hand." Actually, it may be viewed in two ways: as a helpful preventive of attempts to discard the tried, tested, and true, and as a weight that restrains desirable change.

Society has at its disposal several forces that support tradition and inhibit change. The first of these is legal authority. Laws are frequently more easily enacted than they are repealed. Hence, a law that establishes a day a year for the planting of certain trees as an exercise in conservation education may have outgrown its usefulness, but the law is likely to remain on the books anyway. A second force, which is of enduring consequence and which exercises desirable restraint, is generally agreed-upon principles of right and wrong. From our Judeo-Christian tradition we have inherited notions of property rights and individual rights which are virtually immutable. Thus, education in the decent treatment of other people has become, and remains, an objective of the school. A third force, psychological resistance to change, is so potent that it gets full treatment in Chapter 6. Human beings resist change so energetically that, in some areas of their lives, they would rather die than shift their positions. Many a teacher cannot prove that his curriculum and methods of teaching are actually functioning for improved learning, but he will resist to the death any effort to move him away from them.

The curriculum worker must take these and other tradition-assisting forces into account. Almost daily, he encounters people who say, "But we've always done it this way!" In a few instances, his response should be, "I agree that we must continue to work in the same direction, for we are dealing here with an unchanging element of our responsibility." Matters of physical safety and the maintenance of intelligently-derived morality fall within this category. In many instances, however, he should raise questions about the worth of traditionalized practices. There is nothing sacred, for example, in the methods used in the past to teach arithmetic, though the need to teach arithmetic according to some combination of methods will remain a fixed responsibility.

Consider the effect of tradition on the modern secondary school. By tradition, most secondary schools:

1. Organize pupil time in several brief and generally equalized periods;
2. Emphasize a limited number of objectives in education;
3. Tend to use classical content, as in literature and music;
4. Permit pupils to elect subjects rather freely;
5. Yield to established means of evaluation and accreditation;
6. Subject themselves to the rigidities of the Carnegie Unit system; and
7. Add subjects at intervals, but eliminate subjects only with the greatest difficulty.

Curriculum workers who are concerned with secondary schools should look hard at the traditions surrounding the schools. They should ask: Which traditions are imponderables? Which ought to be preserved? Which could and should be eliminated promptly? Surely numerous traditions exist today without justification or validity.

SITUATION 3-1—FINDING TRADITIONS TO CHALLENGE

Imagine yourself to be a curriculum coordinator who, with a committee, has sought to identify traditions that need re-examination. The committee has elicited from teachers and laymen several instances of tradition which they feel should be challenged. Here are six of them:

1. **Teachers in the primary grades should be women.**
2. **Sociology doesn't belong in the secondary school, but history does.**
3. **Teachers are rightly concerned only with how to teach; laymen must tell the schools what to teach.**
4. **The curriculum is appropriately geared to the achievement of the upper classes in society.**
5. **We must continue to put a premium on verbal comprehension and verbal fluency.**
6. **Teachers and school board members properly represent chiefly the middle classes of our society.**

Which of the six stated traditions are actual ones in the schools you know best?

Which of the traditions which exist in the schools you know genuinely need to be questioned? Why?

2. THE EFFECTS OF SOCIAL AND CULTURAL CHANGE

Society influences action for curriculum improvement in a second way: by bringing to bear upon the curriculum those changes that occur in the wider society and culture. Despite the influence of tradition in holding social forces in check, society is constantly changing. Change is accompanied by an instability which a society can tolerate unless and until instability becomes excessive, at which time disorder or revolution occurs.

In many respects, America is moving rapidly:

Science and technology are continuing to advance as new discoveries and breakthroughs are made in physics, chemistry, medicine, and other fields.

Bigness is coming to prevail in nearly everything: in government, labor, business, and agriculture.

Improved transportation and communication have brought about travel at supersonic speeds and the transmission of messages to satellites.

The family has, in some respects, disintegrated. At least, striking changes have been wrought in family patterns of living.

Population seems to be growing out of bounds, not only in our own country but throughout the world.

Social movements which include integration of the races, mobility of our population, and movement of people from lower socio-economic to higher socio-economic status are proceeding apace.

A value crisis has gripped youth and adults, who seem to have become less clear about what they really believe.

Some of the changes affect schools immediately. For example, when the population of a nation is on the move, new faces suddenly appear in school classrooms. About 20 per cent of Americans are now moving each year. Five per cent are moving from one county to another, and not more than 15 to 20 per cent spend their whole lives in the same county.[1] Movement from south to north and from Puerto Rico to the mainland has been especially marked in recent years. Schools in our larger cities have been forced into curriculum reform by the influx of culturally deprived children to whom standardized tests are not applicable and to whom American middle-class experiences are foreign.

Other changes have a subtler, more gradual effect. When family life disintegrates, the school finds itself taking on more and more responsibility which the family previously assumed. Few schools now bathe immigrant children to eliminate lice, but they are faced daily with learning the problems of children whose parents are being divorced, or of children who are feeling the effects of alcoholism in the home.

Teachers are hard put, in society's fastest-moving transition periods, to know what to educate for. Who can foresee the future? Who can do more than identify trends? Fortunately there are always some fixities to cling to, though emphasis among the fixities may change. Education continues its concern for intelligent inquiry, for developing fundamental character traits, and for training children in basic skills. Teachers must stand for principles and ideals in which they strongly believe, meanwhile cooperating with a general public that is anxious and concerned about what is happening to stability in society. More than ever, teachers need to ask themselves what they will accept as truth, for in times of rapid change misinformation quickly appears in classrooms on the lips of teachers and pupils alike. Though diagnosis and application of new developments are difficult, teachers must ask consistently, "What meaning will this change which is appearing in society have for my teaching next week and in the years to come?"

SITUATION 3-2—ASSESSING THE EFFECTS OF SPECIFIC SOCIAL CHANGES

The faculties of the elementary and secondary schools in Raysville thought they noted several changes in American society which have not been mentioned in the preceding discussion. These changes

[1] National Society for the Study of Education, *Social Forces Influencing American Education,* 60th Yearbook, Part II. Chicago: University of Chicago Press, 1961, p. 118.

included an increased desire of parents to send their children to college, an overemphasis in our culture on science and mathematics at the expense of the social sciences and the humanities, and a trend toward internationalism at the expense of American traditions. A panel of administrators, in speaking specifically of the Raysville Schools, noted teachers' tendency to wish to work with upper middle-class children, and pupils' tendency to elect prestige-laden courses like those in advanced mathematics.

Do you believe the comments of the faculties and those of the administrators' panel are either closely or remotely related? How?

How do you react to the faculties' list of changes? What additional ones can you suggest?

Assume that you believe the three changes listed by the faculties are taking place. What impact will they probably have on the curricula of elementary and secondary schools in the United States?

3. THE EFFECTS OF VALUE CONFLICTS

Conflicts in values are inevitable in a society as diverse and complex as ours. As conditions change, so do the people, objects, and ideas we value. Furthermore, valuing depends upon a good many factors, including background, environment, and personality structure. By its diversity, our society has fostered value conflicts which complicate schooling. Nominally, for instance, we value bilingualism, but we discourage "foreignisms" in speech and writing. As teachers, we value grammatical structure at the expense of experimentation with the living, growing English language.

While we misinterpret and misuse value patterns that exist, we are disturbed at the necessity of admitting new values, or even of acknowledging their presence. Social forces have recently pushed upon us new views of old problems, one of these problems being the propagation of democracy in a basically undemocratic society. Nearly all Americans give lip service to democracy as a fundamental value. However, few of us behave consistently in accordance with democratic principles; this is especially true with reference to race and social class.

To see how inconsistent with his profession of beliefs one's actual behavior is, he should list on a piece of paper the names of all the persons he can remember having entertained in his home last year. He should then list on the opposite side of the paper the names of all the people who entertained him in their homes during the same year. The two lists usually show marked similarity, and the persons whose names are listed usually all belong to one race and to one or two social classes, even though the individual nominally believes in maintaining broadly-based democratic relationships. Among several persons of widely differing backgrounds who prepare such lists, the variations in preference for races and social classes are obvious. They betoken the differences in values which teachers find in classrooms with reference to any person, object, or idea they can name. Fortunately, the values of individual pupils change as the pupils are exposed to value-changing experiences. The schools have a special responsibility for helping learners change values which are dangerous and negative.

Today, our society is altering its viewpoints about the place of central government in American life, about the nation's role in international affairs, about strategies to be used in childrearing, about relationships between church and state, about the status of Far Eastern and African peoples, about depersonalization through automation, and about numerous other matters. Upward mobility through the class structure continues. Each serious shift in values requires curriculum leaders to consider the meaning which the shift has for education. At the same time, all teachers need clear values of their own, especially with reference to the role of the school in society. If the school's role is to be large and omnibus, nearly every change in values must mean something to teaching and learning. If it is to be small and limited, many changes in values may be ignored.

Pritzkau has noted that teachers and administrators block the admission of altered values by failing to understand children's environment, by limiting the environment within which children learn, by fearing to deal with certain values that seem inappropriate, crude or immoral, by being unwilling to go beyond the bounds of a teacher's alleged responsibility, and by ignoring differences in values.[2] The result may be instruction in unreality or, as some have charged, effort by the school to prevent learning. The curriculum worker can find many instances of the school's failure to allow for differences in values. In his own teaching experience, for example, he may have faced a pupil population for whom the word "isn't" came naturally. By listening to a new and strange pupil population that has recently come into the schools, he may have learned that, to this population, "isn't" sounds stilted. Outside school, the pupils trade "isn't" for the more natural-sounding "ain't." In a case like this, teachers must decide whether a previously-forbidden word is to be admitted to children's school experience frequently, seldom, sometimes, or never.

[2] Philo T. Pritzkau, *Dynamics of Curriculum Improvement*. Englewood Cliffs, N.J.: Prentice-Hall, Inc., 1959, pp. 176–181.

ACTIVITY 3-1—A SPECIAL PROBLEM IN RECOGNIZING AND MEETING DIFFERENCES IN VALUES

According to Louis Raths, "The evidence is clear that in its [the school's] distribution of rewards and punishments, the former go, out of all proportion, to the middle- and upper-class students; the penalties go, out of all proportion, to the lower social classes. There is evidence that our tests of intelligence are biased in the kinds of problems presented, and in the words chosen to present those problems. The bias is in the direction of favoring the middle- and the upper-class children. Participation in extracurricular activities is shown to distinguish between lower- and middle-class children. Prizes, honors, and awards go, in much higher proportion than their numbers suggest, to the middle- and upper-class children. The high grades on reports to parents and reports to colleges go to the children of the middle and upper classes in much larger numbers than their proportion of the school population. The curriculum materials, represented by the beginning primers and readers, are shown to be a product of middle-class living; hence, probably of more interest to middle-class children than to others."[3]

To what extent do these observations about the realities of school life square with the realities of social class structure in our society? How do you suppose the schools got themselves into the situation which Raths describes?

As a curriculum worker, what concrete actions might you take to develop and use teaching methods and materials designed to correspond more closely to the values held by differing social classes?

4. SOCIETAL PRESSURES ON THE SCHOOLS

Every age brings its own kinds of pressures upon the schools. It is true that some pressures, like the demand to "toughen up" in dealing with children and youth, have remained recurrent if not continuous throughout the history of education. But new times make for distinctly novel pressures. Within recent years, attacks have been mounted against elementary and secondary edu-

---

[3] Louis Raths, "Sociological Knowledge and Needed Curriculum Research," in James B. Macdonald, ed., *Research Frontiers in the Study of Children's Learning.* Milwaukee: School of Education, University of Wisconsin, 1960, p. 21.

cation with enough vigor to have a powerful effect in altering the nature of schooling. Educators have been attacked, said the editor of *Saturday Review* in 1954, for seeking to keep the schools to themselves and for themselves, for using professional jargon to separate and mystify, for shelving or replacing the three R's, for advocating and advancing "Pragmatism," for being anti-religious, and for being disloyal and subversive.[4]

Lately, a major charge against educators has been their conservatism in failing to promote certain reforms in education rapidly enough. The pressure for reform has come, in many instances, from persons and organizations having no official connection with the schools. For whatever the fact implies, ideas and movements in both elementary and secondary education have originated to some extent with individuals and groups who have never taught in or administered a school.

In some communities, the schools have recently been urged to teach "the fundamentals," to restore discipline, to emphasize moral and religious values, to oppose disloyalty to our government, to reduce expenditures, to prepare youth better for making a living, to discontinue preempting the functions of the home, and to return education to the people.[5] Persons from outside the schools who are presently influencing curriculum development have been said to reflect the changing viewpoints of Americans, as well as certain economic forces, our people's deeply-held fears and values, the pressures of a growing population, accelerating developments in science and technology, and events beyond our borders.[6] At the present time, the professionals in education often find their publics indicating that the curriculum is "much too important to be left to educators."[7]

Curriculum leaders usually raise no serious objection to this position, as long as it does not mean lay involvement in matters which school personnel consider to be strictly professional. As they listen to adverse criticism, these leaders tend to forget a significant fact: public opinion remains generally supportive of the work being accomplished by the schools, a fact often confirmed by public opinion polls. Curriculum personnel may well take an openminded attitude toward proposals for educational change. Some of these personnel are insisting, however, that these proposals be tested whenever they can be, lest

[4] Norman Cousins, "The Great Debate in American Education," *Saturday Review*, September 11, 1954, pp. 11–13 and 47.

[5] Frederick W. Terrien, "The Sociology of the Attacks on the Schools," *California Journal of Secondary Education*, March, 1962, pp. 134–141.

[6] Don A. Orton, "Issues Raised by Changes in Secondary Education," *School Review*, Vol. 69, No. 1, Spring, 1961, pp. 1–10.

[7] Louis J. Rubin, "The State of Affairs in Curriculum Development," *Journal of Secondary Education*, Vol. 36, No. 2, February, 1961, p. 95.

inferior innovations be allowed to affix themselves to educational systems which are already overburdened with unjustified traditional practices. Surely educators must help to clarify further the distinction between tasks for professionals and tasks for laymen, a distinction which still remains partially unclear. (The whole matter of the roles of personnel who are inside and outside school systems is discussed in Chapter 9.)

ACTIVITY 3-2—HOW MUCH FEDERAL CONTROL?

One of the current issues in American education is the extent of control of local schools by federal authority. Some educators maintain that, to balance the many pressures on American schools and to provide a stabilizing force in elementary and secondary education, we need a strengthened United States Office of Education, or some other powerful federal agency. Little has been said about what such an agency would do to make its influence felt without infringing upon responsibilities of local boards of education and their employees.

Think about ways, if any, in which you would strengthen federal influence or control in curriculum matters.

Just how far would you go in strengthening federal influence or control? What specific help could the federal government give in balancing the pressures which are now being applied to schools by groups in the society at large?

INFLUENCES WITHIN THE IMMEDIATE COMMUNITY

The individual community has been called the real locus of decision-making concerning the curriculum. In a sense, this is true. In the classroom, one finds teachers and children making decisions that are fundamental, day-to-day curriculum decisions. However, as we have seen, master planning of educational programs in a wholesale manner has recently tended to leave the local scene. Some persons maintain that there is little control of significant matters now being left to boards of education and administrators in local school districts.[8] Other persons, recognizing that every school district does

[8] Thomas D. Bailey, "The Folklore of Local Control," *Education Digest*, Vol. 27, No. 6, February, 1962, pp. 15–17,

have its own board of control, continue to talk freely about the importance of local decision-making.

Actually, the issue revolves about the meaning of the term "significant matters." Certainly communities now have, and will probably continue to have, a great deal to say about the curriculum in their own local schools, especially about the efficiency or inefficiency of the teachers employed. But some important curriculum decisions, *e.g.*, in determining broad educational objectives, may eventually pass from their hands. At present, two state governments—those of Delaware and North Carolina—maintain direct control over the schools within their boundaries, chiefly by keeping a tight hold on appropriation of funds. This system of state control could be extended elsewhere; it could yield to greater federal control of the curriculum; or private groups might spread their influence in the direction of increased, nationwide conformity.

Of course, the school is only *one* of the community agencies that contributes to education. Child development specialists say that more education than we realize occurs before the child is four years old; and observers with a comprehensive view of education report the impact of parents, youth-serving organizations, and other community groups on learners. Curriculum workers are involved in a continuing controversy as to who has responsibility for particular efforts to educate children and youth. In the areas of sex education, religion, driver training, and the social graces, they encounter many differences of opinion about the locus of educational responsibility. With some educators suspecting that the schools have already absorbed too much responsibility for child welfare from the community at large, discussions of the total role of the school are now being conducted in many communities.

As improved communication causes the nation "to shrink in size," more groups of citizens who belong to national organizations promote the programs of these organizations within their own communities. In the view of the National Education Association's chief executive officer:

> Each of these groups is anxious to avoid overloading the curriculum. All any of them ask is that the nonessentials be dropped in order to get their material in. Most of them insist that they don't want a special course—they just want their ideas to permeate the entire daily program. Every one of them proclaims a firm belief in local control of education and an apprehensive hatred of national control. Nevertheless, if their national program in education is not adopted forthwith, many of them use the pressure of the press, the radiance of the radio, and all the props of propaganda to bypass the elected school board.[9]

[9] William G. Carr, "The Public and the Public Schools," *The National Elementary Principal*, Vol. 36, No. 2, October, 1956, p. 19.

Here, Dr. Carr was evidently thinking chiefly of persistent and harmful groups which are affiliated with national interests. Certain beneficent groups, including parents and leaders of industry, do aid schools through their very alliance with national organizations.

It is true that some community groups favor statewide or national uniformity in the curriculum, even though much that is known about learners and learning is solidly against uniformity. Two major advantages of uniformity are said to be certain financial economies and educational continuity when pupils transfer from district to district and from school to school. However, in the American democratic system, development of ideas in local communities and local schools needs to be encouraged, for people grow by participating in planning. Some of the consolidations of school districts which have occurred to date have seriously limited participation in planning at the community level. Presently, America has a wealth of resources and facilities for planning in and through communities, and the nation must decide whether it wishes to lose what DeTocqueville commended years ago: encouragement of groups of our people to volunteer for all kinds of community service.

American communities influence the schools in three basic ways: through the community's own needs, through the limits communities set on the curriculum of the school, and through the community's decision as to who shall receive schooling. The effect of local needs can be seen in rural communities which insist that the pupils in their schools study vocational agriculture. It was also exemplified some years ago in a community in which there was a high rate of school tardiness. Curriculum planners in the community at first suspected that there were too few alarm clocks in the homes, but a more thorough and realistic appraisal of the situation revealed that malnutrition was unusually prevalent. Children simply did not feel like getting out of bed to go to school; consequently, instruction in nutrition, as part of a whole community drive for better feeding of adults and children, became a curriculum mandate. Thus, vocational agriculture in one group of communities and nutrition in an individual community represent the numerous local needs which differ from region to region, from section of city to section of city, and from small town to small town throughout the nation.

Limitations which communities place on their school curricula were indicated recently by public feeling in Los Angeles concerning teaching about the internationalism represented by the United Nations, and particularly UNESCO. The National Council of Teachers of English reports that the writings of Geoffrey Chaucer, William Shakespeare, Nathaniel Hawthorne, William Faulkner, Henry David Thoreau, Mark Twain, Walt Whitman, and other authors have been banned from the schools of many communities. Both school subjects and specific curriculum experiences have been eliminated by boards of education at the instance of community groups. A candidate for an instructional leadership position in a suburban community was known to have prepared a test which made allusion to, but did not recommend, sex education of high-school pupils. "Don't tell the board about your having written this test," the superintendent advised him. "We don't tolerate any reference to sex education in the schools of this community."

The tendency of communities to determine who shall receive schooling is sometimes evident in local unwillingness to establish nursery schools and kindergartens, even when state appropriation of funds encourages their establishment. A less negative example is the current planning of vocational and technical high schools and community colleges throughout the nation.

What a community expects of and will tolerate from its schools can be indicated roughly by surveys of community opinion. An informal questionnaire administered recently in Mamaroneck, New York, included the following items with which respondents were to express agreement or disagreement:

> If a new teaching technique sounds reasonable to our teachers, the school system is justified in trying it out.
>
> Secondary-school students have an ample number of courses from which to choose.
>
> If schools would do a good job of teaching the three "R's," this would be sufficient.
>
> Schools should rate bright children on the same standards as they rate slow children.
>
> Placing fourth- and fifth-graders together in one class might be desirable in some circumstances.
>
> Foreign language instruction as part of the elementary program is desirable.
>
> (From the Office of the Superintendent of Schools, Mamaroneck, New York, undated)

Responses to questionnaires have limited value unless the meanings which respondents intend to express are explored. Determining meaning can be accomplished through interviews and small-group reactions which confirm support for certain projects and provide warnings against launching others.

Inevitably, the curriculum is based firmly in home-school-community relationships, and school-community planning is therefore much needed. The great majority of American citizens live in communities containing fewer than 10,000 people. Many such communities are quite isolated despite improvements in transportation and communication, and where they are not isolated physically the people in them are isolated psychologically, often by their own choice. Both the traditions and the planning that touch people are grounded in local communities, so it seems unlikely that the power and influence of the community in educational decision-making will be forever lost. Such power and influence are enhanced by a psychological fact: learners are best equipped to explore and talk about their own environment; yet they need to have some aspects of it clarified for them. Accordingly, more school assignments should probably be centered in the world of the child, and fewer in the world and the universe at large. "How I Diagnose My Own Fears" might be a more worthwhile composition title than "What the Astronauts Will Find on the Moon." One of the real obligations of the school is to help learners deal with conditions and situations that are in or near them. To this end, community resources should claim learners' attention in the form of resource files, directories to community assets and points of interest, and other aids.

ACTIVITY 3-3—A LIMITED STUDY OF ONE COMMUNITY

Identify a community you know reasonably well. By interviewing several leading citizens, including a board of education member and a first-line school administrator, learn what forces are at work in the community to change the curriculum. Inquire about the relative influence of groups which may be categorized as follows: industrial, labor, political, patriotic, professional, welfare, and health.

What specific groups seem to wield the greatest influence?

How have these groups become so powerful? Who are the persons in the community who direct their activities?

What do you generalize from your findings concerning direction, strength, and necessary control of the community's influences upon the curriculum?

STRATEGIES FOR USING SOCIAL INFLUENCES

Experience and current observation supply the curriculum worker with several strategies which he may use in dealing with society-wide and community influences. The implication here is not that he should seek to resist these influences but that he should use them intelligently as aids to curriculum planning.

First, the curriculum worker needs to be as openminded as he can be about influences that affect the schools. While not all influences are benign, they all deserve hearing and consideration. Too often educational leaders have been said to take a proprietary attitude toward "their" schools, or to be possessive or defensive about existing programs. In the view of some commentators, they have shown too little interest in what the public has had to say, perhaps because they themselves were insecure or were insensitive to the feelings of others.[10] A point of view which may well be taken is that the schools belong to the people, who employ professional personnel to administer and operate them. These personnel, as professionals, should be autonomous in much that they do, but they must also listen to what other citizens are saying and have said. They must work with persons who are living, but their wisdom comes also from their knowledge of the past and their own estimates of the future.

Second, the curriculum worker needs to lead in using social influences. As he welcomes ideas, so also he must help school staffs square the ideas with theory and practice, and must see that assumptions and premises are tested. He should urge citizens who have ideas to spend time advancing them, but he must recognize at the same time that arguments as to whether two and two make four are fruitless, and that persons whose only contact with schools occurred 25 years ago as pupils are definitely *not* educational authorities. When the curriculum worker listens, he should also inform. The need is for dialogue rather than a hearing of witnesses.

Third, the curriculum worker should consider fully the feelings of Americans about education, and should act according to his best diagnosis of those feelings. Generally speaking, Americans take great pride in their schools. Most of the time they are complacent about them, but in moments of real or imagined crisis they become worried and anxious. Someone has said that Americans are satisfied in general with their schools, and are dissatisfied in particular. Accordingly, the curriculum person must serve as a troubleshooter of dissatisfactions—but not, of course, on every occasion. All of us have difficulty in knowing when to counterattack and when to remain quiescent, but school personnel seem to have been oversensitive during recent years to every wind of criticism and complaint. Basically, the public's attitudes toward the schools are more favorable than superintendents and other school leaders believe. The public wants to know mainly whether the schools are moving forward, and in what directions. The curriculum leader should lead the planning for movement, and should cause the plans to be known and talked about.

[10] See, for instance, Logan M. Anderson, editorial in *Phi Delta Kappan*, November, 1955, pp. 57 and 58.

Fourth, the curriculum worker should recognize that he is operating in a special dynamic. The profession which he serves has not been noted for attracting power to itself, probably because teachers behave "like teachers," and are expected to behave thus. In the past, the image of the teacher has been one of a feminine, middle-class, unmarried, white, Protestant, conservative individual without strong community influence. The curriculum person has real responsibility for encouraging teachers to move outside their own milieu, so that they may learn from other institutions, agencies, and individuals, and may contribute to them. One of the teacher's occupational diseases reveals itself in his talking too much to himself and other teachers. The potential of teachers as both contributors and listeners to the community can scarcely be exaggerated. When teachers are seen in a new and better light, other citizens soon help them redesign and reinterpret their role.

Finally, the curriculum leader must realize that he is deep in politics. His is not the politics of the ward-heeling variety but of strategic planning which requires balancing of pressures and cooperative making of policy. Educators should probably stop talking about the administrator's "community relations" and talk instead about his ability as a competent and constructive politician.[11] The curriculum leader is inevitably concerned with pressure groups and with allocations of public funds. These two areas of his responsibility alone thrust him into the realm of politics. Recently Mackenzie has advanced the notion that curriculum development moves through three stages: identification of focus, development of curriculum proposals, and implementation through teaching. These stages correspond to Harold Lasswell's three stages in political decision-making: pre-outcome, outcome, and post-outcome.[12] Mackenzie suggests several propositions which may eventually help curriculum workers understand the politics of their field. For instance:

1. Federal and state personnel are now having increased influence on identification of focus and development of curriculum proposals. (Example: teaching of language under the National Defense Education Act)

2. Local personnel have most influence at the stage called implementation through teaching. (Example: new mathematics programs in the elementary schools)

3. When a single participant has access to influential resources or symbols, curriculum outcomes will reflect his goals. (Example: James B. Conant)

[11] See Thomas H. Eliot, "Toward an Understanding of Public School Politics," *Teachers College Record*, Vol. 62, No. 2, November, 1960, pp. 118–132.

[12] Harold D. Lasswell, *Politics: Who Gets What, When, How.* Cleveland: Meridian Books, Inc., 1958.

4. When two or more participants having access to influential resources or symbols are mutually supportive of one another, speed of movement toward their goals will be increased. (Example: the Trump Plan, sponsored by the National Association of Secondary School Principals and supported by the Ford Foundation)[13]

Additional propositions could, of course, be formulated. Politicians proceed according to tried and tested beliefs about ways in which man as a political animal customarily behaves. Though the idea may offend some individuals, it is possible that curriculum planners will need to become, in future years, minor and benevolent Talleyrands. If they do, making and testing propositions like those above will become one of their conscious tasks. Surely there are signs that curriculum improvement is moving, on a national front, into the realm of politics as big projects develop and as supporting and competing interests vie with each other.

ACTIVITY 3-4—THE SITE AT WHICH POLITICAL POWER SHOULD BE APPLIED

"The most important election is a school board election," said a candidate for the board in his community.

"If I wanted to affect education permanently and importantly," said a candidate for Congress, "I'd try to influence governors, presidents, and Congressmen."

"Times and places determine which of you is more nearly right," said an impartial citizen.

Analyze each of these statements to determine which of them you favor. Give full reasons for your answer.

In the preceding pages, the curriculum worker has been adjured to be openminded about social influences, to exert leadership in using these influences, to understand people's feelings about the schools, to appreciate basic weaknesses in his own profession, and to regard himself as a practical politician. If we return to our initial discussion of society and community as they influence the schools, we see possible strategies for the curriculum worker in another dimension. Beyond the attitudes and understandings he must have, he needs among his strategies certain concrete actions for dealing directly with the influences discussed in the first sections of the chapter.

[13] From a presentation at the Curriculum Crossroads Conference, Teachers College, Columbia University, October 31, 1961.

If tradition is sometimes beneficent, curriculum personnel must find specific traditions that are good, and then see that these traditions are strengthened and used. For instance, certain patriotic observances fall within this category. The curriculum worker's object is to make them more impressive in educating the young in love of country, and then to place them as high as seems desirable on the agenda of experiences which the school provides. Curriculum improvement should never be labeled as action to destroy the desirable learnings of the human race.

Curriculum workers should also take direct responsibility for channelling social and cultural change constructively within the school. For some persons, this action may evade the question as to whether the educator should serve in his own right as a social reconstructionist. Whatever his position concerning his role as a social engineer, he must recognize and use influences that burst upon the school from both ultimate society and immediate community. For example, while he cannot govern the changes in population that occur in his school or school system, sometimes he must provide for children with backgrounds different from any he has known previously.

When social values are unclear to both adults and children, the curriculum worker should urge that much time be spent in helping children clarify their values. In a free society, citizens who do not know what they believe are a danger to the society and therefore to themselves. On key issues of morality, patriotism, and ethical standards, learners should be schooled in the alternatives, but where a decision is inevitably one-way they should know what the way is. Cheating on examinations is dishonest, whatever its causes. Juvenile delinquency is a serious social ill, and alcoholism is a serious personal disease with dire social consequences, whatever may have caused either of them. There is clearly no sense in fencing with hard reality. In order that values may be clear, the methodology of value formation and reformation should be taught. Respect for cause-and-effect relationships, testing of one's present values against evidence, and the origin and development of a philosophy of life are but three of the matters to be treated in a school where creation and re-creation of value structures are a concern.

Sometimes curriculum personnel find ways to turn hostile pressures to the advantage of their schools. Too little is known about this action, though an occasional Horatio Alger-like story is heard about turning inimical forces (which seek to counter the desirable things we know should be done for children) into helpful ones. For example, a violent opponent of a tried and tested reading or social studies program is induced to help study it, and remains to participate in modifying the program and then to support it in its revised form. In some instances, human relations skills of the high order discussed in some of the literature of industrial psychology achieve the desired result. Surely curriculum personnel need to know more and more of these skills. At times, however, they will have to stand and resist, particularly when the subject under attack is in reality a cover-up for dangerous, continuing hostility.

An additional action which curriculum personnel should take is encouraging community members to involve themselves appropriately in curriculum improvement. Though general guidelines to involvement can be developed, the act of skillfully involving people can only partially be described. It is easy to say, for instance, that committees of laymen should be formed for definite purposes and with definite life expectancy, but forming and dissolving them smoothly demands unspeakable human relations skills. One of the special responsibilities of the curriculum worker in his interaction with laymen is to help them think thoroughly about both the local and the nationwide contributions of the schools. Since control of the schools is being divided increasingly among local, state, and national agencies of government, people in American communities should face the need to examine critically the whole range of authority and responsibility for schools, specifically to determine how much control is to leave the grass-roots level to be installed in national centers.

America is entering upon an era in which social forces are likely to influence curriculum planning as never before. Increase in leisure time and still greater ease of transportation and communication will, in themselves, make lay participation in curriculum improvement more and more likely. Finally, social changes will probably multiply rapidly as men, machines, and influences move more speedily in the world of tomorrow.

ACTIVITY 3-5—WHICH WILL YOU HAVE?

Consider the following continuum. Only you can decide your own position along it.

The school isolated ← A position somewhere → The school involved
from the   between the extremes   with and busily re-
community   making the com-
                                                                            munity

With respect to your position, answer these questions:

Shall the school remain as separate as possible from the community?

Shall the school be made to serve as a model of the community as it presently exists?

Shall the school help to remake the community?

Consider and discuss these related issues:

1. What shall the school do about the mores and values which large numbers of community members respect? Provide examples of mores and values you have in mind as you discuss this issue.

2. What shall the school do about treating controversial issues which abound in our society? Be specific about particular issues.

3. What shall the school do about accepting tasks which other institutions and agencies are not performing or are performing poorly? Give examples of tasks.

4. What shall the school do about the social class values which pupils presently hold? Provide examples of values held by two or three different social classes, as listed: upper-upper, lower-upper, upper-middle, lower-middle, upper-lower, lower-lower.

SUMMARY

Social forces have always had a strong effect in the making of curriculum decisions. Some of these forces have originated, and continue to originate, in the wider society and culture in which man lives. Still other forces develop within communities. Curriculum personnel must reckon with social forces without resenting them or their multiple origins, but the educator has a special responsibility to relate them to elementary and secondary education in ways which will benefit children and youth, who are the precious clientele of the schools.

SELECTED BIBLIOGRAPHY

Association for Supervision and Curriculum Development, *Forces Affecting American Education*, 1953 Yearbook (Washington, D.C.: The Association, 1953).

Campbell, R. F., and J. A. Ramseyer, *The Dynamics of School-Community Relationships* (Boston: Allyn and Bacon, Inc., 1955).

Cook, L. A., and E. F. Cook, *A Sociological Approach to Education,* Second Edition (New York: McGraw-Hill Book Co., Inc., 1957).

Havighurst, Robert J., and Bernice L. Neugarten, *Society and Education* (Boston: Allyn and Bacon, Inc., 1957).

Heffernan, Helen, "Goals for Education," *Childhood Education,* September, 1961, pp. 4–10.

Lieberman, Myron, *The Future of Public Education* (Chicago: University of Chicago Press, 1960).

Melby, E. O., *Administering Community Education* (Englewood Cliffs, N.J.: Prentice-Hall, Inc., 1954).

Meltzer, B. N., H. R. Doby, and P. M. Smith, *Education in Society: Readings* (New York: Thomas Y. Crowell Company, 1958).

Menge, J. W., and R. C. Faunce, *Working Together for Better Schools* (New York: American Book Company, 1958).

Mercer, B. E., and E. R. Carr, *Education and the Social Order* (New York: Holt, Rinehart & Winston, Inc., 1957).

National Society for the Study of Education, *Social Forces Influencing American Education,* 60th Yearbook, Part II (Chicago: University of Chicago Press, 1961).

Olsen, E. G., *et al., School and Community,* Revised Edition (Englewood Cliffs, N.J.: Prentice-Hall, Inc., 1954).

President's Commission on National Goals, *Goals for Americans* (Englewood Cliffs, N.J.: Prentice-Hall, Inc., 1960).

Raths, Louis, "Sociological Knowledge and Needed Curriculum Research," in Macdonald, James B., ed., *Research Frontiers in the Study of Children's Learning* (Milwaukee: School of Education, University of Wisconsin, 1960).

Stanley, William O., *et al., Social Foundations of Education* (New York: The Dryden Press, 1956).

Stearns, H. L., *Community Relations and the Public Schools* (Englewood Cliffs, N.J.: Prentice-Hall, Inc., 1955).

chapter four

SCHOOLS HAVE ALWAYS TAUGHT SUBJECT-MATTER. This gratuitous statement would indeed be unnecessary if the notion had not been created during recent years that American schools try to teach *children* instead of subject-matter. It is, of course, impossible to teach human beings without teaching them something.

During the 1950's, Americans lived in an era in which people were becoming concerned about whether subject-matter was "hard" or "soft" and, when it was considered to be soft, what could be done to make it harder. Some schools sought to toughen the curriculum by teaching a greater quantity of the same content more demandingly. This effect was especially noticeable in secondary education, where 40 algebra problems of the same kind replaced the original 20, and where the parsing of 20 sentences was magnified into the parsing of 40. Little was being learned about selection of subject-matter among alternative possibilities because, even before the scare about Russia's Sputnik, a major object was to teach content which had been in the books long enough to be respectable. American teachers had learned that almost anything they taught could be made too difficult for pupils to learn, or so easy as to prove frustrating, but most of them apparently did not believe, with the investi-

Subject-Matter:
Its Role in
Decision-Making

gators in the Eight Year Study, that what one learned was often less significant than the way one went about learning it.

Of course, teachers had to face certain necessary perennial questions about subject-matter. In counseling individual pupils, they had to decide in a given case whether an extra year of science would serve better than a year of home economics. Insightful teachers wanted learners to have "balanced" programs; by this, they meant well-rounded ones. At the classroom level, they were concerned somewhat with improving the quality of teacher-pupil planning, but they showed greater interest in selecting textbooks and other aids to enrich their classroom procedures. Their decision-making about content selection stemmed from two classic sources: the nature of the learner and the learning process, and the impact of society at large and the local community upon the school. Now, in the 1960's, an additional source for decision-making is being consciously tapped: the nature and uses of subject-matter itself. The present chapter will concern itself with the function of subject matter alone in conditioning the curriculum. We shall return, in Chapter 5, to the whole matter of deciding what to teach in terms of bases additional to the nature of subject-matter as a single factor.

A NEW ERA IN THE SCHOOLS

The nature of subject-matter has come to the fore as a criterion of content selection, and thus of curriculum improvement, for three major reasons:

1. Knowledge has exploded to a point at which it is necessary to select for teaching those items of knowledge that seem most significant, and to eliminate much that is inconsequential.

2. Subject specialists have recently had more to say about the nature of their fields, and about the teaching of these fields.

3. Experiments are being directed toward showing that subject-matter, old and new, can be placed in previously unthought-of locations in the life space of learners.

The effect on elementary and secondary schools of each of these factors will be discussed below.

THE EXPLOSION OF KNOWLEDGE

The new era, whose significance in the annals of American education is still uncertain, finds its basis in a monumental explosion of knowledge. A current estimate holds that more gains have been made in the world's knowledge in any recent year than in 100,000 years of the Stone Age, and Robert Oppenheimer says that knowledge is doubling every eight-and-a-half to twelve years. Anyone who views the educational scene at all perceptively can see that there is much more to be known than can possibly be comprehended, more in print than can be read, and much more which no one has time to put into writing or even to express in voice recording. Increase in knowledge is, however, only part of the problem. Knowledge is useless unless it is made grist for the mill of understanding. As knowledge increases, the time available to combine it into usable concepts decreases, so that the learner asks repeatedly, "What meaning can these new findings have for my life and the lives of others?" Quandary develops in the act of finding meaning in a world of too many facts and too many affairs.

Furthermore, the process of increasing knowledge is not merely an additive one. As knowledge abounds, some of that which was known previously is negated and must be discarded. Thus, physics textbooks which were completely usable ten years ago are partially obsolete in a new era of atomic fission, hydrogen weapons, space exploration, and space communication. Unfortunately, the colleges have not prepared students of the subject-fields to distinguish important elements of subject-matter from unimportant ones. The fact is that few college teachers have thought very much about the content they teach. Instead, they find it easier to follow the traditional organization of subject-matter which they themselves received ready-made from their college teachers. Meanwhile large blocks and little pieces of knowledge which are newly-discovered overburden old plans of subject-matter organization, and the teacher becomes more and more perplexed about how he will "cover all the material."

As one looks carefully at the ways in which knowledge is being compounded, he recognizes the multiplicity of these ways: 1) Knowledge which was once a piece of a whole has now become a whole. In mathematics, the theory of sets was once vaguely implied in the solution of certain mathematical problems. Today it is, in itself, a recognized subject-matter entity. Like other new entities, however, its relative position in the whole range of subject-matter is still unclear. 2) Blocks of knowledge which have formerly been accepted are suddenly destroyed as entities. The unaffiliated pieces remain, but they no longer form a context or design. This happened to the construct known as Newtonian physics. Part of what was believed by Newton and those who followed him is valid today, but Newtonian physics as an entity has been superseded by a newer physics which may conceivably be superseded in the future. 3) The number of theories and hypotheses about phenomena is increasing. Though many of them remain untested, those which are being tested suggest new combinations of the items of knowledge. Examples may be found especially in newer fields like psychology, which abounds in theories and hypotheses about individuals, groups, learning, and other concerns. 4) Specialization has become a phenomenon of modern life. More practitioners are engaging in small segments of practice, and researchers are looking more and more deeply into narrower and narrower expanses of content. A case in point is the field of biology, in which specialization has grown strikingly.

THE ADVENT OF SUBJECT SPECIALISTS

Concurrently with this reshuffling of knowledge, subject specialists have concerned themselves directly with elementary and secondary schooling. Previously, they were content to discover knowledge, to report it to other specialists, and occasionally to write textbooks for colleges and schools. Many of the textbooks were written from the viewpoint of the mature scholar and could therefore not be appreciated fully by youngsters in our schools. The explosion of knowledge has, with other factors, caused scholars to think directly about subject-matter content that is truly basic to learning additional content, and to learning in depth. Some of the wisest scholars in subject-matter fields, unlike the professor of chemistry who suddenly became an "expert" in the teaching of arithmetic, tell educators what is most important to be learned in their respective fields, and then leave to the educators the complex task of determining where, when, how, and to whom the content should be taught. Within recent years, however, scholars have been trying their hand directly at designing curricula for children and youth. Says Professor Bruner, who describes the situation that existed in 1959:

> Major efforts in curriculum design had been launched by leading physicists, mathematicians, biologists, and chemists, and similar projects were in prospect in other fields of scientific endeavor. Something new was stirring in the land. A tour of the United States in the summer of 1959 would have revealed a concentration of distinguished mathematicians in Boulder, Colorado, engaged in writing new textbooks for primary, junior high, and high-school grades. In Kansas City, there could be found a group of first-class biologists busily producing films on subjects such as the structure of the cell and photosynthesis for use in tenth-grade biology courses. In Urbana, Illinois, there was a flurry of work on the teaching of fundamental mathematical concepts to grade-school children, and in Palo Alto one might have found a mathematical logician at work trying out materials for teaching geometry to children in the beginning grades of school. In Cambridge, Massachusetts, work was progressing on an "ideal" physics course for high-school students, engaging the efforts not only of text writers and film producers but also of men who had earned world renown in theoretical and experimental physics. At various centers throughout the country, teachers were being trained to teach this new physics course by others who had already tried it. Preliminary work was under way in Boulder on a junior high-school course in biology, and a group of chemists were similarly engaged in their field in Portland, Oregon. Various learned societies were searching for and finding ways of establishing contact between their leading scholars and educators in the schools.[1]

Since 1959, the interest of scholars in school curriculum has scarcely abated. Rather, it has been intensified by national professional organizations and by vast expenditures of funds by foundations and government. The scholars are learning that their publications are sometimes inappropriate or too difficult, that their attempts to influence teachers and administrators tend to be oversimplified and ill-conceived, and that medium-sized and small schools are hard to reach and impress. On the other hand, the scholars' per-

[1] Jerome S. Bruner, *The Process of Education.* Cambridge, Mass.: Harvard University Press, 1961, pp. vii and viii.

sonal prestige helps their cause in an era in which movement for reform seems to originate chiefly outside the school rather than within it. In general, cooperation between scholars in subject-matter fields and professional educators is improving as each group recognizes that the other has a special role and competence. Cooperation is probably poorest in isolated situations like that in San Francisco, in which the "Conservative Revolution" produced a survey report prepared by scholars who prescribed how subject-matter outside their specialties should be taught to pupils in elementary and secondary schools.[2]

EXPERIMENTS IN THE PLACEMENT OF SUBJECT-MATTER

While there has always been a certain amount of experimentation with subject-matter placement, experimentation on a larger scale is now in progress. Obviously large-scale experimentation cannot be left to the individual teacher who, in a lifetime, will achieve only a limited rearrangement of what he teaches. What subject-matter should be moved up the grade scale? What should be moved down? What can children learn that has heretofore seemed beyond their capabilities? These are a few of the questions to which more and more answers are being sought.

Various experiments in rearranging old subject-matter and adopting new subject-matter are under way. Many of these experiments suggest that portions of content might be taught earlier in pupils' development than they have been heretofore, and that teachers are taking longer than is necessary to help children build certain fundamental understandings.

In Denver, five-year-olds are being taught basic reading skills in kindergarten. Reading readiness programs have existed in American kindergartens for years, but few kindergarten teachers have taught children to look at printed words, to listen to the words in spoken context, to think of their initial sounds, and then to decide what the words are. In Denver, parents are being prepared by television and other means to teach their children reading at home.[3]

The curriculum committee of the National Science Teachers Association has recommended that pupils have some experience with all science concepts before they leave elementary school. Part of the content which was formerly taught in junior high-school general science courses is now taught in elementary schools. In senior high schools, science which was formerly taught

[2] *Report of the San Francisco Curriculum Survey Committee.* San Francisco: San Francisco Unified School District, 1960.

[3] *Insight*, a publication of Science Research Associates, Chicago, Spring, 1962.

superficially to junior high-school pupils has been incorporated within more sophisticated science courses.

At the Hamden Hall Country Day School in Connecticut, Omar Khayyam Moore has had two- and three-year-olds teaching themselves how to read and write. He does it by permitting them to play with special electric typewriters until they become curious enough to form and read words. The special typewriter gives the children the sounds of letters and words they form by striking the keys. Soon the children associate what they hear with what they write. Subsequently, some of them listen to words they type from lists. The children learn touch-system typing by having their fingernails painted to correspond in color with given keys of the typewriter.[4]

Other experimentation has led to the tentative conclusion that some subject-matter is being taught too early. In the "new arithmetic," for instance, one conclusion is that children learn certain basic number-concepts with more understanding if these concepts are introduced later in the primary grades.

These are but a few of the experiments with placement of content which are now in progress. Many more will surely follow.

ACTIVITY 4-1—FINDING REASONS FOR CHANGES IN SUBJECT-MATTER PLACEMENT

In a time of fast-moving changes in subject-matter placement, the reasons for changes should be found. It is important to know whether given changes are justified or unjustified.

To learn what changes have occurred, 1) talk with school principals or other persons who see the curriculum as a whole, or 2) compare recently-published textbooks and other teaching materials with materials published ten years ago. To get behind the facts, ask teachers why they have made specific changes in subject-matter placement. Try to learn whether these changes have resulted chiefly from: 1) copying what other teachers have done, 2) falling in with what seem to be national trends, 3) experimenting informally with subject-matter to see whether one's pupils learn it readily and well, or 4) following the results of research which is reported in publications or which is done in one's own professional environment. Learn

---

[4] John Chamberlain, "Reading at Age Three," *The Wall Street Journal,* May 12, 1961. Comments about this experiment by specialists in mental health have been directed recently toward possible hazards to the mental health of the participating children.

whether the teachers feel satisfied with the new placement of subject-matter *as compared with the former placement.*

What do you conclude about the reasons which operate in subject-matter placement?

What, in your opinion, should be done to make changes in placement more judicious?

RECONSIDERING SUBJECT-MATTER AS LEARNING CONTENT

Within very recent years, subject-matter as learning content has been examined more critically than ever before. There is much talk about the role of the various disciplines in learning, a *discipline* being defined by some persons both as a way of making knowledge and as the domain occupied by particularized knowledge. Thus, the phenomena of chemistry have been discovered by a given set of methods which are known to the chemist as a laboratory scientist; and the content the chemist has discovered is distinctively different from the content which has been discovered by the historian or the philosopher, or even by other scientists like the physicist and the biologist. Each discipline, according to the definition, has its own integrity, an integrity that is worth respecting because it has been built by the regulated efforts of so many intelligent and creative persons. A few authors, as they write about the disciplines, seem to be thinking of applications of organized knowledge, as in the field of medicine.

Some of the recent thinking about subject-matter as learning content has followed these lines: subject-matter includes what men know and believe, together with reflections of men's ideals and loyalties; or, subject-matter may validly be selected for use in teaching and learning when it is significant to an organized field of knowledge, when it has proved appropriate down through the years, when it is useful, when it can be made interesting to learners, and when it contributes to the growth and development of our society.[5] Of these criteria, the first is highlighted within the context of the present chapter. The criterion of significance to an organized field of knowledge implies that the items of knowledge within that field can be interrelated so that the structure which the items rationally form can be seen and understood. According to this thesis, there are big and significant principles or concepts on which lesser principles, concepts, and facts depend. A first, major task of the scholar and of the learner alike is to identify clearly these big

[5] B. Othanel Smith, William O. Stanley, and J. Harlan Shores, *Fundamentals of Curriculum Development*, Chapter 6. New York: Harcourt, Brace & World, Inc., 1957.

principles or concepts.[6] Thus, in the view of a leading economist, there are four principles on which all of economics depends. Know these and you have the "hooks" on which the minor principles and the facts of economics hang. The details of economics as a discipline may change, i.e., time may retire some of them, and new details may replace old ones, but the fundamental structure of economics will remain, and it is the fundamental structure that counts. While the fundamentals often develop from observation of details in the first place, the fixity and steadfastness of the fundamentals is a basic consideration in studying the structure of a discipline. Detail is hard to remember unless it is related to the fundamentals. Transfer of training, so long argued in American education, seems to proceed best when learners understand the fundamentals of what they are learning and transferring.

These ideas bring one to the thought that different elements in the structure of a discipline can be taught at different developmental levels. Thus, attention must be given to more than the facts of mere readiness as a function of the human organism. Readiness for *what?* becomes a central question. Piagét has maintained, in Bruner's expression, that "any subject can be taught effectively in some intellectually honest form to any child at any stage of development." This would mean, for instance, that some portions of algebra and geometry can be taught to children in the primary grades. (A few teachers are doing it.) These portions must necessarily be concrete. More importantly, they must accord with the child's perception of the world's phenomena. Piagét points out that children advance through three stages of development in learning subject-matter, and that young children tend to be at the first stage. At this stage, learners perceive phenomena in terms of their own experiences, and they try to establish relationships between their own experiences and the actions which are being taken. At the second stage, they engage in concrete operations with present phenomena, being competent enough to attempt trial-and-error experiments in their heads. At the third stage, they go beyond working with present phenomena to working with hypothetical ones.[7] Each successive stage calls for more abstract thinking, and a prime difficulty in selecting subject-matter is to find content which is abstract enough to challenge without being so abstract as to frustrate. When this is done, even crudely, it is possible to build a "spiral curriculum" in which the same subject, but not the identical subject-matter, is taught on several occasions during one's school experience. For example, selected portions of

----

[6] This idea and many additional ones in this section are developed in Bruner, *op. cit.*

[7] See Jean Piagét, *The Origins of Intelligence in Children.* New York: International Universities Press, Inc., 1953.

Design, with teachers of a subject you know well, several experiences which require pupils to discover the content of that subject. Work with the teachers as they use, refine, and evaluate the results of these experiences. Note, for your own subsequent reference, the ways teachers proceed in freeing pupils for discovery. Note also the materials they need in helping numbers of individuals with the discovery process. Observe what happens to individual pupils as they discover hidden abilities of their own in mastering subject-matter.

NEW DEVELOPMENTS IN SUBJECTS AND SUBJECT-FIELDS

Quite apart from the deeper consideration of subject-matter as learning content which has been described above, new developments have occurred in planning for instruction in subjects and subject-fields. The interest of subject specialists in these developments has been mentioned earlier in the chapter. The exact nature of several major developments should now be considered. First, however, certain general comments can be made about them. One comment is that the developments have often been made with either token or substantial support from foundations and government. Another is that they have taken into account some of the considerations in learning subject-matter which were described in the immediately preceding section of this chapter. Still another is that more of them have occurred in the secondary schools than in the elementary schools. A final comment is that persons who have planned them have given little thought to the process by which teachers are influenced to use new ideas.

The following two tables list pertinent facts about major instructional projects in elementary education and in secondary education. (Some of the projects which received their start in either elementary or secondary education have now become kindergarten-through-twelfth-grade projects, or projects covering a major portion of this span.)

PROJECTS PRIMARILY IN ELEMENTARY EDUCATION

Subject	Title and General Nature of Project	Description of Project
Science	University of California Elementary School Science Project (1959). Purpose: to permit university scientists to aid with curriculum improvement in elementary schools.	Has involved ten scientists and one educator in basic planning. Series of units written by teachers and writers. Tryout of units in elementary schools.

Subject	Title and General Nature of Project	Description of Project
Science	Science Curriculum Improvement Study (1961). Grew from the University of California Project described above.	Has concentrated on experiments in the nature and structure of science, to help pupils learn the points of view of science. Recommends bringing university personnel into elementary school classrooms to teach.
Science	Feasibility Study of the American Association for the Advancement of Science. Covers elementary and junior high-school grades, with a general science approach.	Seeks to build a cumulative elementary-through-junior high-school program with emphasis on discovery. Alternative materials being developed. Tryout of the materials arranged for.
Science	University of Illinois Elementary Science Project (1960). Concentrates on astronomy as an "interdisciplinary science."	Directed by an astronomer and an educator. Has prepared teaching materials on the plan of the universe and on gravitation. Tryout in schools. Teachers' manuals. Pre-tests and post-tests. Materials to be rewritten on the basis of tryout. Liaison with the University of California Project.
Mathematics	Syracuse-Webster Elementary Mathematics Project. Formerly The Madison Project. Now centered at Webster College, Missouri. Aims at discovery of the internal organization of mathematics.	Experimentation conducted in grades 3 through 10. Uses pupil discussions, based on a sequence of questions. Provides unstructured tasks, *e.g.*, finding the height of the school flag pole by methods invented by the pupils themselves.
Mathematics	University of Illinois Arithmetic Project. Designed to help the pupil learn all the mathematics he can.	Experimental classes, kindergarten through sixth grade, bent on discovery of "mathematical frameworks."
Mathematics	The Stanford Studies. Emphasis on the "new mathematics." Subprojects on geometry for the primary grades and mathematical logic for the schools.	Experimental classes using the theory of sets. Books titled *Geometry for Primary Grades*, Parts I and II, and *Mathematical Logic for the Schools*. Institutes for the orientation of teachers.
Mathematics	Greater Cleveland Mathematics Program, sponsored by the Educational Research Council of Greater Cleveland. Emphasizes how and why things happen in mathematics.	Designed for use in kindergarten through sixth grade; to be extended through the twelfth grade. Initial experimentation in three states. Pupil aids, training films, and manuals for teachers, guidebooks for parents.

Subject	Title and General Nature of Project	Description of Project
Modern Foreign Languages	Foreign Languages in the Elementary Schools, sponsored by the Modern Language Association and now endorsed with caution by the Association.	Fifteen to 30 minutes of instruction three to five times a week under direction of competent teachers is recommended by the Association. Project has been plagued by thoughtless adoption of language teaching by school systems. Has conducted conferences, and has prepared teachers' guides and teaching aids; is now using films and television.
Social Studies	Program for Improving the Teaching of World Affairs (1957), sponsored by the Glens Falls, New York, Board of Education and the National Council for the Social Studies, to help pupils understand and appreciate the peoples of the world.	A kindergarten-through-twelfth-grade project. Centered in the school system of Glens Falls, New York. Involves many teachers of this system. Has developed a library of resource materials.

PROJECTS PRIMARILY IN SECONDARY EDUCATION

Subject	Title and General Nature of Project	Description of Project
Science	Physical Science Study Committee, organized in 1957 at Massachusetts Institute of Technology. Purpose: to develop a modern physics course, especially for high-ability pupils.	Has prepared a syllabus, a textbook, laboratory apparatus, laboratory guides, 25-minute films, teachers' guides, and examinations. Has published a science study series in paperbacks. Tries out ideas and materials in schools. Emphasizes open-ended laboratory experiments and basic concepts concerning the universe, optics and waves, mechanics, and electricity. Conducts institutes for teachers.
Science	Chemical Bond Approach Project, organized in 1959 by five chemistry professors to fuse unrelated topics in high-school chemistry courses through emphasis on molecular and atomic structures.	Has a textbook, a laboratory guide, and achievement examinations, the last mentioned having been prepared by Educational Testing Service. Conducts tryouts in schools and teachers' institutes.
Science	Chemical Education Materials Study, designed to produce a variety of teaching materials in	Has prepared a teachers' guide to the materials, a draft textbook, and laboratory experiments, this

Subject	*Title and General Nature of Project*	*Description of Project*
	chemistry. Emphasis on discovery of principles by pupils.	work having been done under the direction of nine chemistry professors and nine high-school chemistry teachers.
Science	Biological Sciences Curriculum Study, instituted in 1959 by the American Institute of Biological Sciences. Develops three approaches to the biological sciences: the ecological and evolutionary, the genetic and developmental, and the biochemical and physiological.	Writing of textbooks, laboratory manuals, and teachers' guides done by 35 research biologists and 35 high-school teachers. Try-outs in schools. Developing "laboratory block" programs, which are experiments in depth. Special materials for gifted pupils. Institutes for teachers.
Science	Study of the Use of History of Science Cases. Develops cases in biology, chemistry, and physics showing science to be a "creative intellectual and social enterprise." Based at Harvard School of Education.	Has prepared teachers' manuals, slides, and the "Test on Understanding Science," revealing pupils' view of the social impact of science. Uses tryouts and regional consultants from nearby colleges.
Mathematics	Commission on Mathematics of the College Entrance Examination Board, which in 1956 designed a mathematics sequence for high schools which goes to analytical geometry and the calculus.	Issued a report and no other materials except a textbook on statistical inference and probability.
Mathematics	Secondary School Curriculum Committee of the National Council of Teachers of Mathematics, one of the few curriculum projects to consider the subject-matter needs of all high-school pupils.	Reviewed trends and proposals in mathematics teaching. Proposed changes in objectives and content. Urged: discovery and reduction of memorization; four years of mathematics for high-school pupils; earlier introduction of elements of algebra and geometry; "growth in depth" rather than a different program for gifted pupils.
Mathematics	University of Illinois Committee on School Mathematics (1952). Insists on the sequential nature of its four-year program, beginning with arithmetic of real numbers and moving to polynomial functions and complex numbers.	Has developed text materials and tried them in classrooms. Emphasizes discovery. Conducts summer institutes and supervisory follow-up of institutes. Is preparing training films on "discovery teaching."

Subject	Title and General Nature of Project	Description of Project
Mathematics	School Mathematics Study Group. Once at Yale, now at Stanford. Aims to introduce modern mathematics and deepen the teaching of current mathematics, especially for college-preparatory classes.	Involves college professors of mathematics, teacher-education personnel, and high-school teachers in preparing textbooks with teacher commentaries. Now writing a series of monographs on topics in mathematics.
Mathematics	University of Maryland Mathematics Project (1957). So far, has emphasized mathematics in seventh and eighth grades.	Involves departments of mathematics, psychology, education, and engineering in guiding preparation of units and teachers' manuals. Emphasizes learning through discovery; also early introduction of units in algebra and geometry.
English	Commission on English of the College Entrance Examination Board. Has highlighted language, literature, and composition.	Is developing "sample curricula" and three series of kinescopes showing teaching methods. Conducting institutes for teachers, with follow-up of teachers who have attended institutes.
Modern Foreign Languages	Modern Language Association's Testing Program. Purpose: to find better ways of evaluating learners' command of foreign language. Aided by subsidies under the National Defense Education Act.	Is developing tests of listening, speaking, reading and writing; especially proficiency tests for teachers and advanced students, which may be used to determine teacher competence and state certification.
Social Studies	High School Geography Project. Formed jointly by the Association of American Geographers and the National Council for Geographic Education.	Is developing a course on tape, with teachers' guides, maps, and other materials. Teachers cooperate with personnel from nearby colleges and universities in tryouts.

The preceding lists describe only some of the instructional projects which have been initiated within the past decade.[12] Most of the projects are in the sciences and mathematics, the subjects in which our teaching has allegedly been furthest behind that of the Russians. In part, study of the teaching of these subjects has been stimulated by appropriation of federal funds under the National Defense Education Act. The subject-field which has

[12] A useful compendium of these and other projects may be found in Dorothy M. Fraser, *Current Curriculum Studies in Academic Subjects* (a report prepared for the Project on Instruction). Washington, D.C.: National Education Association, 1962.

received next greatest emphasis under the Act is modern foreign language. Nearly $8,500,000 were committed by the federal government to 165 language projects during 1959, 1960, and 1961.[13] However, almost none of those 165 projects has received the attention which has been accorded the larger projects in the sciences and mathematics sponsored by private foundations and universities.

Several major projects have not been mentioned above. They include the Science Manpower Project at Teachers College, Columbia University; the Boston College Mathematics Institute; the Developmental Project in Secondary Mathematics at Southern Illinois University; and the Joint Project of the National Council for the Social Studies and the American Council of Learned Societies, in the field of social studies. New projects are constantly appearing. One of the more promising of these is that of the National Task Force on Economic Education, appointed by the American Economics Association and financed by the Committee for Economic Development. The work of this project is likely to influence teaching in both the social studies and business education in the years to come.

Organizations affiliated with the National Education Association are playing an important part in clarifying positions regarding subject-matter selection. For instance, the National Association of Secondary School Principals has issued "position papers" regarding the teaching of the social studies and English. The National Council of the Teachers of English has published a series of books on curriculum content and teaching methods in the English language arts.[14] Recently the Council has published a report, *The National Interest and the Teaching of English*, and more publications will follow.

In a time of national emergency, attention to the curriculum becomes skewed. Recently, we have had our share of interest in science, mathematics, and languages at the expense of the arts, literature, and the social sciences, but changes in the "neglected" fields have occurred to some extent without the presence of expensive projects. Among noticeable trends in the social studies, for example, are these: the non-Western world is receiving more attention; "hopping from country to country" is being discouraged in favor of more intensive study of selected countries; certain content, such as world history, is moving to new positions in the span of grades; and facilities and materials are gradually improving. However, no national commission or group

---

[13] *Ibid.,* p. 69.

[14] See *The English Language Arts.* New York: Appleton-Century-Crofts, Inc., 1952; *Language Arts for Today's Children.* New York: Appleton-Century-Crofts, Inc., 1954; and *The English Language Arts in the Secondary School.* New York: Appleton-Century-Crofts, Inc., 1956.

can be said to have effected a breakthrough in social studies teaching; teachers continue to teach bits of information without direct relevance to concept-development; and most changes in secondary-school social studies have involved merely the addition of a few new courses and realignment of course sequences, as well as minor improvements in materials, facilities, and uses of pupil time. One may, of course, raise the question, "What real improvements within these categories will the projects create?" The answer is unknown, but the assumption has long been that money and effort, properly applied, will surely achieve results.

Recently the Project on Instruction of the National Education Association asked a national sample of elementary-school principals to state the most important change which has been occurring in the elementary schools. Thirty-eight per cent of the respondents said this change was greater emphasis on content, especially in science and mathematics. Twenty-eight per cent said the greatest change was in methods and techniques of teaching; and fourteen per cent, in teaching materials.[15] Apparently, school personnel are much aware of the drive for changes in subject-matter which promises to intensify during the years immediately before us.

ACTIVITY 4-4—INFORMING ONESELF OF NEW PROJECTS IN INSTRUCTION

New projects will come, and older ones will go. To keep yourself informed of these events, turn to central sources which can supply you with information about persons and agencies to whom to write.

1. For current articles and monographs: *Education Index*, available in better-equipped libraries.
2. For general information about live, ongoing projects: The Project on the Instructional Program of the Public Schools, National Education Association, 1201 Sixteenth Street, N.W., Washington 6, D.C.
3. For information about testing programs affiliated with projects in instruction: Educational Testing Service, Princeton, N.J.
4. For information about developments in particular subjects and subject-fields: the subject organizations which are affiliated with the National Education Association; *e.g.*, National

[15] National Education Association, *The Principals Look at the Schools.* Washington, D.C.: The Association, 1962, p. 9.

Council of the Teachers of Mathematics, National Science Teachers' Association, National Council for the Social Studies, National Art Education Association, United Business Education Association, and Music Educators' National Conference. The common address of these organizations: 1201 Sixteenth Street, N.W., Washington 6, D.C. Other organizations have separate addresses: National Council of Teachers of English, 508 South Sixth Street, Champaign, Ill.; Modern Language Association (Program Research Center), 70 Fifth Avenue, New York 11, N.Y.

SUMMARY

Although schools have never existed without imparting subject-matter, the importance of the disciplines and of ordered ways of dealing with them has loomed larger in American education within the past few years. One of the reasons for this emphasis has been the realization that knowledge is increasing at a tremendous rate. Subject specialists have become curriculum planners by demonstrating new placements of subject-matter in school programs, and certain psychologists and educators have begun investigations of the structure of knowledge in a variety of subject-fields. Because of all this activity, the disciplines have been given an unaccustomed role in decision-making about the curriculum—a role which, in the thinking of many persons, places them in equal position with a) the nature of learners and the learning process, and b) the demands of society and the culture in determining what the curriculum shall be.

SELECTED BIBLIOGRAPHY

Association for Supervision and Curriculum Development, *New Insights and the Curriculum*, 1963 Yearbook (Washington, D.C.: The Association, 1963).

Bruner, Jerome S., *The Process of Education* (Cambridge, Mass.: Harvard University Press, 1961).

Foshay, Arthur W., "A Modest Proposal for the Improvement of Education," an address delivered at the 1961 convention of the Association for

Supervision and Curriculum Development; reprinted in *Educational Leadership*, Vol. 18, No. 8 (May, 1961).

Fraser, Dorothy M., *Current Curriculum Studies in Academic Subjects*, a report prepared for the Project on Instruction, National Education Association (Washington, D.C.: National Education Association, 1962).

Phenix, Philip H., "The Use of the Disciplines as Curriculum Content," Educational Forum, Vol. 26, No. 3 (March, 1962).

Piagét, Jean, *The Origins of Intelligence in Children* (New York: International Universities Press, Inc., 1953).

Project on Instruction, National Education Association, *The Principals Look at the Schools* (Washington, D.C.: National Education Association, 1962).

School of Education, University of Wisconsin, *The Nature of Knowledge* (Milwaukee: The Edward A. Uhrig Foundation, 1962).

Smith, B. Othanel, William O. Stanley, and J. Harlan Shores, *Fundamentals of Curriculum Development*, Revised Edition (New York: Harcourt, Brace & World, Inc., 1957).

chapter five

IN THE PRECEDING FOUR CHAPTERS, consideration has been given to separate and distinct foundations for decision-making about the curriculum. The present chapter is meant, in part, to pull together the resources which these foundations provide and, in part, to add other dimensions which should be taken into account as we improve the curriculum. The chapter proceeds in a logical order from the thesis that one must know the direction or directions in which he wishes to move before he begins to improve the curriculum, to the view that he should seek to balance and reconcile the forces which affect curriculum planning, meanwhile attending to the processes by which the curriculum is improved. One of the strong beliefs underlying Chapter 5 is that both substance and process are important in curriculum improvement, and that neither can validly be separated from the other.

Fundamental to a resolution of forces in decision-making about the curriculum are the curriculum maker's beliefs about the nature, education, and destiny of man. In the center of the trilogy nature-education-destiny is education, which expresses what can be *done* with and for man. What can be done with and for him is affected by his nature, and what can be done with

Resolving Forces in Curriculum Decision-Making

and for him in turn affects his destiny. Persons who want to improve the quality of education for themselves and for other people must face an initial question, "What are the sources of the ideas which will determine the kind of education to be provided?" The answers to this question will imply much about the curriculum improver's view of the nature of man. The answers will also suggest what the curriculum improver thinks man should do in the future. Most of all, however, they will bespeak points of view about the substance and process of education.

SOURCES OF IDEAS AS BASES OF THE CURRICULUM

When one thinks about possible sources of ideas as bases for the curriculum, he is forming the foundations of a personal philosophy of the curriculum. Any individual or school faculty wishing to launch upon a program of curriculum improvement should consider the beliefs on which the present program is founded and then consider what modifications of these beliefs must occur if proposed improvements are to be put into effect. The implication here is not that long periods of time should be spent in mulling over and stating in written form a revised philosophy of education. Rather, the implication is that the philosophy will emerge as actions are planned and their probable consequences are assessed. One of the damaging criticisms of curriculum workers has been that they spend too much time talking philosophy and too little time taking concrete action. Philosophy is, of course, too important to be dispensed with. To be useful, however, it should be associated with ongoing action so that the process consists of philosophizing-taking action-philosophizing-taking action-philosophizing rather than philosophizing at length and eventually taking action.

There are several major sources of rationale for curriculum improvement. These are detailed below without strong commitment to any one at the expense of the others. Each has its merits, and each is usable to a major extent in given situations. In general, however, the faculties of most schools would need to draw upon these sources eclectically. In somewhat over-simplified and rigidly-stated form, each of the sources may be described as follows:[1]

1. SCIENCE AS A SOURCE

According to this source, the scientific method is the only reliable method for establishing truth. Students should be taught to solve problems in terms of scientific procedures, and curriculum improvement itself should be accomplished scientifically. That is, valid and reliable data should be assembled in support of any curriculum change that is made. Thus, heavy reliance is to be placed upon rational procedures, according to a definite pattern of rationality, especially as found in problem-solving procedures. Judgment and valuing are of limited usefulness in strict application of scientific methodology because the results gained by them are neither measurable nor certain.

Science as a source of ideas for the curriculum and its improvement enjoys much prestige in an era and a society in which science is assigned so much credence and respect. For years, scientific methods have been used in determining the characteristics of learners, the nature of their growth and development, the extent of their learning, the worth of teaching materials, and, to a degree, the effectiveness of instructional methods. It would be

[1] See B. Othanel Smith, William O. Stanley, and J. Harlan Shores, *Fundamentals of Curriculum Development.* New York: Harcourt, Brace & World, Inc., 1957, pp. 529–544.

possible to take the position that no curriculum change could be initiated until the validity and reliability of the change had been confirmed by research and evaluation. One of the deficiencies of this position is that much of the judging and valuing which curriculum workers prize would be eliminated by the scientific method. Another deficiency is the unwillingness of some persons to accept educational data derived by scientific means as constituting the whole truth. As a matter of fact, researchers in education whose minds are fixed in the methods of the physical sciences often refuse to admit that there is such a thing as curriculum research.

2. SOCIETY AS A SOURCE

Society may be regarded as the ultimate source from which ideas about the curriculum are to be derived. According to this view, the school owes its being to the society which has fostered it, and the school should acquire ideas from the social situation which it observes. When one has said this much, he finds variations in interpretation as to what society is and ought to be. Some persons say that society's views can be determined by gathering a consensus of what people think. This consensus is usually gathered in a local community, and therefore does not show what people who are geographically remote from the local scene, but who are also highly important in a highly mobile society, are thinking. Nevertheless, it would be possible to base a curriculum strictly on a series of opinion polls.

Another variation consists in thinking of government as the spokesman of society. Under this conception, the curriculum would be changed only by legislative enactments and the decrees of the administrative and judicial branches of government. Many persons would say immediately that a society is more than its government, and that curriculum making by governmental authority limits the whole process unnecessarily.

Still another variation assumes that society, in its present state, is to be studied not only by curriculum makers but also by pupils in schools. The object is to perpetuate the present society by involving the pupil in studying it. A curriculum stemming from this view would be devoted to extensive study of the society both in school and out, with details of the society itself forming the subject-matter.

A final variation is known as the reconstructionist. It holds that the school's role is to remake society. The curriculum, then, would emphasize ideas for changing the social order, and curriculum improvement would be bent toward inventing ideas for that purpose. All of these variations make society the central source of ideas about the curriculum.

3. ETERNAL VERITIES FROM THE PAST AS A SOURCE

Eternal truth, in the view of Robert Hutchins and others, has been stated by great persons in the past. This view has recently been expressed in studies of the "Great Books" in adult education and in college curricula, but it has not completely found its way, as a significant emphasis, into our elementary and secondary schools. As held today by the humanists, the notion that lasting truth inheres in the writings of the past depends on human reason for an ordering of truths in primary, secondary, and consequent importance.

A curriculum derived from this source would depend, of course, upon the literature of the past. Any change in the curriculum would call for a reordering of ideas in the hierarchy of truths. Since these truths are considered eternal, they need not be found in new experiences; therefore, reordering them would not involve reflective or creative thinking about present and current phenomena but intuitive and deductive thinking for discovery of first principles, the status of which is allegedly fixed and invariable in any age. The alleged invariability of the first principles does not prevent arguments about them: principles which are put in first position by one authority may well be put in second position by another. Furthermore, the application of fixed principles suggests that the conditions to which they are applied are unchanging, whereas change is a known rule of life. Difficulties of these kinds have prevented eternal verities from man's past from being accepted as a guide to elementary- and secondary-school curricula.[2]

4. DIVINE WILL AS A SOURCE

This position maintains that God has revealed His Will to man through the Bible and through inspiration of the Holy Spirit in the lives of Christian believers. It received support in Colonial New England and was subsequently weakened by the emergence of antithetical viewpoints and the divergent interests of an increasingly less uniform population. A curriculum developed according to these ideas—even if the ideas were modified to accommodate religions other than the Christian—would place heavy reliance upon religious, moral, and ethical teachings found in Holy Writ and church doctrine. Persons who use Divine Will as a curriculum source hold that God's Will encompasses study of secular content so that learners may be prepared to fulfill His Will in their future lives. For public school systems in America, this curricu-

---

[2] For further discussion of this and other curriculum sources, see National Society for the Study of Education, *Modern Philosophies and Education* (54th Yearbook). Chicago: University of Chicago Press, 1955. Also see John S. Brubacher, *Modern Philosophies of Education*, Revised Edition. New York: McGraw-Hill Book Co., Inc., 1950.

lum source is largely unavailable because of legal sanctions against its use. For parochial and certain other private schools, it is a most important curriculum source. The influence of Divine Will as a source is likely to increase greatly if numbers of private religious schools are established as a consequence of the growing secularization of the public schools.

Even a quick review of the four preceding sources shows that no one of them is exclusively acceptable as a basis for the comprehensive schooling which is usually desired by the patrons of our public schools. As has already been said, eclectic viewpoints are needed. These, of course, cannot be widely-applicable, uniform viewpoints; rather, use of the sources must vary from situation to situation and from time to time. Always, the philosophy of a school should be a product of the thinking of the persons who are to subscribe to it. *A philosophy of curriculum sources is, then, a function of the interaction of people as they consider ideas.*

One author has posited that careful consideration of the nature of man can lead to choice of curriculum content, when the choice is undergirded or supported by the psychological, social, and subject-matter considerations described in Chapters 2, 3, and 4.[3] For the public school as an American democratic institution, the most promising view of the nature of man and his education would seem to be the following: Fundamental to the whole educational scene is the *learner*, whose schooling can be improved, in part, by using the best we know and can find out about *ways of learning. Society, the culture, and community influences* help to condition what the learner may learn. So, too, does the *nature of the content* which is set before the learner for his use or mastery. Whether one adopts the meaning of "use" or the meaning of "mastery" with reference to curriculum content makes a fundamental philosophical difference. *Using subject-matter* within a context of a) what is known about learning, and b) the requirements of the social order emphasizes the needs, interests, and concerns of the learner. *Mastering subject-matter* within the same context places emphasis on the subject-matter itself. The central question to be resolved in developing a philosophy is what the individual teacher or the faculty is willing to do for and with learners.

After sources of the curriculum have been drawn upon in developing an acceptable philosophy, general and specific objectives of the school need to be stated. These objectives can then be achieved in light of what we know about the learner, the learning process, social influences, and the nature of subject-matter. According to this line of thinking, the next action of curriculum workers which must be discussed is formulation of objectives.

---

[3] Arthur W. Foshay, "Choice of Content," *Educational Leadership*, Vol. 14, No. 6, March, 1956, pp. 340–343; also, letter to the Editor, *Educational Leadership*, Vol. 15, No. 6, March, 1957, pp. 393 and 395.

FORMULATION OF SUITABLE OBJECTIVES

The philosophy of a school suggests the important values in terms of which the teachers in that school are willing to make their day-to-day decisions. These values in turn suggest certain major objectives which are to be achieved by the school staff. Each objective should be consistent with one or more values stated in the philosophy. Thus, if we say that we value opportunity for everyone to participate in all the activities of the school for which he has ability, energy and interest, we must state at least one objective indicating that we propose to "open" the curriculum to all pupils regardless of such extraneous factors as race, creed, and social class. The objective must be consistent with the philosophy, and it should extend the philosophy into concrete action.

There is real advantage in stating objectives in a uniform way, according to a definite point of view about the uses of objectives. In American education, objectives should be used chiefly to remind teachers, and to remind their pupils, of what the pupils themselves are to do. Thus, if a major objective has to do with learning how to interpret scientific data, we should word the objective in the form of an expected pupil behavior: *e.g., To learn how to interpret data derived from conducting laboratory experiments with electricity.*

Three features of this objective should be noted. First, as has been said, it is written from the standpoint of pupil behavior rather than of teacher behavior. It does not say, "To teach pupils how to interpret data. . . ," though this is a worthy objective for the teacher's private use. Second, the objective indicates a general behavior (interpreting data) in a specific context (laboratory experimentation with electricity). One may show in a general objective the need of his pupils to interpret data of all sorts, but the objective becomes genuinely usable when it has been made specific enough to indicate what kind of data are to be interpreted, where they are to be interpreted, and under what circumstances they are to be interpreted. The objective should indicate both the behavior of the pupil and the content he is to use. Third, both process goals and content goals may be expressed in the same objective. "*How* to interpret data" mentions a process goal; "laboratory experiments in *electricity*" mentions a content goal.

Because learners need comprehensive development, objectives should by no means be limited to two or three types. Teachers have long had as their mission an increase in knowledge in the young. One could add to this their related mission to help pupils build understanding. But for living in our society, learners also need numerous skills, not the least of which are skills in reading and study. Besides, learners need to extend their interests, to develop appreciation, to build desirable social attitudes, and to think critically. Objectives, therefore, are of differing orders and types, and a real contribution of curriculum improvers lies in helping themselves and other teachers to state varied objectives, and then to think how each objective can be achieved by learners through the subject-matter they learn. Tyler has devised a two-dimensional scheme for specifying varied types of objectives according to the subject-matter content and the behavioral aspects of the objectives.[4]

TWO-DIMENSIONAL CHART FOR STATING OBJECTIVES FOR A HIGH-SCHOOL COURSE IN BIOLOGICAL SCIENCE

Content Aspects of the Objectives	*Behavioral Aspect of the Objectives*						
	1. Understanding of important facts and principles	2. Familiarity with dependable sources of information	3. Ability to interpret data	4. Ability to apply principles	5. Ability to study and report results of study	6. Broad and mature interests	7. Social attitudes
A. Functions of Human Organisms:							
1. Nutrition	X	X	X	X	X	X	X
2. Digestion	X		X	X	X	X	
3. Circulation	X		X	X	X	X	
4. Respiration	X		X	X	X	X	
5. Reproduction	X	X	X	X	X	X	X
B. Use of Plant and Animal Resources:							
1. Energy relationships	X		X	X	X	X	X
2. Environmental factors conditioning plant and animal growth	X	X	X	X	X	X	X
3. Heredity and genetics	X	X	X	X	X	X	X
4. Land utilization	X	X	X	X	X	X	X
C. Evolution and Development	X	X	X		X	X	X

Much progress has been made in recent years in stating objectives behaviorally. In 1938, the Educational Policies Commission paved the way for behavioral statement of objectives when it issued a report titled *The Pur-*

[4] Ralph W. Tyler, *Basic Principles of Curriculum and Instruction.* Chicago: University of Chicago Press, 1950, p. 32.

poses of Education in American Democracy.[5] In 1957, French published a study which was sponsored by the Educational Testing Service, the National Association of Secondary School Principals, and the Russell Sage Foundation, and which identified 99 behaviors as being important to secondary education.[6] Previously, the same foundation had issued a widely-ranging description of objectives for elementary schools.[7] Thus, broad objectives are already available in published form. One may, if he wishes, go back to objectives formulated by the *Committee of Ten* (1894), or to the *Seven Cardinal Principles* (1918).

But the point being made here is that, though general, nationally-stated objectives are important referents, the real work of objective-stating should be accomplished near the site of their implementation—in the local school system and in the individual school—with locally-formulated philosophy constantly in mind. The objectives noted in Tyler's chart are of an order to be used in schools and school systems, provided that teachers take time to explore the meanings of the objectives for their own practice. The behavioral objective "ability to apply principles," for instance, is still too general for concrete classroom use.

Teachers need to consider, individually and in groups, both the meaning and the possible implementation of every objective. They need to do so, of course, *as* they undertake curriculum improvement in classroom and school. While they should study and know their objectives before they put them to use, they should test and apply the meanings of the objectives constantly in practice. Curriculum leaders have a special obligation to help teachers with this process in an era in which teachers are easily led astray from realistic objectives by the lure of attractive but unanalyzed practices.

A special relationship between philosophy of education and objectives can be seen in the process by which objectives are determined. Suppose, for example, one is heavily committed to science as a source of educational philosophy, and so uses scientific analysis as a means of determining objectives. It would be possible to formulate objectives following an analysis of pupils' needs, skills, and deficiencies. This has been done in part by Thorndike, when he identified the 10,000 basic words needed by elementary-school children.[8] It would be possible also to formulate objectives after analyzing

[5] Educational Policies Commission, *The Purposes of Education in American Democracy.* Washington, D.C.: National Education Association, 1938.

[6] Will French, *Behavioral Goals of General Education in High School.* New York: Russell Sage Foundation, 1957.

[7] Nolan C. Kearney, *Elementary School Objectives.* New York: Russell Sage Foundation, 1953.

[8] Edward L. Thorndike, *The Teacher's Word Book.* New York: Bureau of Publications, Teachers College, Columbia University, 1921.

the adult activities for which learners are preparing. For instance, Charters studied the arithmetic used by sales clerks in department stores.[9] It would likewise be possible to state objectives following an analysis of curriculum materials. Thus, textbooks and courses of study have often been inspected for their common elements of content. It would be possible, finally, to ask people for their opinions about possible objectives, or to take opinion polls before objectives are formulated. Doctoral studies have sometimes concentrated on asking experts for their reactions to possible objectives. Freely-expressed opinion as a guide was sought by Hand in his studies.[10]

If one proceeds primarily from any one of the other three sources— society, the eternal verities, or Divine Will—he must find means of developing objectives which are consistent with that source. For example, when Divine Will is the major source, revelation must be heavily relied upon. When society is the major source, observation and consideration of social forces are necessary.

ACTIVITY 5-1—THINKING ABOUT SOURCES OF EDUCATIONAL PHILOSOPHY

If an eclectic view of the uses of sources is taken by the curriculum maker, the nature of practical school problems will condition the emphasis to be placed on given sources. Think about the problems listed below. Which of the four sources—science, society, eternal verities, Divine Will—would you utilize in solving each of the problems? Discuss your conclusions with others to discover differing viewpoints and to clarify your own thinking.

The senior class of a high school is planning a two-day trip to a seaside resort. Sponsors of the trip are trying to help the class make a code of social conduct to be followed by class members.

The eighth-grade art class has been invited to submit plans for a new fountain to be erected in the town's public square. Two art teachers are working with five pupils who are superior in art to determine an aesthetically desirable design for the fountain.

During late October, three civics classes are trying to learn about people's motives for voting in the November election. The social studies department is considering what activities and procedures should be recommended to pupils for their use.

---

[9] W. W. Charters, *Curriculum Construction.* New York: The Macmillan Co., 1923, pp. 231–236.

[10] Harold Hand, *What People Think About Their Schools.* New York: Harcourt, Brace & World, Inc., 1948.

ACTIVITY 5-2—MOVING FROM PHILOSOPHICAL SOURCES TO OBJECTIVES

Consider society as the major source of educational objectives. What particular point of view will you take toward the role of society as a source of objectives? That is, should a consensus of citizens' views condition schooling? Or should government be the conditioner on behalf of society? Or should the present social scene? Or should a society which has not yet come into being?

According to the point of view you take, indicate several objectives, stated behaviorally for pupils, which you believe would stem from that point of view. For instance, if you believe that a society which has not yet come into being should condition schooling, you will value experiments by pupils which will lead them to think toward establishment of the new society. Hence, several objectives, written from the pupils' standpoint, might begin with the words, "To design experiments . . ." or "To experiment with . . ." Suppose, on the other hand, you believe that government should condition schooling on behalf of society. You might propose objectives beginning, "To understand legislation . . . ," "To acquire an attitude of acceptance toward regulations about . . . ," and so on. As you state objectives, think of the processes by which pupils are to learn, and also of the content they are to learn.

ACHIEVING A RESOLUTION OF UNDERGIRDING FORCES

A point of view of this book is that what one thinks about the education of man and the philosophy and objectives which stem from this thinking are fundamental to curriculum design and change. Where, then, do the child, his learning, the social order, and the nature of particular subject-disciplines come into the picture? Essentially, they furnish the data which help with living the philosophy and achieving the objectives. In this sense, they undergird 1) the valuing and the thinking which go into building a philosophy and consequent sets of objectives, and 2) the implementing of objectives according to the realities of learners, learning, the social order, and subject-matter.

At the beginning of Chapter 2, there was some discussion of the uses of psychology in putting objectives into practice. In the same way, interpretations of the social order suggest ideas for implementing objectives. So does a study of the various disciplines. No one who is an avid follower of the psychologists, the social scientists, or the subject-matter specialists can afford to ignore the contributions of the other groups. Rather, we validate and support our philosophy and objectives by reference to all three undergirding forces.

As we live and teach, we want the freshest, most accurate knowledge about children and learning. We also want the best influences that society can offer and the best contributions of the disciplines. We want to see phenomena as adults, but we want that freedom to see which belongs to children. "When we are thus free we are able to think of values essential to adult life and yet approach them through essential childhood motivations. We are free to live our way into each of the great disciplines, valuing it tremendously—and yet *using* it unfetteredly for the growth of each individual person."[11] The curriculum is, after all, a body of purposes with the precious human being at the center, influenced by his own nature and nurtured by the world about him, including the subject-matter he is to learn.

The value of each of the forces—learner and learning, social influences, and subject-matter—in making and remaking the curriculum must depend on the nature of the task and the situation surrounding it. The key question is, "For which of these three forces shall we call loudest at a given time and place, so that they become our resources?" Some examples of the applicability of the forces are needed.

I

A committee of teachers and administrators had as its purpose improvement of the listening skills of elementary- and secondary-school pupils. The committee believed that, because so little has been done anywhere to develop listening skills, the members should learn everything possible about listening as art and skill. Inquiries about listening should be made by searching the literature. Eventually, teachers in the district should be encouraged to conduct some experiments of their own regarding listening. In effect, then, the committee said that the methods of science have something to offer in studying problems of this kind.

Having decided the bases on which it would operate, the committee thought somewhat in this order:

[11] Fred T. Wilhelms, "Curriculum Sources," in Association for Supervision and Curriculum Development, *What Are the Sources of the Curriculum?* Washington, D.C.: The Association, 1962, pp. 14–25.

Question: What sort of discipline is listening?
Answer: It is so new to us; we don't know. Let's explore it.

Question: Can anyone possibly object to our studying listening? Are there, for instance, priorities of curriculum study which should delay this study?
Answer: Both questions may be answered negatively. Let's go ahead.

Question: Doesn't the nature of the learner make a difference in learning listening? What if he's a dull pupil? What if he comes from a deprived social class?
Answer: These things worry us. We'd better investigate them.

Question: Are there some listening experiences that ought to come earlier in life, and some that ought to come later?
Answer: This is a matter of readiness that we may be better equipped to deal with if we know more about listening as a discipline. We'll probably find, too, that we'll need to know more about the learning processes which are involved.

This sequence of questions and answers reveals the forces on which the listening committee decided to draw as resources for curriculum improvement. Social influences seemed to this committee to have little bearing on their problem. But the nature of an unknown discipline and serious questions about who learns listening best, and how, concerned them. Therefore, during one year's work, they reckoned chiefly with the discipline itself and secondarily with the nature of the learner and certain of his learning problems.

II

The English department of a high school faced a ready-made curriculum problem. One of its members had drawn the fire of the local post of a patriotic organization for having her pupils read John Hersey's *Hiroshima* without arranging for them to read literature less hostile to America's exploit over Hiroshima near the end of World War II. The teacher in question had been required to appear before the local board of education at both private and public meetings. The matter before the department today was what could be done to assure a balance in the reading diets of pupils with reference to controversial issues. In a period of emergency, this matter seemed to the department members to involve social issues, with a slight overtone of developmental capacity of learners. The questions teachers asked themselves were these:

What is the role of teachers in American society? What is the role of complaining individuals and groups?

> In our community, what can we do to discharge our responsibilities—with safety from unreasonable attack?
>
> What about controversial issues as treated in our schools? What does the State Department of Education say? Where does our board of education really stand? What about our school administration?
>
> How can we find literary materials which can be understood nearly equally well by learners at different stages of development, and which are on all sides of given issues?

Here the force of social influences had predominance. The nature of the learner was secondary. The nature of subject-matter content was involved, but, at the time, it was placed in a tertiary position.

III

A committee of elementary- and secondary-school teachers wanted to stimulate children and youth to write creatively. The committee doubted that old, time-honored procedures for teaching writing would assure the desired results. Accordingly, the members began a search for new ideas in books, articles, and the true experiences of other teachers with whom they corresponded. Eventually they made the hypothesis that, if learners were freed of mechanical restrictions such as neatness of penmanship, correctness of punctuation, and grammatical accuracy, they might create more worthwhile stories, poems, and essays. To test the hypothesis, the committee had to establish criteria of quality in creative writing. This led them to the question, "What does creativity in literature consist of?" Their experiment, then, had to do with the effectiveness of a "brakes off" method of learning in which learning *something* was very important. The committee worried about social influences only to the extent of wondering what parents would say when poorly punctuated, poorly constructed papers came home. The experiment did result in considerably increased creativity according to the committee's criteria. However, the mechanical quality of pupils' writing declined to a point at which an "enforcement period" was used to restore lost mechanical skills.

This is a case in which all three forces were used importantly in curriculum improvement. First, the committee members learned from the literature and from correspondence with experts how pupils learn to write creatively. Since they encountered disagreements, they decided to make a reasoned and reasonable hypothesis of their own with a particular way of learning as its core. To test the hypothesis, they turned to an exploration of the discipline itself as a means of establishing criteria. Finally, their worry about parents' opinions brought social influences to the fore.

Herrick cites several needs for research, the results of which might assist curriculum workers in situations like those described above. First, ways of approaching specific curriculum problems should be thought through. Second, the curricular structures of subject-fields need much further investigation. Third, the roles of persons involved in operating the curriculum should be studied. Fourth, the interaction of teachers and pupils in classrooms needs much study because, at this locus, the curriculum is truly made.[12]

Herrick's reference to the interaction of teachers and pupils is a reminder that decision-making about the curriculum at classroom level depends most heavily upon the nature of particular learners and the ways they learn. When teachers move from their own classrooms to curriculum committee activity, they are faced with additional emphases which have less direct import for them in working with children. In curriculum committee functioning and in in-service activities, teachers tend to hear what the community seems to be thinking and saying and what is happening in the society at large, usually as interpreted by administrators who presumably have wide contacts and are "in the know." They also become cognizant of the availability of subject-matter which may be newly discovered, but which is more likely old subject-matter moved into a newly-prominent position. Pursuant to their participation in in-service and curriculum improvement activities, teachers continue to decide what is to be done with certain social forces and given subject-matter as they face animate learners and the live problems of learning which these learners pose.

SITUATION 5-1—USING UNDERGIRDING FORCES TO PLAN IMPROVEMENT

Professor Morris Shamos of New York University has proposed (*New York Times*, February 14, 1962) that mathematics be presented within the framework of science. In Professor Shamos' view, mathematics should be incorporated within science, with examples in mathematics being "taken from the sciences rather than from the farm or the grocery store; from mechanics, for instance, or from the gas laws or geometrical optics."

If you were to explore this idea further, what, if anything, would you need to know about each of the following:

[12] Virgil E. Herrick, "Sources of Curriculum Development," in Association for Supervision and Curriculum Development, *What Are the Sources of the Curriculum?* Washington, D.C.: The Association, 1962, p. 71.

The nature of mathematics?

The nature of science, with particular reference to physics?

Social demands and influences upon the teaching and learning of mathematics and science?

Relevant principles of learning?

The needs and problems of adolescents who are required to learn advanced mathematics and physics?

Which of these forces would, in your opinion, deserve greatest play in establishing a desirable relationship between mathematics and science? Why?

SITUATION 5-2—INVENTING APPLICATIONS OF THE UNDERGIRDING FORCES

Part of the curriculum terrain is largely unexplored. Such is the case with social studies experiences for primary-grade children. A committee of first-, second-, and third-grade teachers wished to build a social studies program to satisfy the needs of primary-grade children in their community. Key comments by the teachers about considerations to be taken into account are listed below:

"It may be that children's thinking doesn't necessarily proceed from the here and now to the there and then. Does a young child necessarily think more about home and community than he does about definite places in the state, the nation, or the whole world? Does his horizon really broaden according to a set pattern?"

"We need to learn more about children's interests and the needs they presently feel. Shouldn't we, therefore, find ways of studying children which have special relevance to social studies experiences? What could we possibly invent for this purpose?"

"We're free as far as demands upon us are concerned. The community doesn't care what we teach young children in the social studies. (People in the community are much more concerned about reading.) Furthermore, teachers in the fourth and fifth grades don't try to tell us what to do in the social studies."

"We may have to develop some of our own materials to suit the program we devise."

What undergirding force or forces do you consider most significant in solving this kind of problem? Do you take at face value the teachers' comments as they relate to forces?

What inventions are needed for pioneering in applying the forces? For instance, if we do not yet know enough about learning of social studies concepts by young children, what should be done to explore this matter? Also, what could be done to learn more about the interests and needs of these children which could be met by an improved social studies program?

SOME ADDITIONAL CONSIDERATIONS IN PLANNING PUPIL EXPERIENCES

The forces which have been described above are not applied exclusively in the ways which have been indicated. Decision-making about the curriculum involves additional considerations as well. A major consideration is the process of moving from objectives to concrete learning experiences. Both the curriculum committee and the teacher in the classroom have responsibility for transferring wishes into action.

Learning experiences for pupils may be defined as interactions between learners and their environments which create behavioral changes in the learners. The important thing is what happens to the pupils; to have behavioral changes occur in them, they must do something for themselves. This fact suggests a first general principle to be used in selecting learning experiences: *learners should have opportunities to practice the behaviors which objectives imply.* For example, if one wants to learn to interpret data, he must be given data to interpret. If one is to develop wider reading interests, he must be given wider varieties of materials to read.

A second principle to be used in selecting learning experiences is that *the experiences which are chosen must prove satisfying to the learners.* They must get for learners the results which the learners themselves desire to get, and they must accomplish this with a minimum of distaste. Whatever the living disciples of mental discipline and intellectual toughness may say, experience which is unsatisfying or distasteful soon sickens and demoralizes learners.

A third principle is that *the experiences must be within learners' ranges of capability—neither too easy nor too hard.* To find experiences that challenge without frustrating becomes the real problem. It is easy to say, "Begin with the pupil where he is, and lead him onward from there," but accomplishing it requires knowing much more about people and subject-matter than we presently know.

A fourth principle is that *many different experiences can be used in achieving the same objective*. This principle disturbs teachers and laymen who would like to think that one or two stock experiences, used year after year, are the experiences to fill the bill. Creating varied experiences and experimenting with their applications are badly-needed actions.

A fifth principle to be used in selecting learning experiences is that *the same experience will usually bring several results or outcomes*. Inconveniently, learners differ. Specifically, they bring to the same learning task different interests, needs, problems, and abilities. The very existence of multiple outcomes in achieving objectives provides another reason for offering multiple experiences to achieve the same objective.[13]

Some practice has now been had in American schools in fitting experiences to various objectives. These include objectives for increasing knowledge and understanding, objectives for developing interests, objectives for altering attitudes and values, objectives for improving skills, objectives for developing appreciations, and objectives for improving quality of thinking. The commonest kind, of course, is objectives for increasing knowledge and understanding. To assure the achievement of objectives within this classification, the following actions have proved helpful:

1. Arrange for information and understanding to be acquired in the process of problem-solving. Using the problem-solving process will reduce the incidence of rote memorization which results from learning isolated, unrelated facts.

2. Identify the important items of knowledge which most need to be learned. Someone has said that teachers characteristically make pupils become so busy with the little municipal matters that they lose touch with the big federal ones.

3. Cause important matters to be dealt with intensely and intensively. Show in your planning and teaching that these matters really count.

4. Present important information in varied contexts. Plan different sorts of experiences involving the same information.

5. Lead pupils to basic sources of important information whenever time and facilities permit.[14]

Suggestions like these can be developed for designing experiences to achieve other kinds of objectives also. Skillful teachers should be induced to state suggestions which originate in their own educational practice. The undergirding forces—learner and learning, social influences, and nature of

---

13 Tyler, *op. cit.*, pp. 42–44.
14 *Ibid.*, pp. 47 and 48.

subject-matter—should receive continuous, conscious use in applying general principles and concrete suggestions in the selection and ordering of learning experiences.

ACTIVITY 5-3—SUGGESTING CONCRETE ACTIONS IN SELECTING AND ORDERING LEARNING EXPERIENCES

From the following kinds of objectives, select one, and prepare a list of actions which you would take in selecting and ordering learning experiences to achieve that kind of objective:

Objectives for developing interests

Objectives for altering attitudes and values

Objectives for improving skills

Objectives for developing appreciations

Objectives for improving quality of thinking.

Your list of proposed actions will be comparable with the list above for the knowledge-understanding objectives.

This may well be an experience in which you would like to engage with other teachers in a group setting.

PROBLEMS INVOLVED

As curriculum workers think about the whole range of experience which pupils should have in their years of elementary and secondary schooling, they face problems of scope, sequence, continuity, and balance. *Scope* is the latitude or the breadth of the curriculum; *sequence,* the order of time in which educational experiences are to be had. *Continuity* describes the continuousness with which the same kinds of experiences are had over a period of time. *Balance* defines the fit of the curriculum in providing varied but appropriate amounts of experience for learners at given times in their development. Brief consideration will be given here to each of these factors in curriculum design.

Scope——This dimension of the curriculum can be seen in the weekly program of an elementary school. The breadth of elementary-school programs is usually great. Several school subjects and one or two school activities are sandwiched into the week's work, so that the total program accommodates experiences in the language arts, arithmetic, the social studies, science, health, physical education, art, music, planning for and rehearsing an assembly program, and a variety of homeroom activities. The scope is so broad that many elementary-school teachers develop a kind of curriculum schizophrenia, being uncertain as to how they can accomplish all that is expected of them. However, the problem of scope does not end with listing subjects and activities. Each subject and each activity may grow entirely out of bounds. For example, the language arts as a subject-field was once heavy in reading and writing alone. Then speaking as a specific art and set of skills assumed increased prominence. Now listening has been added to the classification. Spelling and penmanship once took much time without conscious relationship to writing; now, in the multitude of other tasks to be performed within the language arts, they may be suffering from underemphasis. Problems of too-broad scope indicate again that the world of education is not afflicted with a scarcity of knowledge; rather, it needs perspective in fitting a profusion of knowledge into limited periods of time at varied stages in the development of learners.

Sequence——Curriculum sequence deals with the question, "What's to follow what?" The problem of sequence must be dealt with in teaching and learning subject-matter in which certain ideas necessarily build upon others. This is the case, for instance, in mathematics and the foreign languages. It is much less the case in the social studies. However, this view of sequence depends upon the importance assigned to subject-matter. If, instead of thinking directly of subject-matter, one were to think of developmental tasks for learners, sequence would be determined by the tasks which learners could be expected to perform at sequential stages of their development. So, sequence might be determined by stages of mental growth; or it might be governed by centers of interest. The latter is one of the determiners of sequence which has been used in creating experience-type curricula.

As has been said previously, sequences that seem clear and feasible according to adult logic seem neither clear nor feasible to numerous learners. Much experimentation is needed in re-ordering experiences in the life space of children.

Continuity——Matters of continuity are inevitably tied to those of sequence. Questions of order of events in learning raise questions about how long certain events should be allowed to continue. Thus, continuity is a vertical matter, in that it affects the continuousness with which certain experiences shall be had during consecutive periods of time. It is also a horizontal matter, in that it affects the continuousness with which given kinds of activities shall be engaged in during the day. An example of vertical continuity is the teaching of a foreign language for three consecutive years. An example of horizontal continuity is the teaching of the social studies during a three-hour block of time on the same day. Continuity also involves large questions of articulation among educational levels of the school system, as among elementary schools, junior high schools, and senior high schools. Like sequence, it is seen in unpatterned ways by children and adolescents.[15] It is patently impossible to plot a uniform plan of continuity for all children. While the experiences of all may be continuous in time, the differences among these experiences need to be conditioned by the differences among individuals.

Balance——If a learner enjoyed a balanced curriculum at a given time, this curriculum would completely fit him in terms of his particular educational needs at that time. It would contain just enough of each kind of subject-matter to serve his purposes and speed his development. General balance in the curriculum can be partly achieved, in the sense that certain kinds of experience can be planned for large groups of learners according to what we know about them and about the subject-matter which is available for them to learn. True balance for individuals, however, is very difficult to attain. For one thing, what constitutes acceptable balance today is imbalance tomorrow. Perhaps the best we can do is to work *toward* balance by being clearer about what is to be valued for the growth of individual learners, and then to apply these values in selecting curriculum content, grouping pupils for instruction, providing for articulation, and furthering guidance programs.[16]

Problems of scope, sequence, continuity, and balance remain largely unsolved. Each of these four factors or dimensions for determining learning experiences must be dealt with according to what is known about learners and learning, social influences, and subject-matter, against a background of values and goals. Learning experiences may also be planned by combining related elements of curriculum content in a plan of *correlation*. Thus, literature about the Jacksonian period in American history may be taught simultaneously with the history of the period itself. In straining correlation a bit, the arts—music, the fine arts, home economics, and the industrial arts— may be partially merged into a core of simultaneous experience. Evidence to support correlation has not appeared in the quantity and quality which were once hoped for. Many educators feel that correlation "fixes" the curriculum too much, preventing teachers and their pupils from planning freely. At any rate, the real problems of curriculum improvement are believed by some educators to be solved less readily by encouraging correlation than by attacking problems of selecting experiences to fit objectives, with the dimensions

---

[15] See Association for Supervision and Curriculum Development, *A Look at Continuity in the School Program* (1958 Yearbook). Washington, D.C.: The Association, 1958.
[16] Association for Supervision and Curriculum Development, *Balance in the Curriculum* (1961 Yearbook). Washington, D.C.: The Association, 1961.

of scope, sequence, continuity, and balance being kept in mind and being brought under further scrutiny.

ACTIVITY 5-4—FINDING EXAMPLES OF SCOPE, SEQUENCE, CONTINUITY, AND BALANCE

Review the curriculum of a school you know well. Notice: 1) the scope of the curriculum for fourth-grade and eleventh-grade pupils; 2) sequences in the language arts and mathematics which extend over series of grades; 3) vertical continuity in a modern foreign language; and 4) balance in the curriculum as seen by a guidance counselor and by a happy, well-adjusted pupil in senior high school. The main object of this exercise is to look at these four dimensions in their affirmative effects. Another object is to understand how much needs to be done to achieve appropriate scope, sequence, continuity, and balance in individual learners' school experiences.

When you have completed your study, ask yourself these questions:

1. How much of this school's accomplishment in achieving appropriate scope, sequence, continuity, and balance seems to have been consciously planned?
2. What actions could be taken immediately and simply to improve scope, or sequence, or continuity, or balance?

SUMMARY

Decision-making in curriculum improvement is a complex task which appears in the classroom where learners are, and also at the site of professional planning where proposals are made for numbers of classrooms. It involves careful and thorough thinking which, particularly at the site of planning mentioned above, may proceed in ways which have been indicated in this chapter. Reference has been made to several classic areas of decision-making in which much progress is yet needed. Professional education is by no means in a position at which decisions about fundamental matters have all been made. Many old and basic problems in teaching and learning need to be solved before curriculum workers invite or search for large numbers of new ones.

HOW DECISION-MAKING RELATES TO PROCESS

For an expanse of five chapters, this book has dealt with decision-making in curriculum improvement. The question now arises, "How does decision-making relate to the process by which the curriculum is improved?"

We have seen that decision-making about the curriculum is in itself a process which involves borrowing from various disciplines —history, psychology, the social sciences, and subject-matter to be taught in schools—and then using insights derived from these disciplines in ways which are peculiar to professional education itself.

Curriculum improvement as an evolving discipline of real power and promise depends so heavily upon process for its own subject-matter that attention is directed in the second part of this book to certain elements of process. In the following chapters, consideration is given to how change and improvement occur, what adequate leadership for improvement consists of, how we get under way in organizing new programs, who makes the curriculum, how communication aids improvement, and what strategies we can use in the improvement process. These matters represent the general concerns of curriculum planners who have been asked to describe the problems which trouble them in their work. Inasmuch as curriculum improvement is greatly facilitated by a thorough understanding of process, this understanding is a necessary concomitant of and supplement to the curriculum worker's knowledge of the bases and methodology of decision-making.

SELECTED BIBLIOGRAPHY

Association for Supervision and Curriculum Development, *Balance in the Curriculum*, 1961 Yearbook (Washington, D.C.: The Association, 1961).

———, *A Look at Continuity in the School Program*, 1958 Yearbook (Washington, D.C.: The Association, 1958).

———, *What Are the Sources of the Curriculum?* (Washington, D.C.: The Association, 1962).

Bloom, Benjamin S., *A Taxonomy of Educational Objectives* (New York: Longmans, Green & Co., Inc., 1956).

Brubacher, John S., *Modern Philosophies of Education* (New York: McGraw-Hill Book Co., Inc., 1950).

Burton, William H., *The Guidance of Learning Activities*, Third Edition (New York: Appleton-Century-Crofts, Inc., 1962, Chapter 6).

Educational Policies Commission, *The Purposes of Education in American Democracy* (Washington, D.C.: National Education Association, 1938).

French, Will, *Behavioral Goals of General Education in High School* (New York: Russell Sage Foundation, 1957).

Kearney, Nolan C., *Elementary School Objectives* (New York: Russell Sage Foundation, 1953).

National Society for the Study of Education, *Modern Philosophies and Education*, 54th Yearbook (Chicago: University of Chicago Press, 1955).

Smith, B. Othanel, William O. Stanley, and J. Harlan Shores, *Fundamentals of Curriculum Development*, Revised Edition (New York: Harcourt, Brace & World, Inc., 1957).

Tyler, Ralph W., *Basic Principles of Curriculum and Instruction* (Chicago: University of Chicago Press, 1950).

part two

Process in

Curriculum

Improvement

chapter six

IT IS OBVIOUS THAT CURRICULUM IMPROVEMENT does not occur automatically. In most school situations, accomplishing it requires expenditure of much time and effort within an environment which is rich in helpful and stimulating influences. Primarily, curriculum improvement results from improvement of individual persons and organizations of people. Their improvement follows a process which can be charted in a general way, a process with which this chapter deals. Subsequent chapters describe certain ramifications of and corollaries to the basic process.

The definition of curriculum improvement given in the first chapter of this book says that the learner's curriculum improves largely in consonance with improvement in his teacher's insights, skills, and attitudes. According to this definition, emphasis needs to be placed on the growth of individual teachers, whether they are assigned to classrooms or whether they rove about as teachers of teachers, bearing the title curriculum coordinator, supervisor, or consultant. *If the curriculum is to improve, teachers must be committed to the significance of self-improvement.* Obviously some teachers are much interested in improving themselves, while other teachers manifest little or no interest in self-improvement. There is, of course, no teacher who cannot do his

The General
Process of
Curriculum
Improvement

work better, and the basic question becomes, then, "How can the teacher who is more or less concerned about his own improvement be helped to improve?" This age-old question still remains partially unanswered, but a few definite answers and additional tentative ones, some of them simply in the form of common-sense cues, are now available.

Improvement with reference to the individual often becomes a very special problem. Consider the case of a teacher named Lucretia and her critic:

> I remember Lucretia. She and I taught in the same high school, though hers was a different generation from mine. I can recall Lucretia's long dresses, straight hair, and wan face that had seemingly never known cosmetics.
>
> "Lucretia's the kind of teacher who defeats school bond issues single-handedly," said a mutual friend. He may have been right. Both her appearance and her attitudes toward youngsters and subject-matter were unappealing.
>
> Lucretia expected much of her pupils, but less of herself. Her understanding of her subject was limited, and she obviously cared little about the adolescents she taught.

I've often thought about Lucretia since those days in Stockville High School. Where should curriculum improvement have begun in *her* classroom? With her—probably! But how, and under what circumstances?

Just incidentally (and maybe it shouldn't be so incidental), I wonder what Lucretia thought of me. How might her brash young neighbor in the classroom across the hall have improved himself so that *his* pupils' experiences could have improved in turn?

The preceding vignette raises some serious questions about the process of curriculum improvement. Among them are these: Granted that Lucretia represents "a type," are there some common ways which can be used in helping people everywhere improve themselves? What different approaches are necessary and desirable for use with widely differing individuals? Are we vain enough to believe that improvement is only for persons outside ourselves? Can a curriculum leader become so preoccupied with the intrinsic worth of a proposed innovation that he forgets that real improvement occurs within *people*, including *himself?*

The dictionary defines improvement as enhanced value or excellence. In a broader sense, it is all of the following: betterment, amelioration, and enrichment. Change, on the other hand, involves a shift in position which may go in either a favorable or an unfavorable direction. One may change, for example, from total innocence of narcotics to drug addiction, but few persons would call this change an improvement. Improvements are labeled as such according to sets of values, and improvement can best be assured by evaluating the true effects of change. In education, many changes have occurred during recent years. Certain persons, using their own systems of values, consider given changes to be improvements when they are regarded as backward steps by many other people. Thus, a lay committee of engineers and scientists who proposed seriously to a board of education that physical education, home economics, and all the arts be eliminated from the curriculum of their local high school made the recommendation because the committee valued a strengthening of the "basic subjects" at the expense of "the frills." In less patent matters, reasonably precise evaluation procedures are needed in determining whether a given change is an improvement. For instance, if a plan for reorganizing elementary schools is to be put into operation, planned evaluation is needed to discover whether the ultimate result has been mere reorganization of the school or actual improvement in children's learning experiences. The two are obviously not the same, though they are repeatedly being confused as American education rushes into change.

In educational literature, curriculum improvement has been termed educational engineering, thus suggesting the existence of a technology of improvement.[1] It has also been termed planned social change,[2] and change in the dynamics of human relationships.[3] Much of what we know about educational engineering is of a practical or common-sense nature. Most of our knowledge of planned social change and the related significance of human relations comes from disciplines other than education. Inasmuch as improvement is really change which is directed toward excellence, betterment, amelioration, and/or enrichment, it should be recognized as especially worthwhile change, but as change nevertheless. Whatever social scientists and educators have learned about the process of change in individuals and groups may be generally applied to the process of improving persons and institutions. With reference to improvement of the curriculum, the educator must, of course, make further applications of the findings of social psychology, sociology, and the other social sciences to his own field.

HOW CHANGE OCCURS

Social scientists have stated that change probably occurs in three stages. The first stage is that of initiation, in which ideas for change are launched and decisions are made regarding the nature, direction, and extent of change. The second stage is said to be one of *legitimation,* in which the sentiment on behalf of change is being communicated. The third stage involves *congruence* of the separate systems of values which are held by the person or persons seeking to create change and by the person or persons who are the targets or human subjects of the proposed change.[4] The process of change may be assisted by permissiveness and support, in accordance with a helpful human-relations approach. It may also be aided temporarily by manipulating extrinsic rewards, such as those of affection, favor, promotion, and additional income. Disaster has sometimes become an easy excuse for making changes seem reasonable and necessary. In the presence or imminence of disaster, action seems necessary, even when the particular action to be taken violates

---

[1] B. Othanel Smith, William O. Stanley, and J. Harlan Shores, *Fundamentals of Curriculum Development.* New York: Harcourt, Brace & World, Inc., 1957.

[2] Alice Miel, *Changing the Curriculum.* New York: Appleton-Century-Crofts, Inc., 1946.

[3] Kenneth D. Benne and Bozidar Muntyan, *Human Relations in Curriculum Change.* New York: The Dryden Press, 1951.

[4] Charles P. Loomis, "Tentative Types of Directed Social Change Involving Systematic Linkage," *Rural Sociology,* Vol. 24, No. 4, December, 1959, pp. 383–390.

principles and values which are long established and widely accepted. In oganizations, including school systems, change occurs as a result of: 1) planning by equals, 2) indoctrination by superior officers, and 3) outright coercion by the same officers.[5] To function enduringly, change should apparently be a "deliberate collaborative process" involving the following features: "a) a joint effort that involves mutual determination of goals; b) a 'spirit of inquiry'—a reliance on determinations based on data publicly shared; c) an existential relationship growing out of the 'here and now' situation; d) a voluntary relationship between change-agent and client with either party free to terminate the relationship after joint consultation; e) a power distribution in which the client and change-agent have equal or almost equal opportunities to influence the other; and f) an emphasis on methodological rather than content learnings."[6]

Change in the individual seems to come about in the following way: Some of the stimuli in one's environment contribute to one's readiness for change by creating a felt need for something different, a dissatisfaction with what now exists. The need is met, at least in part, by a planned or fortuitous experience. Largely as a result of the experience (or series of experiences), one sees himself and his environment in a new light. Consequently he develops new values, and subsequently new goals, which may be closed-ended or open-ended. Sometimes the new goals arouse additional needs, and one finds himself in another orbit of planned change. Encouragement, help, and stimulation are needed during the entire process of change. The nearer one's newly-developed values are to the values he holds dear, the more permanent his change is likely to be. Some persons change rapidly; others, slowly. Differences in rate of change are therefore to be expected.

This brief description, oversimplified as it probably is, contains several ideas which need examination and extension into practice in the schools. When the ideas have passed through the sieve of the educator's experience, they become a set of tentative principles like the following:

1. *People improve with greatest enthusiasm when they detect the desire of the stimulator of improvement to improve himself.* The argument, "You need improving, and I am here to improve you" has slight effect. On the contrary, "We have a common problem; to solve it, we should all improve our competencies" has a pleasanter, more convincing ring.

---

[5] Warren G. Bennis, "A Typology of Change Processes," in Warren G. Bennis, Kenneth D. Benne, and Robert Chin, *The Planning of Change.* New York: Holt, Rinehart & Winston, Inc., 1961, pp. 154–156.

[6] Bennis, Benne, and Chin, *op. cit.,* p. 12.

2. *The direction of improvement should be determined cooperatively.* People's goals differ. However, if they are to work together effectively, they must determine cooperatively the direction their efforts are to take.

3. *To achieve improvement, people must identify and examine each other's centrally-held values.* This action is difficult and time-consuming. It requires the best in communication—the careful listening that Carl Rogers talks about, the careful observing that Daniel Prescott recommends to teachers. It demands lengthy talking together and prolonged watching of each other's behavior, so that the persons involved may truly say, "We know each other."

4. *People improve through experiencing.* The kind of teacher one is may be determined largely by the kinds of experiences he has had. School systems should seek to provide their teachers with the best of in-service education.

5. *Stimulators of improvement should divide their time between contacts with individuals and contacts with groups.* Research and practice show that both individual conferencing and group work are effective in helping teachers improve the quality of their work. The balance between these two general procedures cannot be predetermined; it can be judged only in consideration of given, prevailing situations.

6. *People's resistance to the efforts of others to help them improve constitutes a major individual difference.* Not only are some people more generally resistant than others, but people vary in their resistances to specific new proposals.

7. *Whenever possible, improvement should be induced in situations that involve problem-solving.* People improve most when a stimulator of improvement helps them solve their own problems. Some problems pose a threat, and therefore cannot be dealt with immediately and directly. For instance, teachers who have trouble with classroom control are often unable to discuss their control problems dispassionately. Curriculum workers should do their best to make many such professional problems appropriate ones for discussion and solution.

8. *Stimulators of improvement should try to create and maintain a climate of freedom for those with whom they work.* This statement rests on the thesis that people improve when they feel free to improve. Where there is a feeling expressed in the declaration, "My boss won't let me," that feeling should be eliminated by carefully-guarded words and behavior that point clearly to permissiveness in the whole situation.

9. *Stimulators of improvement should help keep channels of communication open.* Psychological static easily gets between the sender and the receiver of a message. Much of this static can be cleared away by face-to-face communication. Curriculum workers should try to hear what others say by listening carefully, by repeating or rephrasing people's comments, and by trying to understand their messages.

10. *Stimulators of improvement should use their power and influence with great care.* Educational leaders have largesse to distribute in the form of position, salary, approval, knowledge, prestige, disciplinary control, and even affection. Their status often begets in teachers an acquiescence that is easily mistaken for a genuine desire to improve. When the threat or the paternalism is gone, acquiescence disappears too.

11. *Stimulators of improvement should operate on a limited number of fronts at a given time.* Curriculum workers are learning that sweeping, comprehensive improvements rarely take place. Rather, progress is made on a broken front, a little at a time, in manageable form.

The preceding principles should be considered carefully by those who would improve the curriculum. They suggest the following specific actions which the curriculum leader should take:

Work *with* people, not *over* them.
Show that you, too, desire to improve.
Help the people with whom you work know you and know each other.
Help teachers enjoy a variety of in-service experiences.
Work with both individuals and groups, balancing your time between individual conferences and group work.
Recognize that some people improve more slowly than others, both in a general sense and in specific activities.
Try to use problem-solving as a means of improvement.
Help teachers feel free to improve.
Keep channels of communication open.
Use your status, whether it is real or imagined, with great care: you can easily be a threat and an impediment.
Be sensible and modest in your expectations, doing well that which you undertake.[7]

Among the specific factors which assist change and improvement, motivation is evidently much to be reckoned with. At the beginning of the change-improvement process, the person receives his motivation from "dissatisfaction or pain associated with the present situation," dissatisfaction that results from

[7] The principles stated here appeared originally in Ronald C. Doll, "Our Orbits of Change," *Educational Leadership*, Vol. 17, No. 2, November, 1959, pp. 102–105. They are reproduced by permission of the editor of *Educational Leadership*.

"a perceived discrepancy between what is and what might be," external pressures to accomplish change, and an undefined "internal requiredness" that presses the individual to change.[8] After the initial stages of the process have passed, the person to be changed or improved is motivated by a feeling of need to complete the task, and by a feeling of appropriate speed in task completion. He may be motivated further by the existence of desirable relationships between himself and the stimulator of change or improvement.[9] Since these ideas are in no way final, curriculum leaders should check them against their own continuing experiences in dealing with teachers.

Motivation is thought to be inhibited at times by certain "resistance forces." These forces include opposition to any kind of change, opposition to a particular change, desire to cling to ideas or actions with which one is well satisfied, and poor relationships between the person to be changed and the stimulator of change. Sometimes change, no matter how constructive, costs "the client" more than he had originally expected it would, and he becomes discouraged with it. Sometimes, too, he is diverted to other projects, and change is inhibited by the diversion.[10]

Much change and improvement occur through individualized, person-to-person contacts. However, group work is known to have marked effect in changing people. This is true especially when the stimulator of change and the persons to be changed interact consistently in the same group. To be effective as a change medium, the group must, of course, be attractive to its members. The members accept new ideas and values most readily if the new ideas and values relate closely to those which group members already hold. The stimulator of change must diligently seek to cause the pressures for change or improvement to rest within the group itself. Hence, the more the group talks about the need to change, the more pressure for change is built within it, and thus within its individual members.[11]

When they are at their best, groups engage in a high quality of problem-solving. Change is believed to be created most readily by keeping problem-solving openly experimental, cooperative, task-oriented, and educational and/or therapeutic.[12] People who work together may be said to go through three steps in altering their views. They express compliance, usually in an effort to keep or enhance their own reputations. Next, they identify with one

[8] Ronald Lippitt, Jeanne Watson, and Bruce Westley, *The Dynamics of Planned Change.* New York: Harcourt, Brace & World, Inc., 1958, pp. 73 and 74.

[9] *Ibid.*, pp. 75 and 76.

[10] *Ibid.*, pp. 83 and 88.

[11] Dorwin Cartwright, "Achieving Change in People," in Bennis, Benne, and Chin, *op. cit.*, pp. 698–706.

[12] Kenneth D. Benne, "Deliberate Change as the Facilitation of Growth," in Bennis *et al.*, *op. cit.*, pp. 230–234.

or more other persons in their group or organization to achieve "a satisfying self-definition." Finally, they internalize the ideas and values in their environment, making these ideas and values part of themselves.[13]

If change occurred only in one-to-one relationships and in small group settings, it would be difficult enough to understand and accomplish. But it takes place also in large organizations which contain many sub-parts. A particular sub-part—for example, a subject-department in a high school—may be ready for improvement while the remaining sub-parts lag. Another special problem of organizations is the presence of hierarchies and channels through which plans for change or improvement must pass if they are to be acceptable to the organization as a whole. The authors Coffee and Golden generalize that:

> . . . institutions usually develop a formal social structure as a method of performing their work. The structure is characterized by a hierarchy of offices which have distinctive responsibilities and privileges. These are exemplified in a status system which is based on differential prestige and a prescribed set of roles and procedures . . .
>
> The processes of change can be productive within an institution only if conditions permit reassessment of goals and the means of their achievement . . .
>
> The most significant barrier to institutional change is the resistance which persons express when such change seems threatening to roles in which they have developed considerable security . . .[14]

Hierarchies, goals, procedures, and roles are all involved in the process of institutional change.[15] The existence of rigid hierarchies and standardized views of procedures and roles may inhibit change. Cooperative examination of goals does, on the other hand, encourage permanence of change, provided that the altered goals are put into functional use by the hierarchy. At any rate, of the three methods of institutional change which were mentioned previously—planning by equals, indoctrination by superiors, and coercion by superiors—planning by equals seems to have the greatest long-term and desirable effect.

Jenkins has proposed a methodology for encouraging teacher-pupil planning—and for creating other educational changes—which follows four classic steps in social engineering: analyzing the situation, determining required changes, making these changes, and stabilizing the new situation to

---

[13] Herbert C. Kelman, "Processes of Opinion Change," in Bennis *et al.*, *op. cit.*, pp. 509–517.

[14] Hubert S. Coffee and William P. Golden, Jr., in *In-service Education*, 56th Yearbook, Part I. Chicago: National Society for the Study of Education, 1957, p. 101.

[15] See Ray Sorenson and Hedley Dimock, *Redesigning Education in Values, A Case Study of Institutional Change.* New York: Association Press, 1955.

assure its maintenance.[16] Jenkins recognizes the existence of a "force field" (as suggested originally by the late Kurt Lewin) in which there are "driving forces" that push in the direction of change and "restraining forces" that oppose change. The present or current condition in an educational situation is at "that level where the sum of all the downward forces and the sum of all the upward forces are equal." An example of a driving force is the conviction that, if teachers involve their pupils in planning, the teachers themselves will receive greater satisfaction from the act of teaching. An example of a restraining force is teachers' lack of skill in helping pupils plan.

In Jenkins' words, "changes will occur only as the forces are modified so that the level where the forces are equal is changed." To modify the forces, we may: 1) reduce or remove restraining forces, 2) strengthen the driving forces or add to their number, or 3) change the direction of certain forces. For instance, we may remove through training our lack of skill in teacher-pupil planning, strengthen or add to competence in planning, and change the direction by which we achieve the objective "good citizenship" *from* telling pupils how to be good citizens *to* planning citizenship activities with them. In analyzing the force field, the curriculum leader may seek answers to the following questions: What forces are there in the field? Can the directions of some of the forces be reversed or altered in another way? Which restraining forces can probably be reduced with least effort? Which driving forces can probably be increased?

To become permanent, says Jenkins, change must be stabilized: *i.e.*, the stability of the new condition must be assured. This can be accomplished by our being sure that the restraining forces have been made impotent and that the driving forces continue in action.

The qualified comments with which the process of change and improvement must be described indicate the uncertainty that exists about the precise nature of the process. Experience with curriculum improvement activities in school systems has led, however, to development of a lore centering in actions that aid improvement. The more promising of these actions are spelled out in the remainder of the chapter.

SITUATION 6-1—RESISTANCE TO CHANGE: AN APATHETIC FACULTY

Jim Downes, principal of Martinsville High School, had spent two years in his position. Previously he had been in charge of a smaller high school in Townsend Terrace.

[16] David H. Jenkins, "Social Engineering in Educational Change: An Outline of Method," *Progressive Education*, Vol. 26, No. 7, May, 1949, pp. 193–197.

It was October, a month after the start of school during Jim's third year. At the end of the day he came home much discouraged. Sitting in his favorite arm chair in the living room, he looked disconsolate.

"What's the trouble, Jim?" asked Eunice, his wife. "Why don't you come to dinner?"

"I'm discouraged and disgusted," said Jim. "We had a faculty meeting again today. Our curriculum consultant from the college was there, and we thought everything would go well. I say *we*. Sam and I were the only two people who seemed to have any such hopes. If it weren't for Sam and his leadership of the science department, I believe I'd quit. Well, nine-tenths of the faculty members just sat there. When the consultant and I asked what problems the faculty would like to deal with during the coming year, we drew a blank."

"You mean no one said anything?" Eunice inquired.

"Well, practically so. There was a long, dead silence, and then Old Ben Oppenheimer spoke for the group, as usual. 'This is a smooth-running faculty,' Ben said. 'It's been smooth for years, Mr. Downes. It was smo-o-o-o-th before you came. We just don't see any need to manufacture problems.' "

"That was the end of Ben's speech, and practically the end of the meeting. I'm glad the superintendent wasn't there. If he had been, he'd have seen how little I've been able to jar that faculty in two years. . . ."

What might have caused the Martinsville faculty to resist change as it seems to have done?

What dynamics or forces are frequently at work in situations of this kind?

What do you suppose Jim Downes might do to reduce apathy and stimulate change?

SITUATION 6-2—MISDIRECTED CHANGE: THE TENDENCY TO MOVE IN TOO MANY DIRECTIONS AT ONCE

Curriculum change was popping in Plainsburg. The curriculum steering committee for the school system had invited individual teachers and groups of teachers to suggest and prosecute curriculum projects of any sort they wished. No machinery for selecting or screening projects had been established. The consequence was a flood of projects big and little, well-conceived and ill-conceived. Shortly, the steering committee began to express concern as to how many of the projects represented the real needs of the school system, and as to whether there was danger in permitting school personnel "to ride off in too many directions at once."

What is your position regarding control of number and nature of projects which lead to curriculum change?

Which of the ideas about change that appear in the initial part of this chapter relate to the problem of moving in too many directions at once, and should therefore be communicated to participants in curriculum improvement?

FOUR ACTIONS THAT FACILITATE CURRICULUM IMPROVEMENT

Four actions seem to have special effect in facilitating curriculum improvement. Stated in imperative form, they are:

I. Cause the climate and the working conditions in your institution to encourage curriculum improvement.

II. Achieve and maintain appropriate tempo in curriculum improvement.

III. Arrange for a variety of activities that lead to improvement.

IV. Build evaluation procedures into each curriculum improvement project.

Each action will be discussed in some depth.

I. ESTABLISH SUITABLE CLIMATE AND WORKING CONDITIONS

Climate and working conditions, like employees' morale, may be said to result from many little actions and influences. The little actions and influences within an organization may, however, be categorized under larger headings, the chief of which seem to be: the general attitudes of participating personnel; quantity and quality of personnel and especially the competencies they bring to their tasks; physical resources and materials at the disposal of staff members; and absence of undue and detrimental pressure and influence.

Attitudes of participants——Certain attitudes of participating personnel seem to be especially helpful in planning curriculum improvement. One of these is the acceptance of people's right to feel and express legitimate dissatisfaction. Perhaps everyone who strives to progress in his work feels some dissatisfaction with what he is presently doing. His should be a feeling of legitimate dissatisfaction which does not lead to arbitrary complaining but to affirmative action which achieves satisfaction. Curriculum workers should seek to learn the exact causes of dissatisfaction, and should encourage co-workers who feel dissatisfaction to channel it constructively into new activity.[17]

A second attitude relates to acceptance of the contributions of many kinds of people. Not all contributions of ideas and all gestures of helpfulness are of equal worth. Nevertheless, every person who is qualified to belong to a faculty group has a series of unique contributions to make, because he himself is an individual. He is able also to make certain contributions in concert with other members of his group. Curriculum workers should provide ample opportunity for each person to express himself and to offer his own talents.[18]

A third attitude expresses willingness to permit other persons to work on the problems which they themselves identify. Real, live problems are those problems which are real and live to the persons who face them. Imposed or imported problems seldom seem worth solving. Thus, the principal who is concerned with his own problems and constantly requires the teachers in his school to help him solve them may find that the teachers are at first courteous but that they soon become apathetic and even hostile. On the other hand, these same teachers may readily become enthusiastic about solving problems which are clearly their own. Curriculum workers should help teachers clarify and solve problems which the teachers themselves perceive as being well worth solving. The same teachers will then greet with favor occasional opportunities to help solve problems for which they feel no direct personal concern.[19]

A fourth attitude consists of openmindedness about new educational decisions and practices. The improvement process is materially aided by an attitude of openmindedness about the new and different, as well as about the tried and tested. So little in education is known assuredly that any school person is acting presumptuously when he clings to ideas merely because they are supported by tradition. For some persons, openmindedness implies an experimental attitude, a willingness to use the "method of intelligence"—com-

---

[17] Miel, *op. cit.*, pp. 40–47.
[18] Benne and Muntyan, *op. cit.*, p. 315.
[19] See "Who Should Make What Decisions?" *Administrator's Notebook*, Vol. 3, No. 8, April, 1955, p. 4.

monly called the problem-solving method—in dealing with educational problems. For others, it means merely an attitude of "wait and see" while other staff members try new practices. Whatever the degree of an individual's personal involvement in a project, openmindedness is necessary to the project's success, and to prospects for future experimentation.

A fifth attitude is one of willingness to work with other persons to achieve common ends through commonly-agreed-upon means. This attitude affects leaders and followers, *i.e.*, all members of every working group. However significant the contribution of the talented individual who works alone, well-coordinated groups usually prove wiser in plotting both the means and the ends of improvement.[20] Curriculum workers should become well acquainted with procedures that facilitate group work, and should become competent in leading groups of differing sizes and kinds.[21] In addition, they should seek to reconcile the means they use with the ends they desire. One evidence of autocracy is a tendency to use foul means to achieve desirable ends. Competent, sensitive curriculum specialists should consider carefully the means they utilize.

Quantity and quality of personnel——Stimulating, friendly climate and helpful working conditions are aided by the presence of able personnel in sufficient numbers to accomplish worthwhile tasks. Few school systems have too many full-time coordinators, consultants, and specialists in fields like school social work, psychology, reading, and speech therapy. Surveys of the staffing of schools and school systems usually reveal that more work is being accomplished by limited numbers of persons than even the most conservative of personnel analysts expect. However, these persons are often discharging responsibilities which should not be theirs, or they are discharging them in ineffective ways.

While present-day schools are frequently undermanned in the fields of supervision and curriculum services, the quality of assistance which classroom teachers are now receiving could be improved in at least three respects:

1. *The very best available person should be utilized to discharge each major responsibility*, even though employing a new person may prove costly. Too often, teachers or principals with full or partial work loads are being made part-time specialists in reading, art, music, physical education,

20 John W. Thibaut and Harold H. Kelley, *The Social Psychology of Groups*. New York: John Wiley & Sons, Inc., 1959, pp. 256–272.

21 See major references on group work, two of the most useful of which are: Matthew B. Miles, *Learning to Work in Groups*. New York: Bureau of Publications, Teachers College, Columbia University, 1959; and Halbert E. Gulley, *Discussion, Conference, and Group Process*. New York: Holt, Rinehart & Winston, Inc., 1960.

speech, psychology, and other fields in which they may have at one time received limited preparation.

2. *The role of the school in the total community should be examined at intervals* to determine whether all the functions which the school has adopted truly belong to an educational institution. Many teachers, administrators, and laymen suspect that certain "social work" services to children and the community at large have been preempted by the school from other institutions and agencies. Though the school may, in many instances, supply these services speedily and efficaciously, the wisdom of making the school responsible for them in the first place is questionable. Of course, children whose only source of necessary services is the school may legitimately expect the school to continue providing these services.

3. *Special teachers should be assigned in different, more helpful ways.* A recent study by the United States Office of Education has shown that varied and sometimes questionable uses are being made of special teachers in physical education.[22] Reading specialists often devote their full time to helping individual pupils, instead of spending a portion of their time in assisting classroom teachers to become competent identifiers and eradicators of common reading difficulties. Specialists should ask themselves, "How can we provide greatest long-term help to classroom teachers?"[23]

Two additional sources of personnel to improve teaching and learning are: the staffs of universities, state departments of education, and school systems other than one's own; and well-informed laymen. These two sources provide part-time consultants who may be called upon for a few hours' or a few days' assistance at almost any time. The factors that affect the success of consultants have been described in the literature,[24] and alert boards of education and school administrators are making increasing use of consultant services. At the same time, many school systems maintain resource files of community citizens who volunteer their help in instructional fields ranging from the physical sciences and the arts to citizenship education.

No substitute, of course, has been found for competent classroom teachers who work patiently day by day with children. The keys to quality in our schools are the classroom teachers who man them. Consequently, employing

---

[22] Elsa Schneider, *Physical Education in Urban Elementary Schools.* Washington, D.C.: United States Department of Health, Education and Welfare, *Bulletin 1959*, No. 15.

[23] The report of a recent study of schools in New York State by staff members of the School of Education, New York University, has suggested that superior employment practices, careful delineation of the role of the school, and wise assignment of specialist personnel are three of the main keys to school quality in that state.

[24] See Marcella R. Lawler, *Curriculum Consultants at Work.* New York: Bureau of Publications, Teachers College, Columbia University, 1959.

superior teachers and then helping them grow personally and professionally constitute the prime hopes of excellent schooling for American children.

The morale of able teachers can be improved by reducing the load of clerical duties that now burdens many of them. Obviously, professional employment carries with it responsibility for certain routine operations, but studies of the clerical obligations of classroom teachers often reveal numerous and unnecessary clerical loads. Enlightened school administration seeks to free competent persons for activity at their highest level of potential and performance.

The individual teacher tends to feel that his own role is valued if the other teachers within his building are competent. In a time of emergency licensing of marginally-qualified teachers, the problem of maintaining mutual respect and self-respect among staff members becomes especially difficult and important. Yet the effect of quality of personnel upon faculty morale is readily apparent.

Availability of physical resources and materials——Studies of working conditions in schools have revealed the satisfaction teachers feel in having varieties of instructional materials, and in understanding ways of using them. When materials and equipment accord with the needs of the instructional program, and when the persons who use materials and equipment have a major part in choosing them, the usefulness of these resources can usually be guaranteed.

One of the great difficulties with current learning materials is their failure to serve differing ability levels and socio-economic groups. Publishers of textbooks and other materials have only begun to produce instructional aids for the mentally retarded and near-retarded and for the culturally deprived. Furthermore, materials to challenge the gifted have not always been at hand, and many teachers doubt that superior materials exist in quantity for children of any developmental level or status. The school that seeks to improve the curriculum for its pupils searches continuously for materials and equipment that will best take into account the range of individual differences the school encounters. The principal of a school of this sort tries to make physical resources quickly available to teachers by purchasing materials as they are needed and by moving them to points of use as speedily as possible. One of the hazards of modern school administration is the tendency of principals and other administrators to become overzealous about amplifiers and electronic machinery generally, and thus to use precious funds for the purchase of equipment which teachers would gladly trade for materials of more direct use to them.

The classroom library or materials center, the community resource file, the audio-visual center, and the curriculum laboratory all add enrichment and zest to school life. Each of these resources needs further development. Taken together, they need careful coordination so that a functional program of selection, purchase, and use of materials can operate for the assistance of teachers.

Absence of undue pressure and influence——Studies of teacher morale clearly indicate that the effectiveness of a school can be ruined by the conniving and perfidy of irresponsible politicians. Promises that are made and not kept are one of the major sources of trouble. Another is graft, which is now absent from most school districts, but is known to be present in some of them. Tenure laws have generally been successful in preserving teachers' employment, but many teachers are still under pressure to behave in politically "acceptable" ways if they desire salary increments. Unfortunately, some of the more idealistic political scientists now maintain that control of schools should be placed more and more in the hands of municipal and state government officials other than members of school boards. A step of this sort should be taken with great caution because of the dangers of political interference to which numerous teachers are already subjected. The unfortunate effects of undue pressure and influence have been demonstrated over and over again.

Studies of morale in school staffs are not completely conclusive. Nevertheless, they provide additional evidence about the place of good climate and desirable working conditions in schools. Griffiths notes the importance of the administrator's actions in providing better working conditions and salaries, in improving community relations, and in being consistent in orienting, promoting, and placing teachers. In addition, he mentions the significance of personal acceptance and security, of opportunities to participate in team efforts, and of the need for mature personnel.[25]

Yauch gives a final bit of practical advice for improving morale:

Be willing to make haste slowly.
Take the easiest problems first.
Treat people as human beings.
Make their experiences in school pleasant.
Operate on the assumption that teachers can be trusted.
Try a little of the "Golden Rule."
Encourage and accept criticism.
Don't act like a stuffed shirt.[26]

[25] Daniel E. Griffiths, *Human Relations in School Administration.* New York: Appleton-Century-Crofts, Inc., 1956, p. 156.
[26] Wilbur A. Yauch, *Improving Human Relations in School Administration.* New York: Harper & Row, Publishers, 1949, pp. 257–263.

SITUATION 6-3—A SPECIAL PROBLEM OF ATTITUDES

Consider the words of a curriculum coordinator who has a complaint to make:

> Mr. Acornley, our superintendent, came to our K-12 social studies meeting and wanted the whole job we'd been accomplishing for a long time done over. The teachers were all hopped up about some experiments they'd been designing. One of them was describing his plan when Mr. Acornley arrived. After about five minutes of sitting and looking wise, he turned to me and said, "Now I hope you're not misleading these teachers. I think they're getting themselves involved in things that don't concern them. I'm not much in favor of some of the ideas that teachers like to try out on other people's children. Now I'll tell you what we need—and the Board reminded me of it just last week—a good social studies course of study. Preparing one in meetings like this would be more profitable, I'll bet a cookie, than listening to each other talk, especially when the conversation is over the heads of some of the folks anyway. I'll tell you what to do: prepare a course of study and have it ready within two months. Then you'll be making a real contribution." When he'd said all this, Mr. Acornley got up and ambled to the door. Well, you'd have thought a wet blanket had descended on that committee! All we could say was, "It's time to go home."

The effect of this sort of commentary by an important leader is obviously serious and highly detrimental.

What could the curriculum coordinator and the superintendent have done to prevent this outbreak?

Is it possible that the superintendent feels somewhat threatened by the curriculum coordinator's relationship with the teachers, or by the importance of the coordinator's role in instruction? How commonly does this feeling of threat prevail? If it is at all common, what should be the responsibility of curriculum coordinators in preventing it?

What might have been done in this situation to re-establish co-operation and enthusiasm among the teachers?

SITUATION 6-4—SOME CONSIDERATIONS IN EMPLOYING PERSONNEL

"Frankly," said superintendent Smathers, "I'm troubled. People are important to curriculum improvement, especially if they're the right people for a particular job. I don't know what's completely right for our situation. The Board has given us $16,000 to spend for new staff. Here's a list of the principals' and supervisors' suggestions about needed personnel:

a third-grade teacher for Grant School, where the present third grade numbers 41 children;

a high-school chemistry teacher, requested because of an additional enrollment of 52 pupils in college chemistry;

a special teacher in elementary-school physical education, to travel among the elementary schools and teach groups of children whose regular teachers don't feel competent to teach physical education;

a reading consultant to work in the high school and the two junior high schools in improving reading rate and comprehension of groups of secondary-school pupils;

an assistant to the superintendent, with responsibility for recruiting the best teachers available.

"The last three positions on the list would be completely new positions," Mr. Smathers explained.

"With good teachers being paid not less than $5,000 a year, and specialists costing more," continued the superintendent, "it's obvious that we're not going to employ all these people. This is why I've come to my assistant superintendent in charge of instruction. What do you think? Which ones shall we employ?"

Because you, as an outsider, do not know the situation directly or intimately, you cannot be expected to answer the questions. However, if you were the assistant superintendent, much concerned with desirable climate and working conditions as they affect curriculum improvement, what factors would you want to consider before you gave your answers? Why do you consider these factors important?

SITUATION 6-5—SOME COMMON PROBLEMS IN GETTING AND USING INSTRUCTIONAL MATERIALS

Mr. Martinson, the new principal of Clemson High School, looked straight at his assistant. "Henry," he said, "in your 15 years around here have you visited all the classrooms in the building?"

"No," replied Henry, as he fumbled a pad of late-admission slips, "Mr. Davies had me working on administrivia—you know, administrative details—all the time. I hope things will be different under the new regime."

Dodging his assistant's hint, Mr. Martinson explained: "Within the past eight days, I've been in all the classrooms looking for places to help improve working conditions for the teachers. I'm sure we have at least one handle to take hold of. It's the way our teachers are getting and using instructional materials. Here's a list of problems as I see them."

Henry looked at Mr. Martinson's notebook. A half-dozen problems appeared prominently at the top of the list:

1. Most teachers seem to be using a single textbook only. In some classes, there are too few copies of the single textbook to go around.

2. Teachers complain that they must order audio-visual materials a half-year in advance of their use. When films and film-strips arrive, the pupils sometimes say they have seen them two or three times in previous years.

3. A visit to the school library during almost any period of the day reveals that one could shoot a shotgun through the library without hitting many pupils.

4. Workbooks seem to be used mainly to provide busywork or to keep pupils quiet.

5. Teachers say that many of the books their pupils are using are too difficult.

6. There seems to be a feud between the high school's audio-visual specialist and most of the department heads. The department heads charge that the audio-visual specialist is trying to "build her own little empire."

In view of the importance of adequate and well-used materials in achieving desirable climate and working conditions in a school, indicate a) immediate, and b) long-term actions Mr. Martinson and his staff might take in dealing with each of these problems.

II. ACHIEVE AND MAINTAIN APPROPRIATE TEMPO

A second major action which facilitates curriculum improvement is achieving and maintaining appropriate tempo. Curriculum workers are soon compelled to learn that the timing of curriculum improvement activities is vital. Their fundamental problem is one of maintaining balance between gradualism and rapidity. Many school systems work so gradually at improvement that they scarcely make any effort to improve at all. Eventually, groups of citizens in their communities or in the nation at large surpass the professional staffs of these school systems in thinking and planning, and thus are able to create changes in the schools. Too much gradualism, or outright lack of curriculum leadership and action, has contributed to an externally-planned revolution in the teaching of mathematics, physical science, and certain other subjects in American schools. Teachers of these subjects are now making changes in curriculum content which they would probably have been very slow in making if they had not been "pushed." Other externally-planned revolutions are obviously in the making.

The opposite of extreme gradualism is, of course, excessive and ill-founded speed. Many a noble experiment has come to grief because its supporters have moved far ahead of the rank and file of classroom teachers. Many another project has been lost because popular thinking in the community in which it was initiated was not prepared for its appearance on the educational scene. Careful watching of the forces that promote or impede improvement provides the only real guide to appropriateness of speed. Good timing results from responding cautiously to questions like these: "Are we ready for this change?" "How fast can we comfortably move?" "How does the speed at which we are effecting this change relate to the speeds at which we are making other changes?" "If we are not ready for a significant, timely change, how can we develop readiness for it?" "Are there any ideas and actions which could be helpful in sparking change?"

Surely tempo of change or improvement relates directly to the thoughtfulness with which improvement is sought. For instance, a group of teachers may write a course of study during six weeks of occasional meetings, with little effect on the practices of other teachers who are later introduced to that course of study. Instead, an in-service project requiring three years may be directed to the same ends, and the improvement resulting from it may be profound and long-lasting. The distinction between the two activities is not only in duration of time expended but in careful, early consideration of the kinds of activities which might make a genuinely lasting difference. One of the major functions of leadership is to emphasize the importance of certain projects in relationship to other projects. Those which are really important to teachers' growth usually deserve the most time for completion and the most pre-planning of the procedures by which they will be effected. Furthermore, the time of their initiation must depend chiefly upon how soon they have to be accomplished, and upon the number and nature of other tasks which must be performed.

Practitioners of curriculum improvement often face additional problems that affect the tempo of their work. One of these is the varying sizes of the tasks they undertake. An important duty of curriculum planners is to estimate the amount of time particular tasks deserve. If the tasks are large, one, two, or three of them may be all that a school can undertake within a year. Usually, some tasks look small, while others loom large. For instance, considering word analysis in the reading program of upper elementary-school children is a smaller task than determining sequence in the whole language arts program. The former task might be performed rapidly, in conjunction with several other activities. But full consideration of sequence in an important subject-field might legitimately claim a faculty's undivided attention for at least a year. Of course, both big and small tasks are being undertaken in most school systems at the same time. It is important to keep the total number of tasks few enough, according to their size, so that curriculum study is thorough rather than superficial.

A second problem concerning tempo relates to the manageability of projects. Some projects are so large or complicated that they simply cannot be dealt with by the personnel of a single school system. Significant experimentation with educational television, for instance, usually requires large-scale financing and the cooperation of several school systems. Unwise selection of projects which are too large or too involved not only leads to frustration among personnel; it also causes waste of their valuable time.

A related difficulty is, of course, selection of projects which make no real difference in instructional improvement. So many unevaluated tasks are being performed today that little is known about their relative or intrinsic worth. It is a basic viewpoint of this author that one may make expensive rearrangements of personnel and materials, demonstrate them, and advertise them widely, and still not know whether they make a difference to learning. Time spent on unevaluated demonstrations may easily be time stolen from other, more demonstrably useful projects.

Finally, tempo is affected by injudicious rescheduling of tasks which have been performed on one or more occasions previously. One of the common complaints of teachers is this: "Someone has decided that we ought to study the English (or some other) program again. I thought we gave it a good overhauling just three years ago." Teachers become frustrated when curriculum leaders seem to "ride" their own hobbies, calling for restudy of given educational problems at too-frequent intervals. Careful pacing of tasks is a special need in those school systems in which curriculum study has been under way for many years.

The rule, then, about tempo, timing, or pacing may be comprehended in the words: *not too fast, not too slow, not too carelessly planned, not too big, not too insignificant, not too recently considered.* This is obviously a rule easier to state than to live by, but it is extremely relevant to the process of improvement.

SITUATION 6-6—THE EMERGENCIES IN PENNSATONIC

Pennsatonic is a big town geographically, even if it's not a very populous one. The principals of its 16 schools seldom see each other except at monthly staff meetings in superintendent Moody's office. Maybe it's the 20-mile distance from one side of town to the other that makes the problems of the schools so different. Anyway, at last Tuesday's meeting two completely different kinds of problems developed. As a result of them, good old Pennsatonic may not settle down for a long time.

Ned Graves, who's in charge of Adams School, reported that he'd recently been descended upon by a group of parents who wanted to "see the curriculum of Adams School." The group was dissatisfied with the fact that ancient history is being taught in the fifth grade, and with the fact that long division is postponed until near the end of the sixth grade. There were other complaints about the curriculum, too. Ned found some copies of courses of study in the social studies and arithmetic and handed them to the complainants. Now he's sorry he did: the parents soon noticed that the courses of study are nearly 18 years old. Some of the complainants want the teachers to spend their spare time during the next two weeks describing in writing what they teach in these two subjects. Later, they will want the teachers to describe what they teach in other subjects, too.

From the north side of town, Ralph Corson had a different tale of woe. The teachers in his junior high school are up in arms because half of them are expected to do team teaching in a block-of-time

program. Ralph says there is likely to be a strike unless he helps eliminate the block-of-time program and makes an entirely new schedule. A few of the teachers broke up a faculty meeting last week with the complaint that Ralph and two of his "favorite teachers" had planned and installed the block-of-time program during the summer without the knowledge and participation of the other teachers.

State the differences (and similarities, if any) between the two problems presented above.

What could have been done to prevent each of these problems?

What should the superintendent and the principals do a) immediately, and b) long-term to solve each of the two problems? How could they relate their long-term actions to newly-developed system-wide policies in curriculum improvement?

III. PROVIDE FOR A VARIETY OF ACTIVITIES

A third major action which assists the process of curriculum improvement is providing for a variety of activities directed toward improvement. The provision of varied activities has been referred to as a "shotgun approach." When one shoots a shotgun, he is not certain what he will hit with any one pellet. Similarly, curriculum improvers who use varied activities are sometimes unsure who will be attracted to and who will be most affected by each of several activities. The best that one can do is to narrow many possibilities to a few, according to ascribed purposes and the exercise of one's good judgment. If, for instance, familiarity with research procedures is prized for a given group of teachers, an in-service course may be organized for them, an experience in using research procedures in their classrooms may be devised, or an apprenticeship to the research director of the school system may be arranged. Reason dictates that any one of these activities will prove more beneficial than merely inviting the teachers to read about research methods. But which of the three preferred activities should be engaged in by a given group of teachers? If all three cannot be utilized simply because there is not enough time to organize them, or because all three are unnecessary when one would do, which one will have greatest effect on the teachers? Though a curriculum leader may judge that the least sophisticated of the activities may serve best, other considerations affect his decision, and he cannot be sure of the answer to this question.

As Mann says, "Different contents, different methods, different settings, different training units, and different change agents contain different motivational impacts for change. What constitutes the most effective combination for changing behavior in organizations is not known. Few practitioners have really done any bold experimenting; almost none have combined measurement and experimenting to search for the most significant dimensions and variables in the change process."[27] The expedient, for the present, is to use a variety or a combination of activities which seem most likely to serve a given purpose, and then to evaluate their effectiveness to assist decision-making in the future.

As has been said, curriculum improvement may be equated in many respects with supervision and in-service education. Accordingly, the activities used in these three connecting avenues to school quality are fundamentally the same. They exist in some profusion under these headings: group activities, contact with individuals, and use of literary and mechanical media. Following are some of the available activities under their appropriate headings:

GROUP ACTIVITIES

These include meetings of:

committees	conferences	institutes
study groups	work conferences	courses
workshops	clinics	seminars

CONTACT WITH INDIVIDUALS

This refers to:

individual interviewing and counseling	demonstration teaching
classroom observation	intervisitation by teachers
assistance to the teacher in his class-room	course advisement
	directed reading

LITERARY AND MECHANICAL MEDIA

These include preparation and use of:

written bulletins	bulletin boards
research reports	tape recordings of meetings and decisions
policy statements	
course guides	educational television[28]

The reader will probably think of other activities which belong under these headings. Since the days when course-of-study construction was almost the exclusive activity in curriculum improvement, the problem has not been

[27] Floyd C. Mann, "Studying and Creating Change," in Bennis *et al., op. cit.,* pp. 605–615.

[28] Many activities for improving the curriculum are discussed in H. P. Adams and F. G. Dickey, *Basic Principles of Supervision.* New York: American Book Company, 1953; and in Harl R. Douglass, Rudyard K. Bent, and Charles W. Boardman, *Democratic Supervision in Secondary Schools.* Boston: Houghton Mifflin Company, 1961.

a lack of activities but, rather, uncertainty as to which ones should be used in given situations.

Curriculum workers appear to spend most of their time in activities of a group-work nature. They spend the second most time interacting with individuals. In the future they will probably give more attention to the third category, literary and mechanical media, as technology causes the mechanical media to increase. Many curriculum leaders hold that, among all the separate activities, workshops and conferences with individuals achieve most satisfactory results.

McNally and Passow suggest several criteria which may be used to guide selection among possible activities:

1. The particular needs of a situation are met through their (the activities') contribution to desired growth of staff and by the facilitation of work on specific kinds of curriculum improvement tasks or foci of attention.

2. Individual differences in needs, resources, and ways of working among professional staff and school faculties can be taken into account and appropriate provisions made.

3. Necessary resources, both personnel and material, are either already available or can be obtained.

4. The skills, competencies, and knowledge required for effective participation and leadership are studied and, where necessary, training sessions are provided for extending these.

5. Coordination is readily possible so that separate strands of curriculum work can be interrelated for building a consistent, comprehensive educational program.

6. Effective communication among individuals and groups involved in planning, as well as others who are concerned, is strengthened by systematic efforts to inform while work is in process as well as at its completion.

7. Implementation possibilities of program planning are kept visible throughout and the relation between curriculum development and changes in classroom instruction is constantly in focus.

8. Evaluation of both process and product—the procedure and the program change intended—is made an integral part of the undertaking.[29]

SITUATION 6-7—HOMEWORK FOR THE STEERING COMMITTEE

Someone turned on the lights in the curriculum office. It was 5:45 on a Tuesday afternoon, and the steering committee was torn

[29] Harold J. McNally, A. Harry Passow, and Associates, *Improving the Quality of Public School Programs.* New York: Bureau of Publications, Teachers College, Columbia University, 1960, pp. 100 and 101.

between two requirements: leaving for dinner and other appointments, and planning to effectuate four distinct activities within the next two months.

"Since we've rejected the idea of having a sub-committee make the plans," said Dr. Stogdill, chairman of the steering committee, "let's think about possibilities during the next two days and meet here again for an hour on Thursday afternoon."

"I'm not sure I remember all four activities," drawled Herschel Odom. "Ruth, will you put all of them on the blackboard?"

The chalk scraped and clicked as Ruth Hadley listed:

Sensitizing high-school mathematics teachers to new content and sequences in mathematics

Getting teachers' suggestions about names of local citizens to add to the resource file

Hearing from the child-study division of the State Department of Education concerning the topic, "Newer Findings About the Development of Elementary-School Children"

Presenting to all the teachers in the school system a "buddy plan" for the orientation of new teachers next fall

Assume that you are a member of the steering committee. List one or more activities you think you might emphasize in dealing with each of the four problems. Keep in mind the possibility of combining activities that belong to the three categories: group activities, contact with individuals, and preparation and use of literary and mechanical media. Discuss with a group of your fellow students the feasibility of your plans.

IV. BUILD EVALUATION PROCEDURES INTO EACH PROJECT

A fourth major action to help the process of curriculum improvement is building into each project, from its very inception, procedures for evaluating the effects of the project. This action is taken so infrequently that the quality of both older and newer educational practices usually goes unassessed. After a while, the accumulation of unevaluated practices becomes so large that no one can defend with assurance the ways in which schools are operated.

If the chief end of curriculum improvement is improvement of pupils' experiences under auspices of the school, then the significance of every important step toward this end is worth evaluating. The evaluation may, because of the pressures of time and work, be done quite informally, but it should be done nevertheless. The presence of evaluation data lends assurance to practitioners, and it supplies evidence to the people who pay school costs and who want to know whether their money is being well spent.

Evaluation is meant to gauge the extent to which objectives of a project or activity have been achieved. A desirable relationship between evaluation and objectives appears in the following diagram:

OBJECTIVES

ACTIVITIES

EVALUATION

This relationship has already been mentioned briefly in Chapter 5. The diagram suggests that, as soon as the objectives of a project are stated, ways of evaluating the achievement of the objectives should be considered. Activities should then be chosen for their pertinence to the objectives, and also with reference to possible means of evaluation. The thinking process should follow this sequence: objectives, to evaluation, to activities which are useful in achieving the objectives and whose effects can properly be evaluated. Too often, curriculum workers think of activities first, and then either ignore or defer consideration of objectives and evaluation.

Suppose a committee of second- and third-grade teachers wants to develop a social studies program for primary-grade children that is based less on the imaginings of adults concerning what is good for young children generally, and more on the expressed interests of the children themselves in a particular school system. The committee's major objective, then, is to develop a program centering upon the expressed interests of given groups of children. As soon as the committee has set this objective, it should raise the question, "How can teachers know when this objective has been achieved?"

The answer might be formulated thus: "Teachers can know by examining the products of their work in determining children's interests within the field called social studies. One of the products will be the teachers' guide which is written at the conclusion of the study. A more important product will be the choices of social studies content which teachers are observed making in their classrooms. Therefore, while we shall inspect carefully the completed teachers' guide, we shall also conduct before-and-after observations of choice-making by teachers in their classrooms. Both our objective and our methodology of evaluation imply that teacher activities like the following will be suitable: conducting interviews with children, administering a three-wishes test, asking children to draw pictures to express their wishes, recording ways in which children complete unfinished stories, and engaging children in group discussions. In this way, objectives, evaluation procedures, and activities used in curriculum study become closely bound together, and, in fact, evaluation tends to become a continuous process."

More thorough treatment of the evaluation of curriculum projects appears in Chapter 12.

ACTIVITY 6-1—THE PREVALENCE OF BUILT-IN EVALUATION

Review several curriculum improvement projects to see whether methodology of evaluation was discussed immediately after the nature and purposes of each project were described. If you have had no direct contact with curriculum improvement projects, search for a few reports of projects in educational literature, to be identified by using *Education Index* or the specific directions provided by your instructor.

1. In how many instances have plans for evaluation been built into the projects immediately? In how many instances have plans for evaluation been mentioned at all?

2. What do you conclude about the esteem in which evaluation is held by those who believe they are improving the curriculum? What is your own present view of the significance of evaluation?

SUMMARY

This chapter has dealt with the general process of curriculum improvement as it is understood today. The process follows patterns formed by interdisciplinary findings about change in individuals and institutions. Emphasis has been placed upon the importance of cooperative effort in creating improvement, upon the power of motivation, and upon the significance of institutional arrangements. To encourage improvement, curriculum personnel have been urged to pay attention to climate and working conditions in schools, to help

maintain proper tempo of improvement, to promote varied activities, and to build evaluation procedures into each project.

SELECTED BIBLIOGRAPHY

Benne, Kenneth D., and Bozidar Muntyan, *Human Relations in Curriculum Change* (New York: The Dryden Press, 1951).

Bennis, Warren G., Kenneth D. Benne, and Robert Chin, *The Planning of Change* (New York: Holt, Rinehart & Winston, Inc., 1961).

Doll, Ronald C., "Our Orbits of Change," *Educational Leadership*, Vol. 17, No. 2 (November, 1959).

Lippitt, Ronald, Jeanne Watson, and Bruce Westley, *The Dynamics of Planned Change* (New York: Harcourt Brace & World, Inc., 1958).

Miel, Alice, *Changing the Curriculum* (New York: Appleton-Century-Crofts, Inc., 1946).

National Society for the Study of Education, *In-service Education*, 56th Yearbook, Part I (Chicago: University of Chicago Press, 1957).

Sorenson, Ray, and Hedley Dimock, *Redesigning Education in Values, A Case Study of Institutional Change* (New York: Association Press, 1955).

~ ~ ~ ~ ~ ~ ~ ~ ~ ~ ~ ~ ~ ~ ~

chapter seven

THE PROCESS OF CURRICULUM IMPROVEMENT is greatly facilitated by the presence in educational situations of adequate leadership. Ideas about the nature of leadership differ widely. This fact can be demonstrated by citing an incident which occurred at a curriculum conference.

The co-directors of the conference had just completed a tour of the 18 discussion groups which were meeting in a two-day session. They had returned to a central office to discuss the leadership of the groups, with a view to selecting leaders for the following year. The comments which the co-directors made reflect a variety of notions about leadership—notions which suggest that the co-directors do not seem to know what good leadership is. Their comments, arranged seriatim, were these:

"The man in charge of Group 12 is a natural-born leader."

"The members of Group 3 are falling right in behind their leader. He seems to be just what they need."

"The leader of Group 6 is as far ahead of his group as Einstein was ahead of ordinary mathematicians. Maybe he can move them further in their thinking than most of our leaders can move their groups."

"I don't know where we got the leader of Group 11. You wouldn't know he existed. The group goes right ahead without him. I question whether we want so quiet a person next year."

Leadership for Curriculum Improvement

"I don't know what was wrong with Group 4. There just seemed to be a lot of conflict over basic ideas."

Leadership of discussion groups differs in several respects from leadership of large organizations such as schools and school systems. Nevertheless the comments above suggest several pervasive fallacies about the leadership of all sorts of human organizations. They include the following:

1. Leaders are *born*; accordingly, we cannot hope to develop them.

2. Conformity and uniformity in thinking are to be prized.

3. Leaders ought to be so far ahead of their followers in the quality of their ideas that the followers cannot hope to catch up.

4. Leaders should always be found in the act of "leading"; quiescence is for followers.

5. Conflict is necessarily bad, even when it clears the air for further consideration of ideas.

Everyone who has lived consistently in concert with other human beings has seen effective leaders in action. Somehow these leaders create effects which would not have been created had the leaders been absent. Perhaps the epitome of what they do in democratic organizations is to help their co-workers identify worthwhile goals, and then to assist the co-workers in achieving these goals. *What* good leaders do is important, but *how* they do it is also important. Some of the what and much of the how are, in fact, invisible, and are therefore beyond description. Nevertheless, careful study of leadership in varied contexts has resulted in the formulation of several distinct theories of leadership. An initial portion of this chapter is devoted to brief exposition of three of the theories.

Considering the assurance with which the American public accepts certain culturally-based concepts of desirable leadership, the nature of effective educational leadership seems to many persons to remain singularly undefined. One of the culturally-based concepts appears commonly among laymen who visit school board meetings and ask, during debates on school issues, "Why doesn't the administration *tell* the teachers what to do, and then they'd do it?" The monolithic leader who knows all and can therefore tell all still looms in the thinking of the man in the street. Whether or not this kind of leader ever existed very long in any one situation, he is being replaced in some organizations by a leader whose behavior and image are quite different. While no one understands completely the dynamics of leadership, enough has now been learned about leadership as an art and a skill to permit a description of effective leadership for curriculum improvement.

The 1960 Yearbook of the Association for Supervision and Curriculum Development defines educational leadership as "that action or behavior among individuals and groups which causes both the individual and the groups to move toward educational goals that are increasingly mutually acceptable to them."[1] At the present state of knowledge, this is a satisfactory definition. The author of the Yearbook chapter in which this definition appears quickly states, however, that "leadership action is more than words can describe—it is a quality of interaction which takes on added meaning for people as they live it and study its significance."[2] In this sense, effective leadership has a spiritual quality. In commenting on the methods which leaders use in taking action, Mackenzie and Corey classify these methods as force, bargaining, paternalism, and determination of mutually acceptable goals and means.[3] The last-mentioned of the methods accords with the definition of educational

---

[1] Association for Supervision and Curriculum Development, *Leadership for Improving Instruction* (1960 Yearbook). Washington, D.C.: The Association, 1960, p. 27.

[2] *Idem.*

[3] Gordon N. Mackenzie and Stephen M. Corey, *Instructional Leadership.* New York: Bureau of Publications, Teachers College, Columbia University, 1954, pp. 24–30.

leadership which has been quoted above, though effective leaders, because they are human, may find themselves lapsing into use of force, bargaining, and paternalism, just as they themselves are forced, bargained with, and treated like children.

With the definition in mind, consideration should be given to the three major theories which have been advanced in efforts to describe effective leadership. The first of the theories holds that desirable leadership can be had if the leader possesses certain traits; the second, that it can be had as a result of what happens within groups; and third, that it can be had as a result of situations or sets of circumstances within which people are required to operate. Each of the theories will be presented in order.

THE KIND OF PERSON THE EDUCATIONAL LEADER SHOULD BE

More than 100 studies have been made of the traits which leaders should possess. The most disappointing feature of these studies is their failure to uncover a pattern of traits which leaders should invariably have. However, a few individual traits do appear in the studies repeatedly. Most of them seem to bear directly on the selection and the ultimate success of educational leaders. Translated into a version titled "the kind of person the educational leader should be," the commonly-identified traits suggest that:

1. *The educational leader should be empathetic.* He should be able to respond to and identify with emotional needs of the members of his group, and be seen by group members as a person with whom they can readily identify. Their ability to see him as a warm, accepting, affable person is apparently crucial.[4] If they cannot approve him as a person, they are not likely to approve him as a leader.

2. *The educational leader should be surgent.* This means that he should be considered by the members of his group to be enthusiastic, genial, alert, expressive, and cheerful, particularly if he is an elected leader.[5]

---

[4] See, for instance, Graham B. Bell and Harry E. Hall, Jr., "The Relationship Between Leadership and Empathy," *Journal of Abnormal and Social Psychology,* Vol. 49, January, 1954; Raymond B. Cattell and Glen F. Stice, *The Psychodynamics of Small Groups.* Urbana: University of Illinois, 1953; and F. Loyal Greer, Eugene H. Galanter, and Peter G. Nordlie, "Interpersonal Knowledge and Group Effectiveness," *Journal of Abnormal and Social Psychology,* Vol. 49, July, 1954.

[5] Cattell and Stice, *op. cit.*

3. *The educational leader should be a recognized member of the group he leads.* This does not mean that he must be "a regular fellow" or a genuine egalitarian, but that he should be considered a person who conforms to the critical norms of the group and is therefore not markedly "different" or "unusual." Thus, on critical issues, at least, his thinking runs similar to the thinking of most group members.[6]

4. *The educational leader should be helpful to the persons he leads.* Teachers want practical help with the problems they face. They value supervisors who are concerned about these problems, and who either supply direct assistance or arrange contacts which produce it. Studies in industry, politics, and other fields show similar desires of followers[7] to be helped by leaders.[8]

5. *The educational leader should be emotionally controlled.* Persons in charge of instructional projects need serenity and poise to face the tensions, hostility, apathy, and aggressiveness which arise in school situations. Only the steady, unemotional leader who tries to keep his head during crises is respected by his followers.[9]

6. *The educational leader should be intelligent.* The primary reason for this statement is that the great majority of staff members of the schools are themselves intelligent; consequently they have little respect for unintelligent leadership. The educational leader should be academically bright, verbal, and socially adept. (Adeptness in social relationships, resulting from sensitivity to other people, is perhaps one of the prime evidences of intelligence in action.) It is possible, of course, to be so far ahead of one's group in intelligence that group members consider the leader an "outsider" to whom they feel inferior.[10]

7. *The educational leader should be interested in assuming his leadership role.* An effective leader knows what his role involves, and accepts his responsibilities because he desires or welcomes them. If he is half-hearted

---

[6] William E. Martin, Neal Gross, and John G. Darley, "Studies of Group Behavior: Leaders, Followers, and Isolates in Small Organized Groups," *Journal of Abnormal and Social Psychology*, Vol. 41, No. 4, October, 1952, p. 842; also Launor F. Carter, "Some Research on Leadership in Small Groups," in Harold Guetzkow, ed., *Groups, Leadership and Men*. Pittsburgh: The Carnegie Press, 1951, p. 151; and Fillmore H. Sanford, "Leadership Identification and Acceptance," in Guetzkow, *op. cit.*, p. 174.

[7] Though the literature often uses the term "follower," there is evidence that the roles of leaders and followers in democratic groups are often interchangeable.

[8] Daniel Katz, Nathan Maccoby, Gerald Gurin, and Lucretia G. Floor, *Productivity, Supervision, and Morale Among Railroad Workers*. Ann Arbor: University of Michigan Press, 1951, pp. 22 and 23.

[9] Cattell and Stice, *op. cit.*, pp. 93 and 94.

[10] Gardner Lindzey, ed., *Handbook of Social Psychology*. Cambridge, Mass.: Addison-Wesley Publishing Company, Inc., 1954, Vol. 2, p. 886.

about or indifferent to his role, these attitudes will soon become all too apparent to his followers.[11]

We do not know which of these characteristics of the educational leader is most important. However, we are quite certain that these seven do not exhaust the possibility of identifying additional traits. Each of the seven which have been listed might be restated to indicate the importance of the perceptions of members of the group or organization which the leader heads. Thus, the statement "The educational leader should be surgent" might be reworded to read, "The educational leader should be perceived by the members of his group as being surgent." It should be emphasized that, while a leader cannot rely completely on "the bubble reputation," the way he is perceived by others has much to do with his success or failure.[12] For instance, a leader who has control of important information may often forget or refuse to transmit the information to members of his group. The members may easily interpret this lapse, whatever its cause, to be motivated by distrust or self-seeking, and may promptly disown him or lose confidence in him.

One additional point should be made about the characteristics of leaders. What one *is* may assure him a leadership role in one situation, and deny him such a role in another. This is said in anticipation of subsequent comments in this chapter about the importance of groups and situations in determining the effectiveness of leaders.

Following is a situation which highlights personal traits or characteristics:

SITUATION 7-1—CHOOSING THE PRINCIPAL'S ASSISTANT

Woodhaven School District was finally going to give high school principal Matthews an instructional assistant. Matthews had just visited the superintendent, who, busy as he was with the building program and a bond issue, had turned the problem of selecting an assistant over to the principal himself. Back at his office, Matthews shuffled the sets of employment credentials from colleges and universities and came up with two leading candidates.

The basic requirements of the assistantship seemed clear enough to Matthews and to five or six of his staff members with whom he had consulted. They were:

---

[11] Katz, Maccoby, Gurin, and Floor, *op. cit.*, pp. 22 and 23.
[12] Mackenzie and Corey, *op. cit.*

Ability to secure a state certificate in the general supervision of secondary education

A broad educational background

At least two years' experience in a similar position elsewhere

Special competency in leading groups and counseling individuals about instructional matters

Ability to coordinate warring groups and diffident personalities

Matthews and his consultants had been afraid to go further in listing job requirements. Like almost any other instructional position, this would be a difficult one to fill.

As he looked at the list of requirements, the principal muttered to himself, "I think I'll take a new tack: I'll look for the man or the woman who has what it takes to fill the position." Accordingly, he made a list of the characteristics of his two leading candidates by inferences from their credentials and from his interviews with them:

Candidate Smathers	*Candidate Rink*
Very enthusiastic about professional advancement	Moderately enthusiastic about professional advancement
Reserved in her social contacts	Outgoing in his social contacts
Broadly experienced in supervisory work	Somewhat experienced in supervisory work
Excellent academic record	Satisfactory academic record
Fair ability to adjust to differing groups with which she works	Superior ability to adjust to differing groups with which he works
Interested in some of the facets of her past professional work	Interested in most of the facets of his past professional work
Almost icily self-controlled	Sometimes lacking in self-control
Generally well accepted by other staff members	Generally well accepted by other staff members

1. **From your own point of view and on the basis of what you know at present, which candidate should principal Matthews favor?**

2. **What else should Mr. Matthews seek to know about these and other candidates?**

3. **To what extent is knowledge of the characteristics of a leader an insufficient index of his probable performance?**

4. **How do you rate yourself with respect to each of the seven characteristics which appear on pages 153–154?**

LEADERSHIP AS A PROPERTY OF THE GROUP

A second theory of leadership maintains that leadership does not inhere in the traits of individual leaders but in the structure of the group to which the individual leader belongs. To say it directly, "for most groups the inter-individual relationships *within* a single group are determined by the structure of the group to a considerable degree rather than by the personality of the individuals."[13] In developing this theory, researchers gave attention to leadership acts which they observed, described, and classified. Thus they asked, "What are the behaviors of outstanding leaders, whatever their titles or origins?" Leadership, according to this view, therefore, consists of the "performance of those acts which help the group achieve its objective. Such acts may be termed group functions."[14] The acts fall into two major categories: those concerned with achieving goals, and those concerned with keeping the group working happily and productively together. A leader, then, is anyone who engages in the performance of these two types of acts.

Support for this theory comes from the increasing knowledge that leadership is more widely diffused within organizations than people have heretofore imagined it to be. Kimball Wiles reports an interesting experiment in determining pupils' perceptions of potential leaders:

> We did a study of our students in P. K. Yonge High School at the University of Florida. There were 240 students in it at the time. We asked them questions like these: Suppose all the football equipment had burned up— which person would you choose to head a campaign to buy new equipment? Suppose we were going on the radio to explain our school program to the

[13] David Krech and Richard S. Crutchfield, *Theory and Problems of Social Psychology.* New York: McGraw-Hill Book Co., Inc., 1948, p. 401.
[14] *Ibid.,* p. 538.

public—which people would you choose to be on the panel? There were
seven types of activities like this in which a person's leadership could be
identified. We guessed that 25 to 50 students would be selected. Over 200
out of the 240 were identified by their fellows as the persons they would
choose.[15]

The experiment of Wiles and others dealt with the formal tendering or assigning of leadership roles by members of the group. Actually, leadership in
groups—including the large groups we call organizations—is passed in two
ways: formally, as when one receives status from the group or from an outside authority who imposes leadership on the group; and informally, as
when one takes on behalf of the group or accepts from his group a necessary
and often temporary assignment which carries with it little status. Leaders
who are initially given titles and rather precise roles are often called status
leaders; those who "rise to the occasion" are called emergent leaders. One of
the goals of modern administration is to encourage the emergence of leadership, based on the assumption that most tasks within organizations which
are not too specialized or technical can be performed by the rank and file of
the members. This assumption has been held rather widely by theoreticians
in school administration.

If in curriculum matters one acts according to the theory that leadership
is the property of the group, he can derive from the literature of group
process several ideas about what status leaders and emergent leaders should
do to assist small groups and larger organizations in attaining their goals.
The following functions of the curriculum leader appear immediately:

1. *To interact with one's fellow staff members as often as possible.* This
function is basic to the other functions which appear below. One must work
consistently with other people in order to be helpful to them.

2. *To establish a structure that permits broadly-based decision-making.*
Functional structure causes organizations to operate smoothly and effectively.
In democratic organizations, responsibilities should be allocated carefully
among the personnel. After helping to establish structure, leaders should explain the structure and clarify interrelationships among staff members within
it. For instance, when a psychologist is added to the staff for the first time,
the organization of the school or school system changes somewhat, and the
relationships of the new psychologist to principals, teachers, and other personnel needs to be made clear.[16]

[15] Kimball Wiles, "Human Relations Approach to Supervision," an address to
Baltimore supervisors published in *Baltimore Bulletin of Education*, Vol. 37, No. 1,
November, 1959, p. 19.
[16] Lindzey, *op. cit.*, p. 896.

3. *To initiate new ideas and to lend support to other acceptable ideas.* Persons in groups are supposed to do more than merely sit back, keep calm, and maintain the organization's equilibrium. All members of the organization, including status leaders, should be expected to contribute ideas and to examine and support ideas which have already been contributed.[17]

4. *To help the organization reach its goals.* Leadership should help the organization clarify its goals and then move steadily toward them. To accomplish these twin actions, leaders must show insight, skill, cooperative spirit, and ability to stimulate others to perform their tasks.[18] When a leader assists in these ways, he helps his organization to strengthen its morale as well as to increase its productivity.[19]

5. *To develop and maintain good relationships among group members.* Good relationships encourage geniality. Whether a person likes to work in his organization depends largely on the pleasantness of his co-workers and the satisfaction he gets from being a member of their team. From the time of the earliest experiments in worker productivity and morale to the present day, research has shown repeatedly that people's feelings toward each other materially affect both their happiness and their productivity.[20]

6. *To help coordinate activities.* Organizations function best when they are coordinated. This truism has been supported by evidence that coordination reduces antagonisms, moves organizations toward their goals, and settles arguments about ways of working.[21]

7. *To facilitate communication within the organization.* Facilitating communication within schools and school systems can probably be achieved best by keeping lines of communication short, attending to communication among grades or departments within schools, utilizing persons who are adept at communicating, openly approving tested educational ideas, and furnishing the necessary physical aids to improved communication.[22] Special attention to the numerous problems of communication within schools will be given in a subsequent chapter.

[17] Launor F. Carter, "Leadership and Small-Group Behavior," in Muzafer Sherif and M. O. Wilson, eds., *Group Relations at the Crossroads.* New York: Harper & Row, Publishers, 1953, p. 269.

[18] *Idem.*

[19] Nahum Z. Medalia and Delbert C. Miller, "Human Relations Leadership and the Association of Morale and Efficiency in Work Groups," *Social Forces,* Vol. 33, No. 4, May, 1955, p. 349.

[20] John K. Hemphill, *Situational Factors in Leadership.* Columbus, Ohio: Bureau of Educational Research, Ohio State University, 1949, p. 79.

[21] *Ibid.,* p. 97.

[22] Ronald C. Doll, "Communicating Educational Ideas," *Educational Leadership,* Vol. 18, November, 1960, pp. 109–113.

8. *To pay attention to the process by which decisions are made.* Good leadership avoids manipulating people or attempting to sell them answers. It watches the process by which really democratic decisions are made, giving everyone a voice and supplying information which aids decision-making.[23]

9. *To encourage the emergence of new leadership.* In accordance with a broadened concept of educational leadership, organizations improve as they encourage new leadership to emerge. Leadership theory and practice have moved steadily in the direction of spreading leadership responsibilities and utilizing leadership abilities wherever they can be found.

Again, as in the case of leadership traits, one cannot be sure which of these actions are most significant to the process of curriculum improvement. Studies of leadership in varied phases of human endeavor seem to show that good relationships among group members (number 5, above) and coordination of activities (number 6, above) contribute most to the welfare of certain organizations.[24] However, these actions may or may not accomplish the most for curriculum improvement. Nevertheless, these nine actions, taken in aggregate, appear to hold real promise for the leadership endeavors of curriculum workers. Consider which of the nine actions are applicable in the following situation:

SITUATION 7-2—LEADERSHIP WITHOUT EQUILIBRIUM

Leona Riordan was new at her position as elementary school coordinator. In the view of many of her fellow teachers, she should never have been appointed coordinator, but politics had accomplished it. Today she felt newer and more inexperienced than usual. "Something's wrong either with them or with me," said Leona. ("Them" referred to the teachers in Graves School with whom Leona had to work.)

"They tell you a lot of things in college and university that are of no practical use," Leona continued. "Here on the job, someone is always thinking up something for you to do or to avoid. Keeping it all in balance is a real problem. Yesterday I told some of our teachers to meet this afternoon in Room 104. Fewer than half of them arrived for the meeting. In meetings I often run into real trouble. Last week in the meeting on science, one of the fourth-grade teachers asked

[23] See Gordon Lippitt and Warren H. Schmidt, *My Group and I.* Washington, D.C.: Arthur C. Croft Publications, 1952.

[24] Hemphill, *op. cit.*, p. 79.

what I thought of experimentation with electricity in fourth-grade classrooms. I didn't reply. The next day in a meeting on reporting to parents, the question was whether children ought to be compared with each other according to national achievement test norms. What are the teachers trying to do—test *me?* Then, of course, there's the weekly complaint that we don't know what direction we're taking in the elementary schools. And so it goes until I don't know which way I'm expected to turn."

1. How does Leona's conception of educational leadership compare with the theory that leadership is the property of the group? How does it compare with the conception you now hold?

2. What are the basic problems in Leona's situation? If you were in her position, what actions would you take to begin solving them? Consider which of the nine general actions proposed in the preceding pages have any relevance for immediate or long-term use.

LEADERSHIP AS A FUNCTION OF SITUATION OR CIRCUMSTANCE

The third theory of leadership to be discussed and applied in this chapter holds that the situation or circumstance in which the organization and its leadership find themselves is crucial. According to this theory, certain situations call for leadership of a certain quality. Out of the situation and the need it engenders there arises leadership to deal with the situation. Therefore the leadership which is considered competent in one circumstance may not be considered competent in another, and the image of the monolithic leader is thus destroyed. The ingredients or factors in a given situation include the structure of interpersonal relations within the organization, the nature of the organization, the nature of the culture in which the organization exists, and the physical conditions and tasks with which the organization must reckon.[25]

This field or situational theory of leadership has special meaning for the curriculum leader. If he insists on trying to be the center of all activities, he will encounter many frustrations. These frustrations have been known for a long time in the military:

[25] Cecil A. Gibb, "Leadership," in Lindzey, *op. cit.*, p. 901.

A member of an organization who cannot do what is expected of him is immediately confronted by the stress of self-criticism and of criticism, implicit or explicit, from his supervisor and from his co-workers. His self-confidence will diminish, and feelings of inferiority will emerge; he is likely to become hypersensitive and defensive in his social relations, and blame others for his own shortcomings. Emotional stability and motivation will decrease and he may end by spending a large portion of his mental energy inventing excuses to justify his inadequacy.[26]

As the curriculum leader moves from school to school and from group to group within the school system's organization, different situational ingredients operate. According to the situational theory, no single status leader can hope to perform with extreme initiative in all the groups with which he meets, and still perform effectively in many of them. In this sense, the significance of emergent leadership and release of leadership potential in others is forced upon him.

Other cues from the situational theory suggest that the curriculum leader should be a student of good interpersonal relations within his organization, that he should know thoroughly the school system in which he works, that he should have an accurate and comprehensive view of the school and school system in the larger society of which they are parts, and that he must help to improve the work environment for teachers. The work environment needs special consideration with reference to the time needed to do curriculum work, the facilities and materials which are to be provided, and the kinds of tasks to be performed. The importance of these matters has already been seen in connection with the process of change and improvement.

When one discusses the effects on individual leaders of differing situations, he is brought full circle to the importance of personal traits. For this reason, the situational theory has had less support than it might have had. According to a 1957 source, "for a considerable period now the trait theory of leadership has been unfashionable. The pendulum of research and theory on leadership has swung, as we have seen, to the opposite pole, an emphasis on situation or field theory. We are beginning, however, to see a swing back of the pendulum, and strangely enough some of the effective impetus is originating with the situationists themselves."[27] At the present writing, the personal traits theory seems even further on the upswing.

If leadership could be explained adequately by forming a happy combi-

[26] Office of Strategic Services Assessment Staff, *The Assessment of Men*. New York: Holt, Rinehart & Winston, Inc., 1948, p. 456.

[27] Murray G. Ross and Charles E. Hendry, *New Understandings of Leadership*. New York: Association Press, 1957, p. 29.

nation of the three theories, much time could be saved in future study. However, other factors with which the three theories do not reckon enter the scene. Nothing has been said, for example, about the nature of the social organization within which leadership is to be established, about the value systems that exist within organizations, and about differing expectations of leadership behavior and role. In the words of Ross and Hendry:

> Perhaps the best we can say at this point is that any comprehensive theory of leadership must take into account the fact that roles in groups tend to be structured, and that the leadership role is probably related to personality factors, to the attitudes and needs of "followers" at a particular time, to the structure of the group, and to the situation. . . . Leadership is probably a function of the interaction of such variables, and these undoubtedly provide for role differentiation which leads to the designation of a "central figure" or leader, without prohibiting other members in the group from performing leadership functions in various ways, and at various times, in the life of the group.[28]

ACTIVITY 7-1—FINDING SITUATIONAL FACTORS WHICH AFFECT LEADERSHIP

Every curriculum leader who has large responsibility meets with numbers of groups and individuals. In doing so, he encounters situational differences of many sorts. Identify a responsible leader: the principal of a large school, the general supervisor or coordinator in a school system, or other functionary. Ask this leader to recall the events of his professional life during the past week. Make notes while he talks about the differences in situations which seemed to affect the quality of his leadership.

If others in your class or group have had the same experiences, pool your findings with theirs.

THE TASK ORIENTATION OF CURRICULUM LEADERS

Whatever theory or combination of theories of leadership is accepted by persons charged with the responsibility for curriculum improvement, certain general tasks must fall to their lot. These tasks are determined by the nature of the school as an institution, by the kinds of obligations which school per-

[28] *Ibid.*, p. 36.

sonnel are expected to have, and by what we know about the nature of curriculum improvement. According to a recently-developed construct, the tasks consist of defining educational goals, facilitating teaching and learning, building a productive organizational unit, creating a climate for growth and emergence of leadership, and providing adequate resources for effective teaching. They are shared by all professional personnel and by some non-professional ones, and they are believed to be universals, inasmuch as they appear from year to year and from community to community, wherever American schools exist. Because they belong to the instructional milieu of the school, they have little to do with building construction, janitorial service, bus transportation, or other strictly administrative problems. In terms of the previous discussion of leadership, the term "leader" is meant to include anyone within the school or school system organization who helps to define and promote the goals of the organization, and to maintain the organization's morale.

Clarification of the tasks is now in order:

Task I: To help the people of the school community define their educational goals and objectives. In the early days of activity for curriculum improvement, defining goals and objectives was a frequent first step. Because many school systems did not get beyond this step, goal definition fell into some disrepute. The attention of curriculum workers turned to the problem census, the isolated experiment, the demonstration project, and other initial steps as a means of starting improvement. The result has been an absence of purpose-centered education, and an eventual realization in some quarters that without vision the people in schools, as elsewhere, perish. By failing to set goals and objectives, curriculum workers do not know what educational values they stand for, where they are going, or how to evaluate what they have accomplished. Definition of goals, then, is a fundamental task in curriculum improvement; this task is to be shared with laymen.[29]

Task II: To facilitate the teaching-learning process; to develop greater effectiveness in teaching. Task II, which formerly resided chiefly in the central offices of school systems, now belongs more and more in individual schools under the status leadership of building principals. It is accomplished by whatever means the staff decides to emphasize from year to year, *e.g.*, by programs of supervision, by the newer studies of subject-matter, by projects in in-service education, by experimentation and research, by testing programs, and by curriculum committee activity of many sorts. We are in danger of having this task crowded out by bazaars, spring festivals, and cleanup cam-

---

[29] For further discussion of this and other tasks, see Association for Supervision and Curriculum Development, *Leadership for Improving Instruction* (1960 Yearbook). Washington, D.C.: The Association, 1960.

paigns—plans which impede serious study of teaching and learning and of careful follow-up by individual administrators and teachers.

Task III: To build a productive organizational unit. The importance of building organizational structure has been emphasized previously as one of the educational leader's responsibilities. An appropriate organizational unit has as its essentials cooperative planning and group deliberation. It releases people to examine their own and each other's roles, and to decide calmly who has the power and qualifications to assume particular responsibilities. In addition, this organizational unit keeps the channels of communication clear and arranges for finding out how well pupils are attaining the goals which have been set for them and for the schools.

Task IV: To create a climate for growth and emergence of leadership. Much of the previous discussion has stressed the importance of freeing teachers and other personnel to express themselves and to ask for help. In addition, Task IV highlights the importance of providing opportunities for staff members to accept and discharge various leadership responsibilities. It calls for emergent leaders to enrich by their contributions the work of the school, and to free status leaders for assignments which they could not undertake without the help of the emergent leaders. For heavy responsibilities, teachers who emerge as leaders need released time. However, when problems of the school are seen as *our* (the whole staff's) problems rather than *his* (the administrator's) problems, teachers are more willing to share freely in the minute tasks of planning and operating the instructional program.

Task V: To provide adequate resources for effective teaching. Teachers have more resources at their disposal than they realize. Some of these resources are personnel in the school and the community. Others are material in nature—homemade, commercially produced, or borrowed. Leadership must keep alert to lapses in the utilization of presently available resources, and also must search continually for new resources that make teaching live and practical.

These tasks are broad and general enough to fit any situation, and they are shared by many persons. As narrower leadership tasks are talked about, they are seen to belong to specific persons who have strong leadership roles. One of the common expectations concerning democratic leaders is that, while they should share many responsibilities with others, certain responsibilities should be affixed to them as individuals of special competence and with special license to act.

Accordingly, the whole range of responsibilities divides into three categories. Some responsibilities for curriculum planning are shared freely by all who have any stake in the planning. Others are shared cooperatively by status leaders and certain selected or representative staff members, as in curriculum steering committees. Still other responsibilities belong strictly to status leaders who bear the title superintendent, assistant superintendent in charge of instruction, director of instruction, curriculum coordinator, or some other title that suggests comprehensive curriculum leadership; and to other leaders with narrower but more concentrated responsibilities: principals, special subject supervisors, coordinators who bear aegis over a portion of the instructional program, and department heads in secondary schools.

We turn now to a discussion of the responsibilities of two kinds of status leaders: leaders in individual schools and leaders in entire school systems.

RESPONSIBILITIES OF LEADERS IN INDIVIDUAL SCHOOLS

Curriculum improvement must ultimately occur where the pupil is. The status leader who has most direct and immediate access to the pupil is the principal or supervisor in the individual school. As the principal or his assistant works with teachers and their pupils, his leadership skills are brought to bear upon crucial problems which develop in the process of improving the curriculum.

Umstattd describes the leadership roles of principals under seven categories of responsibility:

1. *Interpreter of our culture.* In this role, the principal watches for changes in the culture and the need to balance and re-balance curricular offerings. He seeks to know the school's pupils and their needs with reference to the culture, and to interpret children's needs to teachers.

2. *"Professional leader out beyond."* The principal looks through and across the minor or specialized tasks of the school to major objectives. His vision becomes functional when he secures the cooperation of the staff in driving toward the major objectives.

3. *Director of the curriculum.* In this role, the principal coordinates activities for improvement. In doing so, he organizes personnel, releases teachers for curriculum work, stands aside to permit able teachers to operate freely, maintains an open-door policy in welcoming experimentation, and helps keep his faculty mindful of the relationship of activities to goals.

4. *Supervisor of instruction.* The principal is generally responsible for what happens in the classrooms. He has an interest in educational methods and materials, and he helps assess curriculum practices for their effect on the physical and mental health of children as well as on children's intellectual development.

5. *Public relations officer.* The principal has an important obligation to interpret curriculum changes to the public, which obviously includes more persons than those on the roster of parents whose children attend school. He works with individual parents and groups of parents, and also maintains contact with civic and service clubs, social agencies, business and labor groups, churches, and the press.

6. *Agent of community enlightenment.* To secure long-term benefits for children and youth, the principal shows concern for the general educational level of the community. Sometimes his leadership has greatest effect when, for a time, he leaves the immediate problems of teaching and learning in his school to assist movements for the education of adults, that they may become better parents and citizens and so may facilitate the work of the school.

7. *"Manager of it all."* The principal is general manager of an intricate process—the education of widely differing youngsters. Though his role in professional education is narrower than that of the superintendent, its impact is deep.[30]

The principal who is a truly effective leader in curriculum improvement exhibits certain behaviors which make him distinctive. First of all, he knows the bases on which curriculum decision-making is accomplished: learners and learning; society and culture, with emphasis on his own community; and the contributions of organized knowledge. He understands curriculum design, and he functions well as an organizer and coordinator. A person who keeps activities in perspective and balance, he leads people both within the school and in the community at large. He is close to the needs and concerns of teachers and pupils, and he is able to translate ideals into day-to-day realities. In short, he epitomizes the best in leadership by manifesting executive ability and maintaining desirable human relations, and he accomplishes his work in the most strategically important place in the school system—the individual school.

ACTIVITY 7-2—WHAT THE BEST PRINCIPALS DO

Identify by professional reputation two or three principals who are believed to have done a great deal to help improve the curricula of their schools. Inquire as deeply as you can into the reasons for their reputations. Do this by asking persons who know them professionally what the principals have done to merit recognition as

[30] J. G. Umstattd, "The Principal Interprets His Role in Curriculum Development," *Bulletin of the National Association of Secondary School Principals*, Vol. 43, No. 244, February, 1959, pp. 15–20.

curriculum improvers. Then talk with the principals directly about their accomplishments.

1. What do you conclude that these principals have done to assist with curriculum planning?

2. As you compare your findings with those of classmates who have inquired about other principals, what do you discover the best principals do to make curriculum improvement possible and effective?

RESPONSIBILITIES OF GENERAL CURRICULUM LEADERS

Somewhat different responsibilities commonly fall to the lot of general curriculum leaders—*e.g.*, assistant superintendents, directors of instruction, and general supervisors. Most of these responsibilities are characteristically shared with other personnel. Which of them are shared and which are retained by general curriculum leaders depends so much on organizational patterns in school systems and the personal preferences and whims of the leaders themselves that one cannot distinguish, by general rules, between responsibilities that should be shared and responsibilities that should be retained. One study that has been made of general curriculum leaders' responsibilities shows that leaders frequently engage in these activities:[31]

> Meeting with local faculty groups and supervisors and discussing special problems and programs (*e.g.*, social studies) ;
> Addressing P.T.A., community groups, school groups, etc.;
> Serving as technical consultants to principals and teachers;
> Conferring with supervisors or other curriculum staff members about problems of curriculum and instruction;
> Conferring with commercial, educational, and other representatives visiting the school system;
> Serving as members of various community activities groups;
> Attending and actively participating in meetings of community civic clubs and organizations;
> Attending state and national professional meetings, conferences, etc., and making reports on these to local personnel;
> Developing and distributing a variety of curriculum publications and materials;
> Securing consultants for in-service education programs;

[31] Dwight L. Kirk, *The Role of the Curriculum Director in the Administration of American Public School Systems.* Austin: The University of Texas, 1953, pp. 31 and 32.

Filling questionnaires, information forms, blanks, etc.;

Making periodic oral and written reports to their superintendents on the status of curriculum and instructional programs;

Assisting in the development and execution of policies concerning classification, progress, promotion, and failure of pupils;

Organizing and directing formal in-service education programs;

Observing classroom teaching and conferring with teachers concerned;

Arranging for school exhibits, demonstrations, etc.;

Providing for orientation of teachers new to the school system.

This study, in which 386 persons with general curriculum responsibility in 134 school systems participated, reveals a heavy loading of public relations assignments in the curriculum director's work, and suggests that the generalist in curriculum may be serving largely as an aide to the superintendent, in charge of miscellaneous activities of a curriculum-public relations nature.

To answer the question, "How *should* curriculum leaders spend their time?" a group of leaders in New Jersey conducted a study which they reported in two categories: duties or activities which curriculum leaders considered most important, and activities which the leaders considered "related or adjunct."[32]

Following are the duties or activities which the leaders thought were most important:

1. Planning for improvement of the curriculum and of the curriculum development program.

2. Helping evaluate continuously both the appropriateness of the curriculum and the quality of the curriculum development program.

3. Directing the formation of point of view, policies and philosophy of education.

4. Directing the development of curriculum materials.

5. Using ready-made research data, and promoting local research.

6. Coordinating the activities of other special instructional personnel, *e.g.*, supervisors, librarians.

7. Working with guidance personnel to integrate curriculum and guidance functions.

8. Providing for lay participation in curriculum improvement.

[32] Ronald C. Doll, Harold T. Shafer, Sarah Christie, and Jerome C. Salsbury, "What Are the Duties of the Curriculum Director?" *Educational Leadership*, Vol. 15, No. 7, April, 1958, pp. 429 and 430. See also *The Work of the Curriculum Coordinator in Selected New Jersey Schools.* New York: Bureau of Publications, Teachers College, Columbia University, 1955; and George M. Sharp, "Curriculum Coordinators Study Their Job," *Educational Leadership*, Vol. 12, No. 8, May, 1955, pp. 464–466,

9. Arranging time, facilities, and materials for curriculum improvement.

10. Serving school personnel as technical consultant and adviser regarding curriculum problems.

11. Organizing and directing special in-service education projects.

12. Interpreting the curriculum to the public and, in certain situations, to the board of education.

13. Encouraging articulation among levels of the school system.

Following are activities which the leaders considered related or adjunct:

1. Helping orient new teachers.

2. Making recommendations for the budget.

3. Helping select teachers for appointment.

4. Helping plan new buildings and modernize old buildings.

5. Completing questionnaires dealing with instructional matters.

6. Attending national, state, and local conferences on education, and making reports of these conferences to local personnel.

7. Conferring with commercial, educational, and other representatives who visit the school system.

The last word has obviously not yet been said about the responsibilities of status leaders in curriculum improvement. During the school year 1954–1955, 227 of 348 larger school systems in the nation had assistant superintendents in charge of instruction,[33] and the number seems to be increasing in both small and large systems. This trend calls for genuine understanding by superintendents and boards of education of the appropriate functions of these specialized leaders. Under all circumstances, the major criterion of appropriateness should be the helpfulness of leaders to teachers and other personnel who are on the firing line of curriculum improvement.

Give your reaction to the method of defining responsibilities suggested by the following situation:

SITUATION 7-3—THE RESPONSIBILITIES OF A NEW CURRICULUM LEADER

The president of the Wasson Board of Education turned to superintendent Rogers at the conclusion of the Board's regular

[33] Theron Freese, "Summary of Study of the Position of Assistant Superintendent in charge of Instruction for the School Year 1954–1955," Long Beach, Cal., Public Schools (Mimeographed).

monthly meeting. "What are your specifications for the new position of director of instruction?" he asked.

Rogers was caught flatfooted. "We haven't really determined the specifications," he had to admit.

"Don't you think you ought to—right away?" the president asked.

Early the next morning, Rogers assembled several of his aides to help him establish a set of responsibilities for the directorship. Within an hour or two, they had the basic responsibilities listed to their satisfaction. The trouble came in trying to assign approximate percentages of the director's time to the responsibilities. "Maybe we can't do it very accurately," superintendent Rogers had said, "but I'd like to see each of you put on paper a percentage figure to indicate the amount of time the director should spend on each responsibility." When the proposed allocations of time had been assembled by the superintendent's secretary, they looked like this:

Activities	*Time Allocations*				
	Aide #1	Aide #2	Aide #3	Aide #4	Aide #5
1. Attending curriculum meetings	30%	20%	0%	50%	10%
2. Visiting individual classrooms	10%	2%	40%	8%	60%
3. Conferring with individual teachers	10%	15%	10%	10%	2%
4. Employing new teachers	20%	10%	30%	5%	10%
5. Attending teachers' social functions	3%	2%	0%	10%	0%
6. Reviewing lesson plans	2%	5%	15%	0%	10%
7. Conducting meetings, workshops, and other in-service activities	25%	45%	2%	15%	3%
8. Ordering and assembling materials and supplies for teachers	0%	1%	3%	2%	5%

1. What do you think of the perception of the curriculum director's role which is evidently held by Rogers and his aides?

2. If, as the new director of instruction, you felt obliged to accept the list of activities as constituting your basic responsibilities, how (abstractly) would you want to allocate your time among them? Tell why you would favor your plan of allocation.

RESPONSIBILITY WITH AUTHORITY

Books on school administration often discuss *administrators* and their *authority*. Books on curriculum and instruction tend to discuss *leaders* and their *responsibilities*. Under an ancient concept of leadership, authority resides in the superintendent of schools and those staff members to whom he delegates it. Frequently superintendents have not delegated authority to instructional personnel, though they have delegated it to business managers.

Major modification of this concept is needed. First, authority that is delegated increases "the number of levels of authority and thus results in a pyramidal rather than a flat organizational structure. This type of organization has often been authoritarian rather than democratic and has not promoted a free flow of communication."[34] Authority, a term which is used to describe institutionalized power, should be shared rather than delegated. "Shared decisions make it possible for the staff to be importantly involved . . ."[35] As Whyte puts it, the problem is not that of eliminating authority but of weaving authority and participation together.[36] Inasmuch as, within the structure of American school systems, superintendents are responsible to boards of education for total administration of the schools, superintendents are directly responsible to their boards for instructional programs. If they want the best instructional programs, however, superintendents will share their concerns, responsibilities, and authority for curriculum planning with the members of their staffs.

Furthermore, responsibility without authority tends to be sterile in its ability to produce results. As Caswell says, "It is much more effective to have the responsibility for curriculum work accompanied by authority over matters that fall within the curriculum area. This arrangement will foster cooperative

[34] Roald F. Campbell and Russell T. Gregg, *Administrative Behavior in Education.* New York: Harper & Row, Publishers, 1957, p. 280.

[35] *Idem.*

[36] William F. Whyte, *Leadership and Group Participation*, Bulletin No. 24. Ithaca, N.Y.: New York State School of Industrial and Labor Relations, Cornell University, May, 1953, p. 41.

and effective work in curriculum development."[37] Both individuals, such as directors of instruction, principals, and classroom teachers, and groups, such as curriculum committees, should have authority to plan for and make improvements in instructional programs. The extent and nature of the responsibility and the authority that accompanies it should be made clear to those who are to perform duties in schools. Where there is any possibility of conflict of interest among groups and individuals, the conflict should be foreseen and resolved as early in the life of a project as possible.

SITUATION 7-4—THE CURRICULUM LEADER WITHOUT AUTHORITY

The Branchville Consolidated Schools had an active, thriving curriculum improvement program. Thirteen curriculum committees and five study groups were under way in the eight schools of this consolidated rural district. The curriculum coordinator, Lillian Dinsmoor, was busier than usual now: she had recently helped the superintendent make a cooperative arrangement with the state university to begin curriculum experimentation for which the school district and the university would share the costs. Mrs. Dinsmoor had many responsibilities, but the superintendent saw to it that she was strictly a staff officer.

At 3:30 on a Thursday afternoon, Mrs. Dinsmoor telephoned three of the principals of the Branchville Schools to ask whether they could find substitutes for a previously-selected teacher from each of their schools for the full day one week from the following Monday. The purpose, Mrs. Dinsmoor explained, was to secure teacher representation on a new committee which would help her and Dr. Campbell, of the state university staff, plan for curriculum experimentation in Branchville. The first two principals whom Mrs. Dinsmoor called readily agreed to release their teachers. Mr. McKay, the third principal, refused. "What kind of school do you think I'm operating?" Mr. McKay asked. "We have important things for Mrs. Fineman, our representative on your committee, to do here on that day." Mrs. Dinsmoor knew that she had the responsibility for organizing the committee, which was to meet partly on school time, but

---

[37] Hollis L. Caswell and Associates, *Curriculum Improvement in Public School Systems.* New York: Bureau of Publications, Teachers College, Columbia University, 1950, pp. 81 and 82.

no one had told her what to do when principals refused to release teachers to serve during the school day. She concluded the telephone conversation with Mr. McKay as quickly and as graciously as she could.

1. What, if anything, should Mrs. Dinsmoor do immediately about her problem?

2. What should she do long-term?

3. How should her own actions relate to the possible actions of others in the school system who might help prevent similar situations from developing in the future?

SOME GENERALIZATIONS ABOUT CURRICULUM LEADERSHIP

"Participation in curriculum improvement activities provides opportunities for teachers to exert leadership and to develop leadership competencies."[38] Because opportunities for leadership should be dispersed more widely among the staffs of schools and school systems, one may generalize that:

1. Curriculum leaders should accept present opportunities to decentralize leadership within schools, and should plan for reorganizing schools so that leadership emerges more readily.

2. Curriculum leaders should show maximal respect for individual differences among staff members, so that varied competencies may emerge to season and enrich the program.

3. Curriculum leaders should expect to serve as consultants and guides rather than merely as directors.

4. Curriculum leaders should encourage the use of problem-solving methods in dealing with curriculum problems.

5. Curriculum leaders should prepare and help operate plans for training other curriculum leaders.

To take these actions, curriculum leaders should become competent in:

Practicing good human relations;
Adhering to principles of human growth and development;

[38] Association for Supervision and Curriculum Development, *Action for Curriculum Improvement* (1951 Yearbook). Washington, D.C.: The Association, 1951, p. 187.

Knowing when, where, and under what conditions curriculum change occurs;
Using group process techniques;
Relating quickly to other people;
Developing the creative abilities of other people;
Inventing new plans for organizing personnel and facilities;
Knowing how to solve educational problems;
Seeing themselves as others see them.

Varied conceptions of the roles of curriculum specialists have developed as more and more of these specialists have been employed. Use the following situation to help you clarify your own conception of the role of a "general supervisor."

SITUATION 7-5—WAS HE COMPETENT TO JUDGE?

When the Blankton Valley Schools employed Dave Jenkins as general supervisor, they found the best supervisor in the whole state. Dave seemed to have all the personal qualities, skills, and understandings anyone could ask for in an instructional leader. Members of the Board of Education were impressed with his knowledge of curriculum problems, and so was superintendent Roush. However, Mr. Roush had always had one reservation about Dave. "How," he'd asked several people, "can a man know about instruction from kindergarten all the way through the twelfth grade?"

Superintendent Roush felt that his reservation had been a wise one when the "Adams case" developed at the high school. Miss Adams, a second-year teacher, was, in the words of the high-school principal, "doing only fairly well." The principal asked Dave to visit Miss Adams' French classes, and Dave did so on three separate occasions. Dave concluded that Miss Adams was not doing at all well: she was almost sadistic in her treatment of the pupils, ridiculing and embarrassing them, and assigning them unreasonable loads of work. In addition, she was using antiquated and questionable methods of teaching. Accordingly, he wrote an adverse report and conferred with Miss Adams and the principal about it.

Now Miss Adams, who was the daughter of the town's most influential and wealthy merchant, prided herself on her knowledge of French. Having been in France on nine separate occasions, and having secured a master's degree in the teaching of French, she knew that she was, technically, an excellent French teacher. When she faced Dave in the presence of the principal and the superintendent and, later, in a Board of Education dismissal hearing which was attended by her father's two lawyers, Dave had to admit that he knew no French. The superintendent, the board members, and nearly everyone else in the Board of Education room began to question Dave's competency to judge Miss Adams' teaching.

1. What should Dave have said to the Blankton Valley Board of Education about his qualifications for judging Miss Adams' work? What rather typical lay points of view about teaching and learning was he encountering?

2. To make a well-rounded estimate of Miss Adams' performance in the classroom, what help should Dave have had? Where might he have secured this help?

3. What, apparently, was superintendent Roush's viewpoint about the qualifications a curriculum leader should have? What, then, was probably his view of curriculum leadership?

A CRITICAL LOOK AT PERCEPTIONS OF LEADERSHIP IN SCHOOLS

There are so many gaps in our understanding of instructional leadership that further inquiry concerning it will be needed during the years ahead. One of the greatest needs is for increased discernment concerning the precise roles of elementary- and secondary-school principals in instructional improvement. The roles of principals and other leaders in individual schools will probably be much magnified in the future, inasmuch as the locus of responsibility for instructional improvement has steadily come to be the individual school. Therefore everything possible must be done to build the authority, security, and competence of principals and their assistants. This observation raises the question, "What can be done to increase the confidence and the competence, both pre-service and in-service, of persons who are to lead staffs and programs in individual schools?"

The first question leads promptly to another. Much that has been done in directing instructional improvement programs in the past has included patterning and copying of ideas. There is a growing need for leaders who can stimulate creativity and discovery in themselves and others. The question, then, is, "What ways of thinking and what educational experiences do leaders need if they are to encourage people to create and inquire?"

Next, there is the whole matter of clarifying the meaning of democratic leadership. Evidence has accumulated to show that teachers do not have a clear image of the democratic leader. Actually, they are much better at describing what a democratic leader is *not* than at describing what he *is*. Since they cannot identify him clearly, and since they have rarely given thought to the implications of democratic leadership, can it be that, at the present time, they do not really wish leaders to be democratic? In some instances, teachers seem to want autocratic leaders to do some of their work for them. This is not meant to be a charge of perversity or laziness leveled against teachers: their reaction is often a natural effect of being uncertain as to where an unknown quantity called "democratic leadership" might place them. One may advance the thesis that a leader can be democratic only to the extent to which the staff of the school or school system is willing to assume both new and old responsibilities.[39] These comments return us to some really basic questions:

> What do we mean, in our own times and places, by democratic leadership?
> What responsibilities and obligations might result from enjoying democratic leadership?
> Is democracy in schools really somewhere between autocracy and laissez-faire, as it has often been pictured? Or, is it "softened autocracy" and/or "organized laissez-faire?"

These questions need to be pondered by all persons who aspire to, or who are already engaged in, curriculum leadership.

SUMMARY

Several major theories of leadership have been developed during recent years. Three prominent ones are the traits theory, the group theory, and the situation theory. Taken alone, none of the three is adequate to explain what happens when the leader achieves the maximum in productivity and morale. Five major tasks appear to be the common property of all educational leaders: goal-setting, facilitation of teaching and learning, planning of productive organ-

[39] See George M. Sharp, "The Principal as a Professional Leader," *The National Elementary School Principal*, Vol. 42, No. 2, November, 1962, pp. 61–63.

ization, creation of a stimulating climate, and provision of resources. Within school systems, the role of the principal is rapidly becoming paramount. Meanwhile, demand grows for effective leaders of system-wide improvement programs. Many unresolved issues concerning leadership demand the attention of curriculum personnel who wish to become really competent leaders.

SELECTED BIBLIOGRAPHY

Association for Supervision and Curriculum Development, *Leadership for Improving Instruction,* 1960 Yearbook (Washington, D.C.: The Association, 1960).

Campbell, Roald F., and Russell T. Gregg, *Administrative Behavior in Education* (New York: Harper & Row, Publishers, 1957).

Guba, Egon G., and Charles E. Bidwell, *Administrative Relationships: Teacher Effectiveness, Teacher Satisfaction, and Administrative Behavior* (Chicago: Midwest Administration Center, University of Chicago, 1957).

Mackenzie, Gordon N., and Stephen M. Corey, *Instructional Leadership* (New York: Bureau of Publications, Teachers College, Columbia University, 1954).

Office of Strategic Services, *Assessment of Men* (New York: Holt, Rinehart & Winston, Inc., 1948).

Ramseyer, John A., *et al., Factors Affecting Educational Administration* (Columbus, Ohio: College of Education, Ohio State University, 1955).

Ross, Murray G., and Charles E. Hendry, *New Understandings of Leadership* (New York: Association Press, 1957).

Selznick, Philip, *Leadership in Administration* (New York: Harper & Row, Publishers, 1957).

Shartle, Carroll L., *Executive Performance and Leadership* (Englewood Cliffs, N.J.: Prentice-Hall, Inc., 1956).

chapter eight

"LET ME SHOW YOU OUR CURRICULUM," said the principal to the visitor in his school. Proudly, the principal removed from his desk a mimeographed document which told teachers what to teach, subject by subject.

The visitor scanned the document and replied, "Now let me see your *real* curriculum."

"What do you mean?" the principal asked.

"I mean that I must spend at least a few hours in your school. I need to visit several classrooms at random. I want to stand aside in hallways as the children move through them, and wander through the cafeteria while children are eating and while they're talking freely. If an assembly program is scheduled for today, I want to attend it. And I'd like to visit the library, and then follow the children out to the playing field while they're under a teacher's supervision, and while they're on their own. By doing these things, I'll have at least a limited view of your *real* curriculum."

This anecdote recalls the definition of the curriculum currently used in the literature, but often ignored in practice:

> *The curriculum is all the experiences that learners have under the auspices or direction of the school.*

Initiating Curriculum Improvement

It would not be amiss at this point to recall the definition of curriculum improvement:

> *Curriculum improvement refers not only to improving the structure and the documents of the curriculum but also to stimulating growth, learning, and alteration of perceptions and values on the part of all the persons who are concerned with the curriculum.*

The curriculum involves what happens in classrooms, auditoriums, gymnasiums, hallways, cafeterias, school activities—anywhere the children are under the direction and guidance of the school. It includes informal experiences as well as formal ones. It is as big, broad, and all-inclusive as the lives of people in any major American institution.

THE NATURE OF CURRICULUM PROBLEMS

What, then, is a problem for curriculum study? Is it merely a problem associated with science, mathematics, language, and the other subject-fields?

It *is* indeed subject-centered problems of all sorts, but it is also problems of pupil attitudes toward teachers, learning, and subject-matter; problems of behavior in school corridors; problems of pupil participation in school government; all sorts of problems once considered to be on the periphery of school experience.

Perceptions concerning what constitutes a problem for curriculum study vary from group to group. Young children view curriculum problems differently from the way adolescents view them, and teachers often see them differently from the manner in which supervisors see them. Problems that seem pressing in one school appear insignificant in another. Always there is much to be done to improve the program of a school if one will but look about him with care, perceptiveness, and sensitivity. Anderson has listed 47 typical problems for curriculum study. To see their variety, note the following samples:

> Studying selected children and adolescents in order to gain a better understanding of them.
> Providing for individual differences.
> Making a follow-up study of dropouts and graduates.
> Making case studies of pupils from minority groups.
> Selecting a variety of books for classroom libraries.
> Obtaining community reactions to the school.
> Planning for and making home contacts.
> Developing a program of citizenship education.
> Improving the music program.
> Planning a work experience program.
> Correlating developmental reading with the rest of the school curriculum (secondary school).
> Planning for the exceptional child in the regular school program.
> Developing a program and organization for the use of audio-visual aids.[1]

The reactions of classroom teachers, especially beginning teachers, to a list of this kind might be that the problems are big and general, thus not concrete enough to concern the teacher "where he lives." Another reaction coming from nearly anyone with close knowledge of elementary and secondary schools might be worded thus: "None of these problems seems to be of concern to us just now. However, I can name a currently 'hot' and significant problem." School personnel should recognize that having problems is natural and legitimate, that not to have them means that one is professionally or intellectually quiescent. The alleged size and importance of a problem, whether large or small, should not make its proponent ashamed of it. If a problem

---

[1] Vernon E. Anderson, *Principles and Procedures of Curriculum Improvement.* New York: The Ronald Press Company, 1956, pp. 155 and 156.

proves to be either too large or too small to manage, subsequent consideration of it can serve to modify it in desirable ways. In the process of problem-solving, identification is a necessary first step. Definition or refinement of the problem constitutes an equally necessary subsequent step or series of steps.

These facts remind one that "teachers and administrators frequently voice their problems in a form that is more respectable than real. For example, the teacher may say that the principal's office bothers him with frequent interruptions of his classroom routine, and that because of these interruptions, his pupils lose interest. When this respectable statement of his problem has been 'pushed back' far enough, one may find that the teacher is really troubled by his own failure to vary his teaching procedures. Obviously he needs help in clarifying and stating his true problem (which is in part his relationship with the principal), and especially in accepting it as being respectable and worthwhile."[2] Rationalism about the respectability of problems can often be achieved in group settings, when the proponent of a problem realizes that other persons have the same or similar problems.

Numerous curriculum problems crosscut the specialized fields of supervision, in-service education, and curriculum improvement. A common question is, "When should a problem be identified as a problem of curriculum improvement rather than of supervision or in-service education?" Actually, by the process of subdividing the content of university courses and varying the activities of school systems in improving teaching and learning, an unrealistic trichotomy has come to exist among supervision, in-service education, and curriculum improvement. If the major objective of these three strategies is seen to be the improvement of teachers in service so that the experiences of their pupils may be improved, in turn, the substantive distinctions among the strategies become less sharp. Their interrelationships may be diagrammed thus, with a large amount of overlap among them:

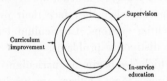

The distinctions among the strategies affect process much more than they affect substance. Therefore they may be regarded simply for what they are: differing strategies for the solution of curriculum problems. The prob-

[2] Association for Supervision and Curriculum Development, *Research for Curriculum Improvement* (1957 Yearbook). Washington, D.C.: The Association, 1957, pp. 260 and 261.

lems themselves should be analyzed carefully; then strategies should be selected for their solution. For instance, if lack of variety in teaching methods has caused an eighth-grade social studies program to become lackluster, activities under the traditional headings of in-service education (exposure of teachers to methodological ideas that are new and different to them) and supervision (follow-up and help in executing the ideas) may be in order. Curriculum workers should feel no self-consciousness about the category into which a problem falls. Activities in supervision, in-service education, and curriculum improvement are complementary means of implementing solution or amelioration. The focus of attention should be placed on the problem itself.

Some administrators, perhaps because they tend to see the curriculum as a whole and simultaneously lose contact with the day-to-day classroom scene, often become enamored of grandiose plans for improvement. This fact is demonstrated at national conventions when panel programs on educational television, block-of-time programs, administrative grouping, and team teaching enroll many participants and observers, while programs devoted more directly to ways of meeting the needs of individual children in classrooms are under-attended. Administrators need to meet frequently in problem-identification sessions with classroom teachers who have a realistic view of those actions that mean the most to effective teaching and learning.

Thus, a basic principle in getting started toward curriculum improvement is to *give attention to matters that concern teachers in their daily work.* These matters often have to do with methods of "reaching" individual pupils, selection of content for teaching particular groups of children, classroom organization of children and facilities for better learning, and ways of assuring the motivation of children to learn.[3] Master planning of facilities and organizational arrangements with which administrators are frequently preoccupied can make a genuine and lasting contribution to children's experiences under school auspices. However, teachers are not likely to show deep interest in such problems and proposals when they face their own distinctive problems at their respective teaching stations. Curriculum leaders should generally plan to begin with these distinctive problems.

Problems with which to begin a curriculum improvement program emerge from many settings. Some of them are products of given classroom situations and groupings of pupils; others are peculiar to individual schools; others stem from the developmental levels at which children are living and learning, and can thus be categorized as grade-level problems; others extend

---

[3] See L. A. Van Dyke, "Perspective and Priorities in Curriculum Planning," *School and Community,* Vol. 46, No. 6, February, 1960.

from kindergarten through the top grade; still others come from community pressure groups; and still others emerge from the mandates of state governments and from the exigencies of the national scene. In beginning a program of curriculum improvement, it is important to determine *who* should be charged with the solution of *what problems.* Nothing can frustrate teachers more severely than to work many days to solve problems which actually belong in the province of other individuals or groups. Master planning is needed in determining which problems are beyond the scope and control of persons on the local scene; which problems may appropriately be dealt with immediately by local personnel; which problems may be solved by the same personnel over long periods of time; and which problems have been so poorly identified that, in their present state, they are merely wrong perceptions of real situations.

One of the forces which has impeded curriculum improvement in the United States is the tendency of local school districts to participate in projects superficially, without appropriate expenditure of time and money. Some projects need heavy underwriting and support. Many of these can be conducted by federal and state governments and by regional groups. Examples are the conferences for administrators conducted by the Department of Education, State of New Jersey; the cooperative school system studies directed by the Metropolitan School Study Council, Teachers College, Columbia University; and many of the activities sponsored by the Southern Association.[4]

Reference has already been made to the two major steps in starting toward problem-solution: identifying a problem, and then defining it. The discussion to this point has centered about some basic considerations in problem identification. Attention should now be given to the second step, problem definition. Actually, the first step merges into the second. A problem, whatever its source, is likely to be in a decidedly raw state when it is first proposed. It expresses the concern of an individual or a group about a school situation which is believed to need attention. The problem need not relate to a situation which is serious or especially troublesome; rather, it may relate to a situation which has within it great prospects for improvement because it has already proved profitable in stimulating learning. Once again it must be said that the fact of having problems need have no negative implications.

As one looks critically at problems in their originally-proposed state, he sees that they are frequently too big in over-all size or that they have too many dimensions to be manageable. For instance, problems of child study are frequently proposed in such comprehensive form, with so many sources of

---

[4] See American Association of School Administrators, *American School Curriculum* (31st Yearbook). Washington, D.C.: The Association, 1953, pp. 97 and 98.

data being used in gathering initial evidence, that one does not know where to take hold of them or how to handle them. On the other hand, problems are often too narrow or limited, particularly as they are seen by classroom teachers, who tend to be so close to daily problems that they become myopic. Moreover, problems suggested by persons far removed from classrooms may have, for teachers, a totally unrealistic ring, so that teachers resist dealing with them. The object of the initial stage in problem definition is to limit the scope of oversized problems, to extend and bolster narrow ones, to make certain that problems are real and practical, and, in general, to assure the manageability and usefulness of the problems to be solved.

As definition by staff groups proceeds, discussion of the meanings of problems can become boring and impractical, while group members complain that a given problem is "being beaten to death." Or the problem may fall prey to persons with axes to grind, or with predispositions to view the problem in traditionalized rather than fresh ways. Some of the difficulties in problem definition can be solved by following a plan which proceeds thus:

1. The already-identified problem is defined until it is judged to be single rather than multiple, manageable in size, and worth solving—this being the initial step mentioned above.

2. The problem is thought about further, with a view to formulating hypotheses concerning what could be done to solve it.

3. When several promising-looking hypotheses have been formulated, they are tested intellectually through discussion, and those which do not seem fruitful or relevant are eliminated.

4. A new problem focus now forms around the hypotheses that remain. These hypotheses are tested by accumulating evidence which confirms or denies their worth in solving the problem. The evidence stems from the forces in decision-making: children, their development and learning; social forces that affect the schools; and the nature and structure of subject-matter.

5. Now that the problem has been reasonably well defined, tasks in testing hypotheses are assigned to staff members on the basis of their competence and interest.

6. Inquiry of this kind often leads to at least a minor redefinition of the problem as staff members find hidden factors and influences which they have not previously considered. The danger here is in "going off on strange rabbit trails" which may lead too far afield, perverting the original intent of the inquiry.

7. Problems often prove to be interrelated, so that recognition of one of them speedily leads to recognition of another. This fact makes curriculum improvement a fascinating activity.

The procedures which have been listed above need not, of course, be followed seriatim in all situations. The indispensable ingredient in the processes of problem identification and definition is careful, critical thinking about the meanings of problems and about ways of solving them. There is no reason why neighboring schools and school districts should not join in using these processes in solving problems on which they are often working in ineffective independence and isolation.[5] Surely it is possible meanwhile to conduct basic inquiry nationally, without subjecting the schools to the dangers and the unrealism of a national curriculum.

The scope and range of curriculum problems suggest the following situation which you should consider before you read about the forces and agencies on page 189.

SITUATION 8-1—SORTING THE PROBLEMS

The Curriculum Steering Committee of the 68-teacher Cormorant Unified School District was conducting its second meeting since the time of the Committee's formation three months previously. At its first meeting, the Committee had decided to poll all the teachers in the district to determine what pressing curriculum problems and concerns the teachers could suggest. Forty-nine teachers had responded to a simple questionnaire which asked for one or more open-ended statements of problems and concerns that should receive prompt attention.

When the returned questionnaires had been read, and the responses had been interpreted and categorized by a sub-committee of the Curriculum Steering Committee, the following problems and concerns were listed in rank order:

$$N = 49$$

Item	Frequency of Response
Excessive clerical work required of teachers	30
Scarcity of locally-developed curriculum guides	23
The prevalence of gum-chewing in our classrooms	18
Frequent interruption of classroom work because of announcements, drives, campaigns, and essay contests	17

[5] See Fred M. King, "A Trend in Curriculum Development," *Education*, Vol. 80, No. 7, March, 1960, p. 433.

Item	*Frequency of Response*
Too much interference from community members not connected with the schools	17
Children's weakness in language skills	16
Lack of knowledge of what teachers are doing in grades above and below us	15
Failure to concentrate sufficiently on the three R's	14
Children's poor study habits	12
Uncertainty about what the principals want us to do	9
Poverty, as lack of richness, in the arts—music and the fine arts, particularly	7
Poor discipline in some classrooms	6
A top-heavy emphasis on football	3
The presence of certain incompetent teachers	2
A weak science program	2
Poor arithmetical skills	2
Lack of supplies when we need them	1
Too many chiefs and too few Indians	1
Ineffective leadership by the administrators	1
Limited funds for audio-visual aids	1

1. If you were a member of the Curriculum Steering Committee, how would you contribute to a further categorization of these problems and concerns? For instance, which of them seem to relate closely to teachers' own feelings about their jobs? What other categories can you find?

2. Which of the problems and concerns seem to you to be respectable cover-ups for *real* problems and concerns? Why? How could you be reasonably sure that you are right?

3. Select one of the problems or concerns that interests you particularly. What would you do to help teachers begin solving or ameliorating it?

4. If you have an opportunity to do so, conduct a similar questionnaire survey in a school with which you are familiar. Then consider actions you can take in exploring teachers' initially-expressed problems to determine the full and accurate meanings of these problems.

FORCES AND AGENCIES THAT IMPEL CURRICULUM STUDY

The seeds of curriculum improvement are planted consciously in numerous places. Still other seeds drop fortuitously on fertile soil. Chapter 6 has described the process by which teachers learn to improve themselves. The present section lists some of the forces and agencies which, sometimes intentionally and sometimes unintentionally, contribute to initiation of curriculum improvement.

Most of these forces and agencies exist within school systems. Always they include alert superintendents, curriculum coordinators, and principals who want to see the schools move forward in using the best available knowledge of children, learning, teaching methods, subject-matter, and the requirements of a changing society. In addition, each school is likely to have its unofficial or emergent leaders who stimulate other personnel to improve their practices. Nearly every teacher can name at a given time one or more problems, even if they are other people's problems, which he would like to see acted upon. Pupils themselves, the live consumers of education, demand attention which often leads to curriculum improvement. Many a promising improvement program has resulted from administering standardized tests, though the data derived from the initial testing may have been of doubtful worth. Teachers and other personnel become carriers of ideas from meetings, conventions, intervisitations, and college and university courses. Professional literature is now so profuse as to challenge any teacher to read it currently, even in his own teaching field. These are but a few of the forces and agencies that sponsor improvement from within the school organization.

Ours, however, is an era in which demands for change, if not always for improvement, come from many voices outside the school. The roles of individuals and groups both within and outside school systems will be discussed in Chapter 9. Here are some of the outside voices:

Agencies of the federal government;
Educational testing organizations which develop tests and other evaluation
   devices for sale;
Popularly-written books and articles;
Regional associations of colleges and secondary schools;
Individual subject-matter specialists and groups of specialists;
Patriotic organizations, trade associations, labor unions, and industries.

The truth of a statement which was made years ago by curriculum specialists is now being realized: the school that avoids improving its own curriculum will soon have its curriculum "improved" for it. Many school systems have been so negligent in planning for curriculum improvement that they have become fair game for numerous competing interests outside the schools. Without question, many individuals and groups external to the schools are performing beneficent and valuable services for education, but they should not be allowed to become entire substitutes for school personnel who are working with children and youth day by day. McNally and Passow point to several actions which personnel of school systems can take in initiating curriculum improvement:

> Regular discussions for sharing common concerns, to make significant problems visible, and for exchanging ideas.
>
> Development of channels for communicating instructional problems to a central planning and coordinating group.
>
> New materials to be sent to individuals and groups, keeping them abreast of new developments.
>
> Opportunities for individuals and groups to have contact with new ideas and practices through conferences, meetings, and school visitations.
>
> Study of practices and procedures to gather pertinent information about the educational programs.
>
> Encouragement and support of experimentation and research in the classroom by furnishing necessary aid (*e.g.*, consultants, materials, and skill training).
>
> Periodic evaluation of learning and teaching, and analysis of results for leads to improving program quality.[6]

Consider the following situation relative to forces and agencies that impel curriculum study:

SITUATION 8-2—WHOSE CONCERNS SHOULD HAVE PRIORITY?

Orangeville Elementary School was a brand new school in a desert which had recently been made to bloom by irrigation, and which was accordingly attracting numbers of young families. Most of the fathers of Orangeville's children worked in industrial plants in the city 30 miles away. A few were skilled laborers, but the majority were scientists, engineers, or highly-specialized technicians.

When the School opened a year ago, Bill Ransom, the principal, organized the Curriculum Improvement Council to identify curric-

---

[6] Harold J. McNally and A. Harry Passow, *Improving the Quality of Public School Programs.* New York: Bureau of Publications, Teachers College, Columbia University, 1960, pp. 78 and 79.

ulum problems and to begin dealing with several of these problems immediately. During its ten months of operation, the Council had met face to face with all the teachers who were not Council members, and had identified two pressing concerns which seemed worth exploring in depth. One of these was the need to choose enriching materials for a school that had little more than basic textbooks. The other was the need to develop programs in art and music, inasmuch as these subjects were being largely neglected in favor of the three R's, science, and the social studies. The Council was certain that the teaching staff was committed to pursuit of these two concerns.

Then lightning struck. A committee of parents, intent upon the opportunities of their children for college admission, called upon Bill Ransom and insisted that the previously-publicized concerns of the teachers be overridden in favor of the following alleged needs:

Homogeneous grouping at all grade levels from first through sixth.

Investigation of why some children do not learn to read as rapidly as others.

Establishment of special coaching classes in the three R's.

The teaching of "ninth-grade general science" in the fifth and sixth grades.

Increase in homework assignments.

Greater competition among children in the primary grades.

Later that week, the commander of a patriotic organization discussed with Bill the importance of eliminating the social studies from the curriculum, of returning to separate teaching of history and geography, and of requiring every sixth-grader to memorize the Declaration of Independence.

1. Indicate the degree to which you respect each of these concerns, according to the origin of the concern and its intrinsic nature.

2. In this situation, what should be done by the following personnel: Bill Ransom, the Curriculum Improvement Council, and the faculty as a whole?

3. The Orangeville Elementary School was new, and had scarcely had an opportunity to get under way. How do you account for the presence of virulent, external forces at this stage of the school's career?

4. What principles might apply in balancing and reconciling the internal and external forces in a situation of this kind?

PROCEDURES FOR GETTING UNDER WAY

Several major procedures have been developed for getting under way in curriculum improvement. They include the problem census, in-service media, cooperative studies and surveys, experimentation, formal evaluation, and the development of philosophies and sets of objectives. Each of these procedures will be discussed in turn.

THE PROBLEM CENSUS

A time-honored way of initiating curriculum improvement programs is to ask teachers and other personnel to state their problems orally or in writing. At best, this procedure should be operated on a face-to-face basis in an informal, unstructured situation. At the Norwich Free Academy, for instance, teachers "free associated" in voluntary curriculum committee meetings about possible study topics. In this small independent school, 90 per cent of the faculty attended meetings of the curriculum committee at one time or another.[7] A more formal way of inventorying problems and concerns is to ask in writing for open-ended statements, or to present a written list of problems to be ranked in order of importance. In Corpus Christi, Texas, the Council on Instruction gathered from school staffs statements of 27 problems, and returned the whole list to the staffs for rating.[8] Another school used a ready-made inventory form, the *Illinois Inventory of Teacher Opinion*, which was developed in connection with the Illinois Curriculum Improvement Program.[9]

IN-SERVICE MEDIA

Institutes, workshops, and conferences have sometimes provided opportunities for problem identification. At an institute, a challenging talk by a

---

[7] George E. Shattuck, "The Curriculum Committee Goes to Work," *Bulletin of the National Association of Secondary School Principals*, Vol. 43, No. 244, February, 1959, pp. 65–67.

[8] Corpus Christi Public Schools, *Curriculum Bulletin* (mimeographed), October 2, 1951, p. 1.

[9] Arthur C. Hearn, "Columbus High School Organizes for Curriculum Development," *Bulletin of the National Association of Secondary School Principals*, Vol. 43, No. 244, February, 1959, pp. 67–72. This form appears in Harold C. Hand, *What People Think of Their Schools*. New York: Harcourt, Brace & World, Inc., 1948, pp. 195–217.

curriculum specialist may be followed by productive group discussions. Capitalizing on another medium, Belleville, New Jersey, has utilized workshops as a means of identifying problems which transcend the themes of the workshops themselves.[10]

COOPERATIVE STUDIES AND SURVEYS

Sometimes a start is made toward curriculum improvement by a faculty's engaging in informal study of professional books, or by its facing an unknown and novel situation. The staff of newly-organized Oakcrest High School, in Atlantic County, New Jersey, knew little of its pupil population. It decided to conduct bus tours of the "sending districts" and to study the pupil population from records and other data as an initial step in developing a program to meet the needs of learners. Self-surveys of schools, *i.e.*, surveys conducted by staff members themselves, and cooperative surveys involving school systems and college staffs, like that conducted several years ago in Great Neck, New York, with the cooperation of Teachers College, Columbia University, yield important topics for further study.

EXPERIMENTATION

Experiments conducted by teachers individually or in small groups have led to the exploitation of bigger fields for study. By beginning a program with isolated instances of experimentation, a school system can maintain a valuable "broken-front" approach to improvement which has been described as "a little improvement here and a little there." For years, the Horace Mann–Lincoln Institute of School Experimentation, Teachers College, Columbia University, has sponsored experimentation based on the interests and desires of personnel in local school systems. So, in general, has the Illinois Curriculum Program. A more recent development, the Physical Science Study Committee at the Massachusetts Institute of Technology, has encouraged physics teachers to try a pattern of teaching which was originated by the Committee. Thus, experimentation varies in nature from the free and unstructured to the prescribed and limited.

FORMAL EVALUATION

The results of administering tests and inventories, particularly tests of pupil achievement, have touched off numerous curriculum improvement activi-

---

[10] Frank M. Durkee, "Organizing for Growth in Service," *Educational Leadership*, Vol. 17, No. 6, March, 1960, pp. 336–339.

ties. Item analysis of test results can be especially helpful in indicating weaknesses that need correcting. Harold Hand states the importance of evidence in showing teachers that "the facts of the present situation are disturbingly out of line with their picture of what a good school ought to be doing."[11] When teachers readminister in October the final examinations they have given the preceding June, they often discover how shockingly ineffectual their teaching has been. In general, teacher-made tests, administered after a delay of several weeks or months, do more to convince teachers of learners' needs than do "national" tests prepared by remote commercial agencies.

DEVELOPMENT OF PHILOSOPHIES AND SETS OF OBJECTIVES

For a time, development of philosophies and lists of objectives fell into disrepute because this procedure is time-consuming and is sometimes said to keep teachers from dealing with live, flesh-and-blood problems. Subsequently, a reaction occurred when so many school systems appeared to operate in a "rudderless" way, devoid of acknowledged objectives. A few recent reports have indicated that teachers sometimes go beyond simply making pious statements of objectives to experimenting with the meanings of the objectives for practice. Aberdeen, South Dakota, has done some work in implementing objectives. Lewis reports a study in Minneapolis in which four elementary schools developed lists of objectives for their respective schools, stating the objectives in terms of pupil behaviors. They then found or made situations in which children's behavior, according to the objectives, could be studied; observed children's behavior to determine achievement of the objectives; and analyzed the results to effect program changes.[12] Promising as these approaches are, many curriculum workers tend to shy away from stating objectives because of the time required and because of the uncertainty of ways to transfer the statements into practice. The importance of preparing both philosophies and sets of objectives remains, of course, undiminished.

In the realm of techniques for the curriculum worker, West has suggested numerous specific ways of getting programs under way. Following are several promising ones:

Help teachers identify one general area of emphasis for the year.
Set aside a day a week. Call it "Teacher Day" and use it for conferences with teachers about their problems.

---

[11] Harold C. Hand, "How Can the School Be Organized for Curriculum Improvement?" *Bulletin of the National Association of Secondary School Principals*, Vol. 38, No. 202, April, 1954, pp. 273 and 274.

[12] Arthur J. Lewis, "Cooperative Self-Evaluation Can Aid Curriculum Development," *Educational Leadership*, Vol. 11, No. 8, May, 1954, pp. 482–485.

Utilize a school and community pupil-personnel survey.

Keep publications like the *Encyclopedia of Educational Research* handy for teachers' use as they puzzle about problems.

Display recent books and other materials and aids where teachers can see them.

Encourage teachers to develop small experimental projects in their classrooms.[13]

Even the smallest school is likely to be too complex an institution to rely very long on just one of the procedures for initiating curriculum study. Teachers with searching minds think of varied ways of pursuing the common objective of improvement. Following are narratives concerning the beginning stages of three improvement programs:

Program I: The curriculum coordinator conferred with the superintendent and other administrators regarding the budget, aims, and underlying principles of the new program, and concerning the present condition of the curriculum. A council of administrators prepared a general plan for the program, and "study committees" consisting chiefly of teachers identified problems for study. A "pilot committee" then looked for materials which would be helpful in solving the problems. In addition, a review of the present curriculum was undertaken.[14]

Program II: The faculty of a high school formed a Curriculum Improvement Committee, which was charged with referring specific problems to special committees. In its first year, the Curriculum Improvement Committee made several proposals for curriculum revision, reviewed present course outlines, led several research-type projects, revised school brochures, helped plan an in-service program, tried to keep abreast of national developments, and served in a continuing curriculum advisory capacity.[15]

Program III: In its early stages, this program featured a concentrated effort to locate needs and resources of the school system. Its leaders accomplished their purpose by conducting a census of teachers' problems, consulting administrators, utilizing testing programs, sponsoring classroom visitations, conferring with individual teachers, using parent contacts, and analyzing personnel records.[16]

The variety of approaches employed in these programs helps to show how unwise it is to pattern one program after another. Varying times and

[13] Jeff West, "Improving Curriculum Procedures," *Bulletin of the National Association of Secondary School Principals*, Vol. 43, No. 244, February, 1959, pp. 77–82.

[14] Itrice E. Eubanks, "Initiating a Program of Curriculum Improvement," *School and Community*, Vol. 46, No. 9, May, 1960, p. 21.

[15] Eugene Kitching, "Curriculum Improvement in Action," *Educational Administration and Supervision*, Vol. 43, No. 3, March, 1957, p. 165.

[16] Jack Rand and Robert Burress, "Case Study of a Curriculum Improvement Program," *School Executive*, Vol. 73, April, 1954, pp. 50–53.

places call for creation of new ideas and use of differing combinations of procedures.

Initial identification of problems is often a crude and invalid process. To analyze problems with some care, and to accept and reject them conscientiously, criteria must be established. Among the possible criteria are these:

> Will solution of the proposed problem prove worthwhile? Is it worth the necessary expenditure of time? How meaningful will the process and the results be to the participants?
> Can the problem be solved at this time? Is the timing of its proposed solution appropriate?
> Is solution of the problem within the competence of the participants?
> Is the problem of such size and scope as to be manageable?
> If help is needed in dealing with the problem, is competent help available?

Staffs of schools and school systems have real difficulties in determining priorities of problems and concerns to be dealt with. The values of participants in curriculum study are very important in the process of determining priorities. These values should be permitted to appear during lengthy periods of probing, questioning, and conferring. Great danger to morale and productivity lies in assuming that values emerge quickly and that the problems which are finally identified are really being considered in their appropriate order of importance. In their haste to get projects under way, curriculum workers must not fail to take time for adequate initial deliberation.

SITUATION 8-3—PROCEDURES TO FIT THE SITUATION

Glovers Central School District has been in operation 72 years. Recently a superintendent of 28 years' tenure has retired. During his regime, only occasional and sporadic activity to improve the curriculum has occurred. The following additional facts have also become evident:

1. Few of the 329 teachers have taken any in-service courses within the past five years.

2. The community has recently experienced a wave of conservatism, which has resulted in the defeat of two bond issues to pay for new school buildings.

3. A local resident has created disturbances at board of education meetings about the presence of "radical" textbooks in the schools.

4. The teaching staff likes to think of itself as a collection of individualists.

5. John Dewey's name is generally despised in the schools and, where it is known, in the community at large.

6. Teachers' concerns are directed largely toward improvement of reading and of English composition.

7. An evaluation committee from the regional association of colleges and secondary schools has recently called the Glovers High School "25 years behind the times in program and in understanding by teachers of what constitutes a modern program."

1. Assume that you have been appointed curriculum coordinator, in charge of the school system's curriculum program, and that the teachers' concerns for reading and for English composition are bona fide. What would you do to probe these concerns in depth?

2. Which of the procedures enumerated in this section of the chapter would you think might prove most helpful in opening a wedge to improvement?

3. Whom would you need to work with in making decisions about the procedures to be used? How, exactly, would you hope to proceed?

ORGANIZATION TO INITIATE IMPROVEMENT

At about the time problems for study are being identified, organization to initiate and thence to facilitate improvement needs to be established. There is obviously no point in organizing personnel merely for the sake of organizing them. Organization becomes useful only when it facilitates group endeavor. It serves best when it is functional, when it permits widespread participation and free-flowing interpersonal relationships, when it fulfills the institution's own purpose, when it provides for continuity of problem-solving, and when it arranges for coordination among groups.[17]

One of the theses of this book has been that curriculum improvement occurs chiefly where the teacher *is*—in the individual school. This would imply

[17] Alice Miel, *Changing the Curriculum.* New York: Appleton-Century-Crofts, Inc., 1946, p. 64.

that most organizational arrangements should be centered at the building level. To a large extent, this is true. However, the need for developing programs vertically for the sake of sequence and continuity, the importance of articulation among educational levels, and the necessity for teachers to associate with teachers in other schools at the same grade or educational level make organization for curriculum improvement bigger than the mere organizational structure of an individual school.

Thus it is unwise to center organization either in individual schools or in central offices. Rather, a centrally-coordinated approach is needed in facing both those problems which originate in the individual school and those problems which are of concern to the total system or to a level within the system. The centrally-coordinated approach encourages activity in both the central office and the local building, in accordance with the kind of problem being attacked. For example, the central office may be concerned with teacher morale throughout the system, while the local school wishes to develop a social studies program for children of a given socio-economic background.[18] Small school systems containing only one or two schools tend to operate according to a local building or decentralized approach, and some traditionally-oriented systems retain strong central control. But the centrally-coordinated approach is commonest today.

In individual schools, teachers organize in grade-level groups, departments (secondary school), teams, school councils, planning committees, and working (ad hoc) committees.[19] Sometimes, as in Fairfield, Connecticut, large schools are broken down into schools within schools. In the individual school, the leadership of the principal is obviously very important. Committees in individual schools develop resource units, adapt outlines and course guides to the school's needs, consider schoolwide problems like the quality of assembly programs and the power to be given pupil government organizations, and perform a multitude of other local functions.[20]

In whole school systems curriculum planning is initiated by means of systemwide faculty organizations, central steering committees as well as vertical ad hoc committees, lay advisory committees, and central office supervisors, to mention only a few of the groups in the organization. Central organization often provides guidelines for planning, general curriculum lead-

[18] Ronald C. Doll, A. Harry Passow, and Stephen M. Corey, *Organizing for Curriculum Improvement.* New York: Bureau of Publications, Teachers College, Columbia University, 1953, pp. 1–10.

[19] Leon S. Waskin, "Organizing for Curriculum Study," *Bulletin of the National Association of Secondary School Principals,* Vol. 43, No. 244, February, 1959, pp. 41–45.

[20] Edward A. Krug, Chester D. Babcock, John Guy Fowlkes, and H. T. James, *Administering Curriculum Planning.* New York: Harper & Row, Publishers, 1956, p. 94.

ership, machinery for getting under way, duplicated or printed curriculum materials, and means of evaluating the programs. The public schools in Philadelphia have been especially adept at organizing for systemwide activity.[21]

CENTRAL STEERING COMMITTEE

Centrally-coordinated organization makes almost mandatory the formation of a central steering committee, sometimes called a district-wide or central curriculum committee. Much attention has been given in the literature to the functions of central steering committees and to ways of forming them. Common tasks for these committees are:

Surveying curriculum needs;
Getting action started;
Facilitating communication;
Approving the accomplishments of ad hoc committees;
Locating help—personnel, facilities, time, and materials;
Coordinating activities;
Arranging for and guiding evaluation;
Maintaining relationships with individuals and groups outside the committee
    and also outside the school system.

Advice concerning the formation of central steering committees has been given as follows:

1. Committee members should know why they have been appointed. Some of the members should help in the preliminary exploration of possible purposes. Statements of purpose should be specific enough to set direction, but general enough to allow latitude.[22]

2. Committee members should be chosen for definite terms, possibly on a rotating basis. Interest in curriculum problems should be a major factor in the selection of committee members. The matter of representation should depend on one's view of curriculum improvement and of the committee's function.[23] Representation can be arranged, for instance, by region, by position, or by educational level.

3. Whether the committee is appointed, elected, or chosen from volunteers, it should have the approval and support of personnel throughout the

---

[21] American Association of School Administration, *American School Curriculum* (31st Yearbook). Washington, D.C.: The Association, 1953, pp. 81–91.

[22] Paul M. Halverson, *Group Work in Cooperative Curriculum Development* (doctoral dissertation). New York: Teachers College, Columbia University, 1952.

[23] Association for Supervision and Curriculum Development, *Action for Curriculum Improvement* (1951 Yearbook). Washington, D.C.: The Association, 1957, pp. 122–124.

system.[24] Without approval and support, curriculum activity lags. Administrators should probably not be in the majority in any committee membership.

4. Laymen usually serve best on an adjunct advisory committee. Generally speaking, they do not perform comfortably or competently as members of the steering committee itself.

5. The size of a steering committee should be guarded with care. Six persons may prove too few for idea development, whereas 60 persons become a nearly unmanageable reaction group rather than a discussion group.

6. Steering committees serve an important enough function to be granted released time for at least some of their meetings.

7. If agenda-planning sub-committees seem necessary, they must be kept sensitive to problems as the whole group sees them.[25]

8. A steering committee functions best when its members pay attention to the current agenda and help to plan agendas for future meetings.[26]

9. The *spread* of participation in steering committee meetings is as important to morale as the *quality* of it.[27]

AD HOC COMMITTEES

Committees to perform special functions, called ad hoc committees, should be organized to fulfill clearly-defined purposes, such as preparation of a system of reporting the work of junior-high-school pupils. Obviously, these committees should arise from definite, pressing concerns, and should not be organized because of a preconception that they are essential to a thriving program. Membership should be based on competence and interest, and it should terminate at a definitely-prearranged time. Someone has said that it is easy to form committees but difficult to get rid of them. Committee members should be helped to see their task broadly, in the context of a program that has other facets.[28] Furthermore, they should know the scope and the probable duration of their task.

Ad hoc committees come in varied sizes and organizational forms. Some are short-term task forces. Others study problems of such importance that they become long-term enterprises. Manitowoc, Wisconsin, has had two basic kinds of ad hoc committees: "A" committees, which are grade-level committees for

[24] Krug, Babcock, Fowlkes, and James, *op. cit.*, pp. 64–66.
[25] Halverson, *op. cit.*
[26] *Ibid.*
[27] *Ibid.*
[28] Hollis L. Caswell and Associates, *Curriculum Improvement in Public School Systems.* New York: Bureau of Publications, Teachers College, Columbia University, 1950, pp. 90–94.

elementary schools, and subject committees for secondary schools; and "B" committees, which work on selected problems or themes.[29] An interesting study by Lowe revealed that no apparent difference exists among the process problems faced by vertical, horizontal, and building committees; and that, in programs based on volunteering for committee membership, there are several levels of involvement, with persons who carry out interim assignments being most involved. Lowe found also that ad hoc committees of four to ten members, which meet for about five hours a day and are task-centered, give greatest satisfaction. As might be expected, ad hoc committees tend to deal with problems of substance or content and ignore problems of process.[30]

Ad hoc committees will continue to be the backbone of curriculum improvement programs, so much more attention should be given to the quality of their functioning.

ORGANIZATION OUTSIDE THE LOCAL DISTRICT

In a few states, the influence of state departments of education in initiating curriculum improvement remains potent. In recent years, Pennsylvania, for example, has directed curriculum projects of various sorts, and Virginia has continued its statewide study groups.

However, the county unit has assumed new importance in curriculum leadership, sometimes as an intermediate structure between state and local units, and sometimes as a thriving and somewhat independent organization which is geographically proximate to the local districts within it. Arlington County, Virginia, Dade County, Florida, and Los Angeles and San Diego Counties, in California, have impressed the nation recently by coordinating administrative units within them and providing resources which small, independent school districts might be unable to afford. Frazier notes the process by which Davidson County, in Tennessee, organized a countywide program:

1. The county superintendent called a meeting of the principals who served in local school districts.

2. The principals helped to identify subject-fields for possible study.

3. Individual schools chose the fields they wanted to emphasize, and then combined their efforts. For instance, personnel from a school that was

[29] Krug, Babcock, Fowlkes, and James, *op. cit.*, p. 74.
[30] Elizabeth Lowe, *An Analysis of the Activities of Three Curriculum Committees* (doctoral dissertation). New York: Teachers College, Columbia University, 1952.

interested in a child-development problem met with personnel from other schools who were interested in the same problem.

4. Articulation and communication were given attention through "sharing meetings," bulletins, and newsletters.

5. The county organization then chose a curriculum council to serve as a steering committee.[31]

In Hunterdon County, New Jersey, county superintendent of schools Kenneth Woolf used funds provided by the State Department of Education to organize kindergarten through twelfth-grade articulation committees in four regions of the county, and to foster the curriculum studies in the language arts and citizenship education which the articulation committees identified as being most significant to teachers in local school districts. Experimentation with organization in counties and regions is likely to continue rapidly during the decade ahead.

The issue concerning how to organize so as to facilitate rather than impede progress can be illustrated by the following situation.

SITUATION 8-4—THE SHORTCOMINGS OF THE CURRICULUM STEERING COMMITTEE

To listen to the teachers in the Mannheim School District, one would think that everything was wrong with the newly-organized Central Curriculum Committee. In teachers' rooms and other out-of-the-way places, the comments went like this:

"Who ever said we needed a big committee to tell us to do what we're already doing?"

"It's the group of administrators who thought of the idea. I notice that no teacher was in the group that made the decision to have a Central Curriculum Committee."

"I think each school can take care of its own business. We don't need a big central committee, even though there are 12 schools in the system."

"There is some need for a central committee. I say that because I believe every fifth grade all over town should be doing the same thing at about the same time. Someone or some group has to police the teachers."

"The big trouble with a group like the Central Curriculum

---

[31] Eva Frazier, "A County Plans for Curriculum Improvement," *Bulletin of the National Association of Secondary School Principals*, Vol. 44, No. 258, October, 1960, pp. 180–186.

Committee is that it becomes a debating society—all talk and no action."

"Why doesn't the superintendent spend his time preparing the principals to do their jobs? Then they could take the leadership in developing curriculum instead of having the leadership centered in a group like this."

"In the eight months it's existed, the Committee hasn't done a thing to help the eight groups that were already started in an informal way before the Committee was organized. I know. I'm a member of the committee on reporting to parents."

"I guess someone on the inside is bucking for promotion."

1. Which complaints seem to you to be best justified as representing the *real* shortcomings of the Committee? Why?

2. How do you account for the presence of each of the comments which you have rejected?

3. What democratic principles of organization for curriculum improvement can you adduce?

THE EFFECT OF PERSONAL FEELINGS

The preceding case leads conveniently to a discussion of personal feelings. The initial stage of organized curriculum improvement, like the course of true love, does not always run smooth. As we have seen in Chapter 6, people tend to resist change in varying degrees in different areas of their living. At the same time, most persons wish to appear desirous of conforming to vogues which have the support of superior officers. Teachers find conforming behavior less troublesome and upsetting than resistance.

Because of these facts, 1) locating problems that represent real concerns is difficult; and 2) interest in curriculum study is often feigned. In many a school, the following sort of dialogue has passed between teachers:

Teacher A: Why did you volunteer to join the social studies committee? Were you really interested?

Teacher B: No, I wasn't interested, but sooner or later I'll have to accept a committee assignment of some kind. This might as well be the one.

It is easy to say that persons like Teacher B should be removed from our schools if they persist in their present attitudes. However, an educational challenge lies in helping teachers become alert and alive, so that they do more than "keep school." Besides, we must recognize that some of the attitudes curriculum leaders encounter have resulted from their own fumbling, from the unproductiveness of much curriculum work in the past, and from already adverse attitudes toward certain school administrators. For example, a study of curriculum improvement in selected elementary schools showed that the teachers received little satisfaction from curriculum meetings because they were antagonistic to the school authorities. These teachers were pleased with their own classroom goals, but not with the goals which administrators tried to set for them.[32]

Actually, curriculum leaders have oversimplified the reasons teachers become involved or fail to become involved in new curriculum projects. The reasons are numerous and complex.[33] Leaders should make it easy for personnel to accept or reject specified opportunities for service. Often staff members are already performing important responsibilities other than the one immediately at hand, and they may justifiably reject new responsibilities.

Practical experience with the emotional element in initiating curriculum improvement leads to these conclusions:

1. Nothing of significance is likely to happen until teachers' real concerns come out. The climate of the school and school system can contribute greatly to the emergence of these concerns.

2. The behavior of educational leaders can help or hinder both initial and eventual progress.

3. The notion must be conveyed that educational engineering requires time and persistence.

4. The whole spirit must be one of working *with* people, rather than of causing people to work.[34]

5. Feeling tends to improve as curriculum groups become "in-groups" to which the members feel that they belong.[35]

A particularly sore spot in the feelings of personnel appears in the conflict between principals and those central office personnel who "invade" school buildings. Supervisors from central offices have not always been discreet in their work with teachers, sometimes by-passing principals and denying them their prerogatives as instructional leaders in their own schools. On the other

[32] Maurice J. Eash and Robert E. Chasnoff, "Framework for Effective Curriculum Improvement," *Overview*, March, 1960, p. 65.

[33] Margaret M. Stuckey, "Involvement in Curriculum Improvement," *Clearing House*, Vol. 30, No. 7, March, 1956, p. 407.

[34] See De Graff Platte and Edwena Moore, "Curriculum Improvement, Ltd.," *Clearing House*, Vol. 34, No. 3, November, 1959, p. 155.

[35] Kenneth L. Husbands, "Changing the Curriculum: a Point of Departure," *Educational Administration and Supervision*, Vol. 40, No. 2, February, 1954, pp. 144–154.

hand, principals have often been known to operate schools as their own little empires, ignoring the advice and help of supervisors. Certainly, in every school district the roles of various personnel should be clearly enough defined to avoid major conflict. More will be said about role definition in the next chapter.

The situation which follows is an actual one taken from a study of teachers' feelings about curriculum improvement.

SITUATION 8-5—HOW THE TEACHERS FELT

William A. Fullagar conducted an investigation of teachers' feelings about a newly-started curriculum improvement program.[36] **Among the statements he collected from teachers were these:**

"Look at the beginning of the program. It didn't come from any suggestion of ours. It was thought up by the board of education or someone else at the top. They get the ideas but expect us to do the work."

"After the program was decided upon, no one gave us any clear picture of what it was all about. . . ."

"We would have gotten more out of our program if we could have met in groups made up of those who teach the same grade. . . ."

"Speaking of the administration, they contributed their share of problems for us. Some of our principals were quite open in their hostility to the program and criticized the ideas which we brought back from our meetings. . . ."

"In a sense we were our own worst enemy. We were suspicious of the motives of those who were working with us, that is, the consultants and the administrators. . . ."

1. On the basis of your own experience with teachers, select one or two of these comments that sound most like remarks made by teachers you know. How, in your opinion, are feelings like these acquired?

2. What other feelings might teachers be expected to express at the start of an improvement program? Which of these feelings are legitimate and completely to be expected?

---

[36] William A. Fullager, "The Teacher and Curriculum Improvement Programs," *Educational Administration and Supervision*, Vol. 40, No. 2, February, 1954, pp. 110 and 111.

EXPECTATIONS TO BE KEPT IN MIND

The success of curriculum improvement programs will most likely be assured if certain expectations are held at the outset:

1. Persons in local schools and school systems should accept responsibility for curriculum improvement. This responsibility should be dispersed among numbers of people.

2. Feelings of personal security and worth, as well as satisfactory interpersonal relations, are essential.

3. Adequate time, facilities, and resources should be provided.

4. Curriculum workers should attempt to solve problems that seem real and important.

5. Effective communication about plans, policies, procedures, and achievements should be established and maintained among persons who have a stake in the projects.

6. Curriculum development should be considered a continuous, normal activity, and not a stop-and-start activity.[37]

7. All of the persons concerned in a given project should be involved in it in some way.

8. Nothing of real importance should be undertaken without developing an understanding of its purposes.[38]

9. Continuous evaluation of improvements should be built into the design of each project.

10. Balance must be achieved in both the loci and the types of activities to be performed.

11. Consistency must be maintained between the means and the ascribed ends of each project.

Persons who undertake curriculum improvement should not expect that great changes will necessarily occur within a period of a few months. Initially, growth may come only in the form of people's sensitization to themselves, to each other, and to the nature of the curriculum and its changes.[39] Values,

[37] The preceding six expectations have been taken from Doll, Passow, and Corey, *op. cit.*

[38] Maurice R. Ahrens, "Planning for Reorganization of the Secondary School Program," *High School Journal*, Vol. 37, No. 8, May, 1954, pp. 229–233.

[39] William M. Rasschaert, "A Descriptive Analysis of a Departmental Curriculum Improvement Project in an Urban Junior High School," *Journal of Experimental Education*, Vol. 27, September, 1958, pp. 37–48.

attitudes, and skills change to some extent almost immediately, but progress of lasting significance takes time.

SUMMARY

This chapter has dealt with some of the characteristics of curriculum problems and forces that provide impetus to curriculum study. It has then moved to direct consideration of procedures that can be used in initiating programs of curriculum improvement, and of ways to organize personnel for undertaking curriculum projects. The chapter concludes with an emphasis on the feelings of professional staff and on expectations which need to be considered in the process of initiating activities for improvement.

SELECTED BIBLIOGRAPHY

American Association of School Administrators, *American School Curriculum*, 31st Yearbook (Washington, D.C.: The Association, 1953).

Anderson, Vernon E., *Principles and Procedures of Curriculum Improvement* (New York: The Ronald Press Company, 1956).

Association for Supervision and Curriculum Development, *Action for Curriculum Improvement*, 1951 Yearbook (Washington, D.C.: The Association, 1951).

———, *Research for Curriculum Improvement*, 1957 Yearbook (Washington, D.C.: The Association, 1957).

Doll, Ronald C., A. Harry Passow, and Stephen M. Corey, *Organizing for Curriculum Improvement* (New York: Bureau of Publications, Teachers College, Columbia University, 1953).

Krug, Edward A., Chester D. Babcock, John Guy Fowlkes, and H. T. James, *Administering Curriculum Planning* (New York: Harper & Row, Publishers, 1956).

McNally, Harold J., and A. Harry Passow, *Improving the Quality of Public School Programs* (New York: Bureau of Publications, Teachers College, Columbia University, 1960).

Miel, Alice, *Changing the Curriculum* (New York: Appleton-Century-Crofts, Inc., 1946).

West, Jeff, "Improving Curriculum Procedures," *Bulletin of the National Association of Secondary School Principals*, Vol. 43, No. 244, February, 1959.

chapter nine

As A CURRICULUM IMPROVEMENT PROGRAM BEGINS, the question soon arises, "Who shall participate in curriculum planning?" In our day, problems of defining roles of participants in curriculum improvement loom larger than they ever have before. Some of the key issues concerning participants' roles are: What responsibilities should various personnel take in planning and improving the curriculum? What special backgrounds, skills, and abilities do they need? How may the talents of participants be used in coordinated ways? These and related issues are sharpened by massive and widespread criticisms which have been leveled against the schools. Persons who have worked for years in professional education are sometimes replaced in curriculum planning today by non-professionals whose programs for changing schools and school curriculums receive wide publicity. Indeed, some of the most complex problems of teaching and learning are being made to look easy enough for professional educators to have solved years ago. However, as broadly-based participation in curriculum planning increases and intensifies, it causes intelligent participants to show more respect for the complexity of problems with which they must deal.

Misjudgments about roles in curriculum improvement are easy to make. In times of real or imagined emergency, people assume roles which, on re-

Participants and Their Roles in Curriculum Improvement

consideration, seem entirely inappropriate for them. Also, in times of emergency, more people accept roles than in times of calm, and the role-takers come from more varied backgrounds. When Russia's first Sputnik blasted off in October, 1957, excitement about the curriculum of American schools created novel categories of curriculum improvers, mostly in the ranks of individual subject-specialists, educational foundations, and uninitiated laymen. As the number of people showing interest in the curriculum increased, the possibility of maintaining productive dialogue among them diminished. In general, participants in curriculum improvement today fall into two large classifications: those who operate outside local school districts, and those who operate within them. It is possible, of course, to identify other classifications, such as those of professional and non-professional personnel, but the crucial issues of the times increasingly center about the respective roles: 1) of persons beyond the confines of local communities, and 2) of community personnel, both professional and lay, who are willing and able to exercise local control. Therefore, the following discussion will divide into consideration of the roles of personnel outside local school districts, and of the roles of personnel within these districts.

First, however, the meaning of the term *role* as it is used in this chapter needs clarifying. Social scientists have defined roles to mean: 1) *positions* within organizations or hierarchies, 2) *behaviors* of the performers of tasks, and 3) *expectations* concerning work to be accomplished by role-takers.[1] The present discussion is confined primarily to application of the second definition, and also to limited application of the third. Consequently, a first question to be answered is, "What do persons and organizations *do* to fulfill their roles, especially as they themselves visualize these roles?" A second question is, "How can differing and sometimes conflicting roles be assigned and balanced so that curriculum improvement may proceed most satisfactorily?" The first question is answered in the next two major sections of this chapter; the second question, in the last major section.

ROLES OF PERSONS AND ORGANIZATIONS OUTSIDE LOCAL SCHOOL DISTRICTS

. The literature of curriculum improvement contains ascriptions of role to certain categories of curriculum improvers, *e.g.*, to administrators and laymen working at the local community level. It tells almost nothing about the roles being assumed today by persons new to the educational scene. So much has happened to shift roles and to create new ones that recent history and the current scene provide the best sources of information about who is making curriculum decisions. A random list of role-takers outside local school districts would surely include:

> State legislatures, state boards of education, and state departments of education;
> Regional accrediting associations;
> Colleges and universities;
> National and state pressure groups;
> Producers of sponsored teaching aids;
> Textbook authors and publishers, testmakers, and manufacturers of other devices and materials;
> Consultants from colleges and universities;
> Specialist groups in subject-matter;
> Laymen who author books and magazine articles;
> The federal government;
> Professional organizations in education and individual educational leaders.

---

[1] Neal Gross, Ward S. Mason, and Alexander W. McEachern, *Explorations in Role Analysis*. New York: John Wiley & Sons, Inc., 1958.

Several years ago, much was being said about the influence of state departments of education and of colleges and universities. These and all other role-takers in the preceding list continue to be important, but the attention which school people formerly gave them has been partially shifted to other participants. For instance, the federal government has become more powerful in determining the curriculum by increasing its expenditures for education; James B. Conant has become the most frequently-mentioned educator on the national scene, as an informal inquiry by Dean Lindley Stiles of the University of Wisconsin clearly indicates. Subject-specialists and specialist groups, whose work is reported in Chapter 4, have affected the curriculum. On the other hand, laymen who write books about education seem to be writing fewer of them. So the tides of participation ebb and flow. Because all the participants listed above are likely to remain on the scene for a long time, each of them will be discussed briefly. Altered classifications of participants which will, in the opinion of this author, carry greatest weight during the next decade will, however, be discussed initially and at greatest length. Though making predictions is dangerous, rapid shifts in roles seem to require some prophecies about future developments.

THE FEDERAL GOVERNMENT

Prominent among the newly-potent influences is the federal government, which was once mainly interested in vocational education and in disseminating educational ideas from the United States Office of Education. Amid demands for establishment of a central organization to develop a national curriculum, this branch of government has increased its aid to schools under the *National Defense Education Act,* which has spent money chiefly to improve the teaching of languages, the sciences, and mathematics, and to strengthen guidance programs. Indirectly, the government is influencing the schools by granting funds to colleges and universities for research projects. It is also providing financial aid for school construction and purchase of facilities.

The United States Office of Education, historically weak, is likely to become much more potent in the future. Additional federal monies will be spent for education, and whether control of the curriculum occurs directly or subtly, federal control will probably increase. Many educators already foresee danger in the distribution of federal funds for narrow and specific purposes. They favor, instead, broad-purpose expenditures which have less direct bearing upon the curriculum, *e.g.*, for building construction and teachers' salaries.[2]

[2] Glen Robinson, "Legislation Influences Curriculum Development," *Educational Leadership,* Vol. 19, No. 1, October, 1961.

Some of them see local control being seriously reduced, with an enhanced uniformity and rigidity quickly following.[3] Possibly the federal government will find its ultimate role in supporting basic curriculum research and in preparing guidelines for curriculum improvement which can be implemented in local school districts. Whatever it undertakes, its role can become one of the most significant because the government has both size and money. It needs only changes in point of view about its appropriate role, and these could be legislated almost overnight by a zealous Congress, with quick approval by the President.

NATIONAL ORGANIZATIONS

The term "national organizations" is meant to include all organizations, professional and lay, which can affect the nation as a whole, which have ample funds at their disposal, and which have a definite and comprehensible program to sell. Some of these organizations already exist—the great foundations and the National Education Association, with its affiliated groups. Other large organizations are almost certain to be established in the future. If foundations continue to be protected by tax laws, their influence will increase. The National Education Association is only beginning to find itself in new fields of professional leadership. There is much room for professional-lay cooperation in newly-created organizations for basic study and inquiry which can immediately affect practice.

Any potent, new organization will need to go considerably beyond the kinds of activities sponsored during the 1950's by the National Citizens' Commission and the White House Conference. It will have to develop national impact, and it will therefore need large financial support. First, however, it must advance a program which has realism and which makes sense to numerous people. Such an organization cannot be partisan or narrowly supported by patriotic groups, industries, businesses, or labor unions. It will promptly face a decision as to the support it will give to public schools versus private schools, and as to its stand regarding several other controversial issues in education. If it can create a broad, forceful program, it will replace certain small, regional organizations which already exist. Ours is notably an era of organizations rather than of individual leaders. Earlier in the century, individual leaders—Kilpatrick, Bagley, Bode, and others—had great independent influence. Today the individual leader usually finds his role within the complex of organizations, and he may find it there even more so in the future.

[3] Elaine Exton, "Meeting the Emerging Threats to Local Community Control," *American School Board Journal*, Vol. 141, November, 1960, pp. 38 and 39.

Participant	Current Status
	how to work with less well prepared people than themselves. Can have much influence in setting directions for study.[10]
8. Specialist groups in subject-matter	Strong today in influencing certain teachers, especially at secondary-school level. Receive their support from foundations, universities, and government. Groups are in the publishing field independently, and engage in inservice education of teachers. Less concerned with the process of change than with the intrinsic good sense of their proposals. Impact is chiefly on the more wide-awake teachers in populous centers.[11]
9. Laymen who author books and magazine articles	Temporarily, at least, are rather quiescent. Appeal to the popular interest in education, and fall prey to the notion that anyone who inquires briefly can state truisms about the curriculum. Some books, by strong-minded laymen and quasi-educators, have had a lingering effect on the schools.
10. The federal government	Aiding the schools through the *National Defense Education Act,* and in a few minor and often indirect other ways. Its aid to universities encourages development of experimental projects. Except for failure of legislation in Congress, would be assisting the schools much more.
11. Professional organizations and individual leaders in education	Chief activity occurring among organizations affiliated with the National Education Association. Leadership by individuals mainly submerged within the organizations. Alliance of two or more organizations to promote particular projects is becoming more common.

ACTIVITY 9-1—DEVELOPING A PERSPECTIVE CONCERNING OUTSIDE AGENCIES

The agencies that operate in differing times and places assume varied roles. For instance, in your community this year, the three agencies of greatest power to remake the curriculum may be a regional accrediting association, a powerful industry, and the state board of education. In a community 50 miles away, however, the three most powerful agencies may be wholly or partially different.

[10] See "Employing Consultants" (Editorial), *American School Board Journal,* Vol. 139, December, 1959, p. 42.

[11] Paul M. Mitchum, "Curriculum Planning by Subject Matter Groups," *Educational Leadership,* Vol. 19, No. 1, October, 1961, pp. 11–15.

Analyze your community situation by methods of inquiry and reflection. Then respond to the following questions:

1. Which three of the agencies listed in the chart above have the most powerful influence in remaking the curriculum?
2. Which two or three have changed most in role and function during the past five years? What are the directions of these changes?
3. Which two or three agencies would you like to see strengthening their roles during the next few years? Why?
4. Compare your responses with those of other persons.

ACTIVITY 9-2—IDENTIFYING NEW AGENCIES AND COMBINATONS OF AGENCIES

It is possible that in your community additional agencies or combinations of agencies are forming to participate in curriculum planning. If so, what are the nature and status of these independent or combined agencies? If not, are there additional or combined agencies you would like to see forming? Why? How, at this point, do you view the contributions and the dangers which come from the actions of persons and groups outside local school districts?

ROLES OF PERSONS AND ORGANIZATIONS WITHIN *LOCAL SCHOOL DISTRICTS*

Though outside agencies are affecting the schools in important ways, the heart of the improvement process still resides in the American community. Even an outright dictatorship would have difficulty in forcing uniformity upon systems of education that have long been free and independent.

Involved in the educational process at the local level are school boards, individual laymen and groups of laymen, school administrators and supervisors, teachers, and pupils. The roles of these persons and organizations will be examined briefly.

SCHOOL BOARDS

Boards of education are legally responsible for the schools under their direction. Formed of laymen, they provide responsible lay participation in legislating for and guiding the schools. With reference to the curriculum, the responsibilities of board members are twofold: 1) to inform themselves about the curriculum so that they can intelligently determine objectives for teaching and learning, and 2) to make policies and to vote funds which will ensure progress toward these objectives.[12]

Intelligent board members soon learn how complex teaching and learning really are. If they are to make wise decisions, they must learn from members of the staff (other than superintendents and principals) by attending teachers' meetings, in-service courses, and informal discussions of school problems, and by browsing in professional libraries.[13] In the process of decision-making about school subjects and subject-matter content, board members need to develop criteria like the following:

Does the subject or content satisfy legislative and other requirements?

Does it fulfill educational purposes to which the board and its employees subscribe?

Does it have value for the pupil and for society?

Can the finances, personnel, and organization be supplied to include it in the program?[14]

When boards of education use criteria like these for making curriculum decisions, they are likely to serve their communities and states well by resisting the pressure and caprice which have caused many boards to blunder into unwise judgments.

INDIVIDUAL LAYMEN AND GROUPS OF LAYMEN

Laymen other than members of boards of education have been assuming increasing roles in guiding the destinies of American schools. Most practitioners in the public schools would agree with Misner that the feasibility of lay participation is no longer a debatable issue.[15] Community sharing in the making of major curriculum decisions *is* desirable because changes prove more durable if they are understood and supported by the public, and because

[12] Fred G. Thatcher, "School Boards and Curriculum Decisions," *Educational Leadership*, Vol. 19, No. 1, October, 1961, pp. 16–19.

[13] James B. Jackson, "How Boardmen Can Evaluate the Curriculum," *American School Board Journal*, Vol. 142, February, 1961, p. 17.

[14] John P. Sullivan, "Curriculum Guide for School Board Members," *American School Board Journal*, Vol. 142, June, 1961, pp. 9a and 10.

[15] Paul J. Misner, "Citizens and Teachers Plan the Curriculum," *National Parent-Teacher*, Vol. 50, May, 1956, pp. 26 and 27.

those who are to be affected by policies should rightfully share in their development.[16]

The question, then, is not *whether* laymen other than board members should participate, but *to what extent* and *how* they should participate. Certainly no group of laymen "without portfolio" should constitute itself a rival board of education. In their relationships with the board, lay groups should serve as aides, resources, and advisers. The generalization has been made that lay groups should work on real problems, be sponsored by boards of education or school administrators, elect able officers, maintain a supply of resource personnel, agree on their own recommendations, and submit their findings directly to the board of education or to sponsoring administrators.[17]

But laymen have become more than adjuncts to boards of education and administrators. They often work closely with the professional staffs of schools in improving the curriculum. Insightful laymen soon perceive the levels at which they should be involved. They do not seek to preempt the authority, either intellectual or legal, of persons who have made the study of the curriculum their life work; otherwise, there would be little point in employing specialists in education.[18] They do only those things that intelligent amateurs can validly do. Occasionally, of course, one encounters laymen who have been reading unrealistic books and articles about education, who have learned in their own school experience to dislike teachers, who have come to the view that educators plot against the welfare of children, or who oppose high taxes on general principles. Curriculum workers need special patience and skill in working with persons who base their actions on motivations like these.

Many of the current difficulties with lay participation result from failure to think about the extent and manner of participation. Much lay participation has occurred on too broad a front, with inadequate definition of both the nature and the duration of committee assignments. Furthermore, school officials have too often involved laymen merely to defend present practices. When these same laymen have suggested possible improvements, the officials have resisted mightily, and the laymen have gone away saying, "Educators are too hard-headed; we can't work with them."

If one remembers that the schools belong to the citizens, and that co-

[16] See B. Othanel Smith, William O. Stanley, and J. Harland Shores, *Fundamentals of Curriculum Development.* New York: Harcourt, Brace & World, Inc., 1957, p. 452.

[17] William J. Cravatts, *Lay Committee Activities in Public School Districts in New Jersey* (unpublished doctoral dissertation). New Brunswick, N.J.: Rutgers University, 1959.

[18] See D. H. Wilkinson, "Some Factors That Complicate Lay Participation in Curriculum Development Programs," *Educational Administration and Supervision,* Vol. 45, pp. 173–178.

ordination between the schools and other community agencies has become a genuine necessity, four levels of involvement seem reasonable and workable:

1. Involvement on as broad a front as the *White House Conference* (central, lay committees on the curriculum perform this function on a continuing basis, making some of their best contributions in helping to determine objectives).

2. Provision of resource help by laymen (human resource files have become common in the larger school systems).

3. Participation in decision-making in individual schools (lay cabinets and advisory committees constitute prime examples of this mode of participating).

4. Utilizing lay assistance to teachers on a regularized basis (the help which mothers give in school libraries and elsewhere in the school has sometimes proved indispensable).

Surely lay participation that exceeds the potential and the responsibility of laymen is of no kindness or help to anyone. The bounds of participation must be set and maintained with increasing care.

SITUATION 9-1—HOW FAR SHALL LAYMEN GO?

The new curriculum improvement program in Terrytown had been under way for nearly a year. Ned Stanley, the curriculum coordinator, had recently told the curriculum steering committee that he felt the need of lay participation, but that he didn't know quite how to get it.

"Let's begin by informing our PTA's about the five study groups we've organized," one of the members of the steering committee had suggested. After some discussion, the other members of the committee had concurred. Accordingly, a "package program" containing a common message to the PTA's had been prepared. For 20 minutes, three or four members of the steering committee were to tell each association what the teachers and administrators had been doing to improve the curriculum in the Terrytown Public Schools.

Tonight was the third time Ned Smith had spoken to a PTA. As usual, Ned told about several interesting study projects, about the released time that teachers were receiving for doing their curriculum study, and about the favorable attitudes of participants. Then he asked the same question he'd asked twice before: "What do you parents think of what we're doing to improve our schools?" Result: two or three harmless and noncommittal replies. Then the vice-president of the Terrytown Trust Company responded: "I don't think we laymen know whether you're doing anything worthwhile or not. Why don't you professionals decide things like this for yourselves?"

1. What kinds of curriculum projects could the banker legitimately say belonged exclusively to the professionals?
2. What kinds of projects naturally call for the participation of parents?
3. Think of two differing situations in curriculum planning: one in which parents should be involved continuously, and another in which parents should have absolutely no part at any time. Think of still another situation in which parents should be involved to a certain point.

ADMINISTRATORS AND SUPERVISORS

Administrators and supervisors of school programs have very special roles to fill. Though they administer the curriculum remotely while teachers administer it directly and immediately, the impetus they provide has an important effect in making programs succeed. Evidence has been accumulating that the power of money in stimulating curriculum improvement has its definite limits. When additional money, expended for a variety of purposes, no longer makes any real difference, forward movement can be had chiefly by bringing new and effective leadership personnel to the task. Truly effective administrators and supervisors know teaching-learning processes, have an understanding of learners and of the intellectual disciplines, and possess knowledge and skill as educational engineers.

In the forefront of administrators and supervisors is, of course, the superintendent, who must simultaneously keep things going and inspire change. He or she provides opportunities for participation in curriculum planning, lends active support to curriculum projects, aids communication among personnel, and values efficient problem-solving.[19] Specifically, the superintendent must establish organization for improvement; interpret the revisions in program to the board of education; seek funds, personnel, and materials; and

19 John D. McNeil, "A Deciding Factor in Curriculum Improvement—the Superintendent's Attitude," *School Executive*, Vol. 77, July, 1958, pp. 46 and 47.

facilitate lay participation.[20] If improvement programs are to work, superintendents must give them personal attention. When superintendents see themselves almost exclusively as business administrators, trouble tends to develop in their instructional programs.[21]

As has been indicated in Chapter 7, general supervisors and curriculum coordinators are assuming special roles, frequently as superintendents' delegates. These functionaries now exist in about ten per cent of American school systems. General supervisors and coordinators have been called by some observers the most active and important agents of curriculum change.[22]

However, the *real* gatekeeper of curriculum improvement is the school principal. His proximity to teachers and pupils makes him so. In a broad sense, he serves as interpreter of the culture, professional leader on the educational frontier, supervisor of instruction, stimulator of local community enlightenment, and manager of a crucial educational enterprise.[23] In a more specific sense, he tries to employ able teachers, arranges reasonable teacher loads, orients new staff members, encourages teachers to evaluate their performance, supports changes, stimulates teachers to in-service growth, helps his staff understand their goals, and in every way possible facilitates the improvement process.[24] Such a listing of roles and responsibilities assumes more understanding and ability than many principals now possess. The heavy instructional responsibilities which superintendents and community members place upon principals call for quality of preparation which colleges and universities have too seldom provided.

The roles of assistants to principals are changing rapidly. One group of assistants, department heads in high schools, has been replaced in certain school districts in the Southwest and in a few more limited areas with coordinators whose roles, though newly-assigned, are often better understood than are roles in the older position, the department chairmanship.[25] Depart-

[20] James J. Jones, "The Superintendent Must Lead in Curriculum Development," *Educational Administration and Supervision*, Vol. 45, March, 1959, pp. 91 and 92.

[21] See Wayne L. Sorenson, *Crucial Issues in School Administration* (unpublished doctoral dissertation). Palo Alto, Cal.: Stanford University, 1959.

[22] William S. Vincent, "Educational Administration in Relation to Curriculum Change—U.S.A.," in *The Secondary School Curriculum* (International Yearbook of Education). New York: Harcourt, Brace & World, Inc., 1958.

[23] J. G. Umstattd, "The Principal Interprets His Role in Curriculum Development," *Bulletin of the National Association of Secondary School Principals*, Vol. 43, February, 1959, pp. 15–20.

[24] Audie J. Lynch, "The Role of the Principal in Improving Instruction," *High School Journal*, Vol. 42, pp. 131–135.

[25] Benjamin J. Cook, *A Study of the Department Head in the Comprehensive High School* (unpublished doctoral dissertation). New Brunswick, N.J.: Rutgers University, 1961.

ment chairmen have too often become very minor figures in the administrative hierarchy.

Perceptions of administrators' roles differ widely. A recent study indicates that principals do not have accurate perceptions of the total role-concept held for them by their staffs and by their superintendents; that closer agreement exists between the principal and his staff than between the principal and his superintendent regarding concepts of the principal's ideal role; and that principals are seen by their staffs as overemphasizing public relations and strictly administrative functions at the expense of curriculum functions. Role definition, as it affects principals, will need stronger clarification in the years to come. Already, principals have much autonomy in instructional matters, but they are both unclear as to their roles and overinterested in "housekeeping" functions.[26] Superintendents and other persons who supervise the work of principals should decide whether principals are to be *nomothetic* leaders, who emphasize institutional requirements and conformity to role expectations, or *idiographic* leaders, who minimize role expectations in favor of the requirements of individual personalities.[27] Idiographic leaders are likely to be much less "neat" in their administration of schools, and to behave less as "good boys and girls," according to the perception of the central office.

TEACHERS

There is little need to re-emphasize the fact that classroom teachers largely determine the curriculum. Regardless of grandiose curriculum plans, when the classroom door is closed, the insight and skill of the teacher determine in largest measure the quality of learners' experiences.

Teachers perform three major tasks that make them effective improvers of the curriculum: 1) they work and plan with pupils; 2) they engage in individual study; and 3) they share experiences concerning the curriculum with other teachers. Thus, by learning from children, from books, and from each other, they grow in insight and skill so that they may provide better experiences for their pupils. Among these three tasks, teachers most often prefer group activity with other teachers. Teachers in elementary schools

[26] Leo Weitz, *The High School Principal in New York City; a Study of Executive Responsibility in Theory and Practice* (unpublished doctoral dissertation). New York: New York University, 1961.

[27] See Donald J. Willower, *The Development of Hypotheses from a Theoretical Framework and a Test of Certain of Them Concerning Idiographic and Nomothetic Leaders' Perceptions of Subordinates* (unpublished doctoral dissertation). Buffalo: University of Buffalo, 1959.

like grade-level meetings; teachers in secondary schools, department meetings.[28] Perhaps the loneliness and isolation of the teacher's life cause this predilection for group work with peers. To influence curriculum planning on a broad front and in favorable ways, teachers need to pool their thinking, for only as they know, accept, and promote the goals of their schools can they be lastingly helpful in curriculum planning.[29] Group thinking, of course, does not always result in wise decisions; but it does create higher morale, maintenance of interest, and willingness to change. The quality of group problem-solving, including the nature of the evidence collected during the problem-solving process, makes for quality in decision-making, and hence for improvement.[30]

What happens in the group should transfer, in part, to the classroom and to the privacy of the teacher's study; by the same token, what happens in the classroom and the study should enrich the life of the group. In performing his three tasks, the teacher should keep a central goal in mind: to improve the quality of his decision-making as he comes to the educational crossroads on frequent occasions during each day. Much more needs to be learned about ways in which the teacher's ability to make decisions can be improved and enriched both by pre-service and in-service.

PUPILS

Children and youth are the "consumers" in the educational process. As such, they deserve to be consulted at intervals as teachers plan with them. Also, they may be consulted more formally and lengthily at intervals in curriculum planning.

Consultation with pupils may take several forms, beginning with oral question-asking: *e.g.*, "How do you feel about . . . ?" At times, pupils may be requested to fill out questionnaires, or to engage in group discussions of curriculum proposals, or to subject themselves to intensive interviews. The older the pupil, the more formal and sophisticated his participation may become.

But pupils can do more than give quick reactions. They can participate for periods of time in certain curriculum studies. In a junior high school in which the teachers felt especially secure, selected pupils who had suggested

---

[28] Catherine M. Broderick and Barbara T. Mason, "What Questions Need We Ask About Staff Participation?" *Educational Leadership*, Vol. 15, March, 1958, pp. 343–346.

[29] See Maurice J. Eash and Robert E. Chasnoff, "Framework for Effective Curriculum Improvement," *Overview*, Vol. 1, March, 1960, pp. 64 and 65.

[30] Kimball Wiles, "Does Faculty Participation Produce Curriculum Improvement?" *Educational Leadership*, Vol. 15, March, 1958, pp. 347–350.

that they and other pupils were sometimes disorderly because the teachers "talked too much" in their classroom lectures were asked by a curriculum committee to help the teachers find ways of reducing their lengthy oral contributions in classrooms. The consequent study resulted in teachers' discovering teaching methods which they had not previously considered or tried.

Schooling that ignores what learners think and feel creates more than deep-lying resentment: it limits the learning that is possible when the teacher knows the thoughts and values of the learners.

SITUATION 9-2—ACHIEVING BALANCE IN PARTICIPATION

Monegan High School had just been evaluated by its regional association of colleges and secondary schools. Its school plant had undergone some serious criticism, as had the adequacy of its teaching staff and its library. Among the subjects taught at Monegan, the social studies had been listed as being in greatest need of improvement. According to the evaluators' report:

"1. Teachers are using single, antiquated textbooks, and are using them to excess. Supplementary reference sources are badly needed.

"2. Classroom procedures need varying: the lecture method predominates.

"3. The social studies program should be in reality a citizenship education program. Youth should involve themselves, under auspices of the school, in community affairs. They should learn at first hand what active citizenship means, not merely within their school but in the community at large."

Which of the following groups have roles to assume with regard to the above-mentioned three curriculum needs?

Pupils

Teachers

Administrators

Laymen in general

The Monegan Board of Education

State your perception of the role of each group which you believe to be involved.

ASSIGNING ROLES AND ACHIEVING
BALANCE AMONG THEM

The varied roles and role-perceptions which appear in the preceding sections of the chapter suggest how difficult the tasks of assigning and balancing roles can be. Role-adjustments and reallocations need to be made at the site of role-performance. From the point of view of this chapter, the site of adjustment and reallocation should usually be the local school district..Teachers and administrators, aided by boards of education and other adult citizens, should determine what functions, originating either within or without the school district, should be discharged by the schools, and then who in the schools should discharge them.

When the locus of authority for role-assignment and balance is the school system, personnel in each system can take three important steps in establishing roles:

> They can plan to assure coverage of all necessary assignments, according to their view of the purposes of the schools.

> They can strive to remove conflict among role-takers and duplication among the roles themselves.

> They can seek to assure convergence of perceptions regarding particular roles.

Ways of taking each of these steps will be discussed briefly.

ASSURING COVERAGE

American schools badly need a re-examination of their purposes. A few school districts have followed the work of "Little White House Conferences" in their communities with a careful plotting or replotting of purposes. Most districts, however, have tended to drift and shift with the pressures, without benefitting from comprehensive planning. Only when purposes are known can roles be listed. Curriculum leaders in many communities need to help local personnel decide the directions in which the schools should go, and also to help them see what specific tasks the purposes imply, and who should perform the tasks. By agreement during meetings, staff members who share an area of responsibility can divide among themselves segments of the area which are to be assigned to individuals.

For example, when a guidance director was first employed in the West

Orange, New Jersey, Public Schools, the superintendent assembled all persons who were concerned in any way with guidance as an area of responsibility. In a series of meetings, these persons determined the bounds of guidance responsibility and allocated portions of the responsibility among classroom teachers, counselors, librarians, principals, the guidance director, and assistant principals. For each major classification of staff members, *e.g.*, for counselors, two levels of responsibility were assigned: primary responsibility, which was exclusive to persons in that classification, and cooperative responsibility, which was to be shared with persons of other classifications. Allocations of responsibility were put in writing, and were altered as changing conditions required.

REMOVING CONFLICT AND DUPLICATION

"The best laid plans of mice and men . . ." However carefully-conceived the plan of allocation, differences are likely to arise among staff members who have differing perceptions of their roles and who also differ temperamentally. One of the major disputes among curriculum personnel has now become almost a classic: the dispute between new curriculum coordinators and veteran principals. Whenever a new position is created, conflicts about roles are likely to arise. The need is for recognition and acceptance of the differences, and development of a reasonable plan of action.

> An example of this is to be found in the case of a newly appointed helping teacher who came into conflict with a veteran reading consultant because the helping teacher had begun to assist elementary school teachers with grouping and materials in reading. The director of instruction met with the two specialists involved in the conflict. He asked each specialist to state her perception of her own function with respect to reading, as well as her view of any other areas of present or potential conflict. As the two staff members talked about their perceptions of their distinctly different roles, they found their own grounds for agreement, with little help from the director of instruction. They seemed to find satisfaction in recognizing their differences in perception, and then in testing these perceptions against reality. They succeeded in citing instances in which overlapping efforts to help teachers had confused the teachers. At their second and third meetings, they agreed on specific actions concerning instruction in reading which each would take, and they then role-played the methods they would use in referring teachers from specialist to specialist for assistance.[31]

---

[31] From material supplied by the author for use in the 1960 Yearbook of the Association for Supervision and Curriculum Development. See Association for Supervision and Curriculum Development, *Leadership for Improving Instruction*, pp. 84 and 85.

Not all stories of this sort end so happily. In this situation, there was no hidden agenda of smoldering dislike, since neither specialist had known the other very long. At any rate, reduction of both conflict and duplication can be had, it appears, only by giving the warring parties enough opportunity to talk about their differences. Sometimes they can settle the differences alone; at other times they may need the intervention of a third or a fourth party, or even of a policy committee. It is often the duty of administrators to mediate disputes of this kind. One should realize that conflict about roles is not necessarily unfortunate: it often serves to clear the air and to eventuate in a more definite clarification of roles. By troubleshooting in cases of conflict, curriculum leaders can assure greater balance and harmony among roles.

ENCOURAGING CONVERGENCE OF ROLE PERCEPTION

The present chapter has referred at intervals to varying perceptions of a given role. Each occupant of a role, if he becomes sensitive to problems of role-perception, asks himself interrelated questions: "How do I see my own role?" "How do others see my role?" "How do I think others see it?" Perceptions can be converged through study of similarities and differences in perceptions. When direct attention is given to areas of difference, these areas often tend to diminish.

The difficulty in getting perceptions to converge is demonstrated by the confusions which pervade complex organizations. These confusions result from such factors as changed and changing situations, differing personality patterns and self-concepts, the inadequate preparation of role-occupants, the tendency to assign several roles to one person, and the presence of sub-groups within organizations.[32] Case studies and sociodramas, as well as discussion of role-perceptions, should be used in causing differing views of roles to merge, so that staff members will be able to work together with less conflict and greater productivity.

ACTIVITY 9-3—THE CONFLICT BETWEEN PRINCIPALS AND CURRICULUM COORDINATORS

"I thought curriculum planning was *my* job!"
This statement is frequently being made simultaneously by

---

[32] See J. W. Getzels and E. G. Guba, "Structure of Roles and Role Conflicts in the Teaching Situation," *Journal of Educational Sociology*, Vol. 29, September, 1955, pp. 30–40.

principals and curriculum coordinators in the same school districts. Interview one or more principals and one or more curriculum coordinators to learn their respective perceptions of ways in which this conflict has arisen.

When you have assessed the situation, state what you believe might have been done to avoid conflict. State also what actions should be taken in the future to prevent additional conflict.

SUMMARY

In a day in which roles of improvers of the curriculum are becoming amplified and confused, the problem of who is to assume specific responsibility for improving the curriculum becomes an especially difficult one. Whereas curriculum improvers were once found mainly within local school districts, persons outside these districts are now assuming more and more responsibility. This chapter contains a prediction that the federal government, certain national organizations, state and regional professional groups, producers of teaching materials, and teacher educators will occupy enhanced roles during the next decade. The chapter also emphasizes the important roles of professional personnel and laymen within local school districts: boards of education, individual laymen and groups of laymen, administrators and supervisors, teachers, and pupils. Assigning and balancing roles require coverage of assignments, removal of conflict among role-takers and of duplication of roles, and convergence of perceptions regarding particular roles.

SELECTED BIBLIOGRAPHY

Association for Supervision and Curriculum Development, *Forces Affecting American Education*, 1953 Yearbook (Washington, D.C.: The Association, 1953).

Getzels, J. W., and E. G. Guba, "Role, Role Conflicts, and Effectiveness," *American Sociological Review*, Vol. 19, April, 1954.

———, "Structure of Roles and Role Conflict in the Teaching Situation," *Journal of Educational Sociology*, Vol. 29, September, 1955.

Gross, Neal, Ward S. Mason, and Alexander W. McEachern, *Explorations in Role Analysis* (New York: John Wiley & Sons, Inc., 1958).

National Society for the Study of Education, *Social Forces Influencing American Education*, 60th Yearbook, Part II (Chicago: University of Chicago Press, 1961).

Storen, Helen F., *Laymen Help Plan the Curriculum* (Washington, D.C.: Association for Supervision and Curriculum Development, 1946).

"Who Should Plan the Curriculum?" special issue of *Educational Leadership*, Vol. 19, No. 1, October, 1961.

chapter ten

WE WORKED A WHOLE YEAR, but no one knew about it."

"How can I convey to the other teachers in my school what I've learned in recent months?"

"All that we do in Ramsey Elementary School seems to involve very few people."

The preceding comments are typical of the many remarks one hears about lack of communication among the staff members of American schools. If it is true that many years are required for an educational idea to move from its source to common practice, it is also true that many promising ideas are lost annually because they are never launched into communication channels of any sort. How can ideas move freely within schools and school systems, and then move out into the educational world at large? How can countering ideas be fed back to the sources of the original ideas to modify, correct, and improve them? In brief, how can we have the news about developments in education distributed so quickly and easily that practice will evolve with the speed that befits a thriving profession? Providing appropriate answers to these questions could aid materially the process of curriculum improvement.

~~ ~~ ~~ ~~ ~~ ~~ ~~ ~~ ~~ ~~ ~~ ~~ ~~

The Massive
Problem of
Communication

COMMUNICATION: A COMPLEX ENTERPRISE

Human communication, which has been defined as transmission of facts, ideas, values, feelings, and attitudes from one person or group to another, has been called the number-one problem of school administration. It may also be the greatest problem of curriculum improvement. Merely transmitting the simplest of information from sender to receiver without undue loss or confusion becomes a major task. The complexity of messages about the curriculum, the intertwining of networks through which messages move, and the uncertain readiness of receivers to accept the messages all increase the problem.

The process of human communication has been described by Wilbur Schramm as conforming to the model which appears on page 234. The model suggests something of the complexity of communication. Like most complex problems, however, human communication has been oversimplified by laymen. "The prevailing thought is that all the sender has to do now is transfer his ideas from his mind to the receiver's mind. He bundles his ideas into a neat little package and sends them off on an unperilous journey to be opened and digested whole."[1] Actually, the model reminds one of Harold

[1] Fred R. Dowling, "The Teacher and Communication Theory," *Education*, Vol. 81, No. 3, November, 1960, p. 182.

A Source ⟶	"Encodes" a ⟶ Message	And Tries to ⟶ "Transmit" It	To "Receivers" ⟵ Who Try to Decode It	And Respond
You have facts or ideas you want others to understand	You select words, gestures, or pictures to prepare a "message" you hope others will notice and understand	You try to convey your message by means of conversations, discussions, letters, bulletins, newspapers, magazines, television, radio	Those who notice your message interpret it in a framework of their interests, attitudes, and group relationships	They may decide to think about your message, to discuss it with you, to support your idea, to oppose it, or to do nothing about it[2]

Lasswell's pithy question: "Who says what to whom via what channel with what effect?" The question suggests the agents of and elements in communication: *who,* the sender; *what,* the message; *whom,* the receiver; *what channel,* the communication medium and the structure of human relationships through which the message is transmitted; and *what effect,* the evaluation of results. The first four of these agents or elements can either facilitate or impede communication.

Barriers to effective communication in schools have been identified by several students of the problem. Culbertson notes three substantial barriers: variable meanings of words, perceptions of the communicator which are held by persons who receive his messages, and the motivations that affect receivers of the messages.[3] To be specific, specialized vocabularies, different social backgrounds, multiple definitions of words, and the unique experiences of individuals cause inaccuracies in communication. The communicator may threaten other persons by his personality, his status, or his behavior. He may seem impatient, gruff, or harsh. He may engage in duplicity or attempt to manipulate others. In some phases of his work, he may seem incompetent. Meanwhile, receivers of communications, called *communicatees,* are affected by fatigue, conflicting demands on their time, varying backgrounds of experience, and anxieties about the status of communicators. In the face of such formidable barriers, it is remarkable that communication proceeds as well as it does.

The dimensions of communication can be viewed in at least two ways.

2 Gordon McCloskey, "Principles of Communication for Principals," *Bulletin of the National Association of Secondary School Principals,* Vol. 44, No. 257, September, 1960, pp. 17–23.

3 Jack Culbertson, "Recognizing Roadblocks in Communication Channels," *Administrator's Notebook,* Midwest Administration Center, The University of Chicago, Vol. 7, No. 7, March, 1959.

First, some communicatees desire messages that are thorough and complete, while other communicatees want messages that are superficial and only generally informative. Messages of the former sort are intended for persons who are deeply involved in the task with which the message deals. Messages of the latter kind are for persons who merely want to hear about what is happening, without becoming too directly involved in it.

A second way of viewing the dimensions of communication has been expressed in the Citizenship Education Study as 1) spreading *facts* that everyone wants to know, and 2) conveying *assumptions, values,* and *philosophy* that provide the seedground for new insights and thence new procedures.[4] According to this viewpoint, a message may differ not only in the depth but also in the nature of its content. Facts may be communicated by means of a letter, a book, a bulletin, or a speaker. Assumptions, values, and philosophy, which are much more difficult to convey, require multiple "interaction media" like leisurely meetings and workshops, role-playing, and demonstrations. That is, multiple media are needed for reinforcement, and most of the media involve direct contacts among human beings. Either a simple or a complex message may be subject to differences in perspective. These differences occur not only with reference to the differing roles of communicator and communicatee, but also according to the position which each occupies in the organizational hierarchy.[5]

Research in human communication, within the fields of political science, psychology, semantics, and sociology, suggests additional ideas about the nature, importance, and complexity of communication in schools:

1. Much communication occurs informally, outside the neat, formal channels we prepare.[6] We should expect this situation to exist as a plain fact of human behavior.

2. True communication occurs only when we have given ample opportunity for feedback of ideas from communicatee to communicator. Benefit from feedback accrues to communicator as well as to communicatee. Alex Bavelas has shown, for instance, that "as the exchange of ideas, or feedback, increases, speed, accuracy, and morale of the communicators also increase."[7]

3. Communication does not automatically teach. In Cincinnati, "an extensive, long-term effort to familiarize the population with the United Nations

[4] Citizenship Education Study, "A New Look in School Administration," *Educational Leadership*, Vol. 6, No. 5, February, 1949, pp. 302–309.

[5] B. Othanel Smith, William O. Stanley, and J. Harlan Shores, *Fundamentals of Curriculum Development*. New York: Harcourt, Brace & World, Inc., 1957, p. 468.

[6] Wilbur Schramm, "Educators and Communication Research," *Educational Leadership*, Vol. 13, No. 8, May, 1956, pp. 503–509.

[7] Dowling, *op. cit.,* p. 184.

achieved very little new learning, in spite of maximum use of radio, press, films, and other media."[8] The process of curriculum improvement (Chapter 6) requires teaching of the highest order. Thus communication for curriculum improvement must emphasize effective teaching, the methodology of which needs careful study and development.

Ideas and sets of values seem to be conveyed faster and more accurately in "settled" professions like medicine than they do in education. Several reasons for this phenomenon might be advanced: a vast body of respectable learnings, against which new ideas must be evaluated, has been accumulated; sources such as the leading professional journals command great respect; practitioners, though they frequently work alone, work cooperatively on certain important occasions; and the practitioners themselves are less secretive about professional lore. Teachers "talk shop" almost unremittingly, but they talk much more about problems than about reliable solutions to problems. In a new profession, especially in one that involves the uncertainties of the social sciences, respect for what is communicated comes slowly. This is a fact with which communicators in education will have to reckon for a long time to come.

The following situation is meant to enhance your sensitivity to the seriousness of communication problems:

SITUATION 10-1—COMMUNICATION BACKFIRE

Bill Akers, the superintendent of schools, was talking with one of his assistants about a communication mixup in the school system.

"But I never said that," bellowed Mr. Akers.

"*I* know you didn't," his assistant replied. "The committee of teachers and principals doesn't know it, though. Someone told the committee that you said their plan for improving the arithmetic program was ridiculous, and now the committee members believe you said it."

"What I said by telephone to one of our principals was that organizing a lot of meetings of teachers to talk about what's new in the teaching of arithmetic is largely unnecessary. Maybe we need an occasional, short meeting, but nothing as elaborate as the committee wants: three workshops, each two days long, and partly on school time besides. The Board won't stand for it, and I won't stand for it,

[8] W. Phillips Davison, "Modern Mass Communication—Trends and Prospects," *National Elementary Principal*, Vol. 39, No. 6, May, 1960, pp. 40–43.

either. Not when we have good teachers' guides that explain the new ideas in the arithmetic textbook series. I maintain that any teacher who can read will get ideas from the guides, and then can put them into practice on her own initiative. How long are we going to spoon-feed teachers and try to redo what the colleges are supposed to have done?"

"I guess you'll have to put more of your thoughts in writing," said the assistant.

"I suppose so," replied Mr. Akers. "When you're in a position like mine, you're likely to be wrong, whatever you say and however you say it. The trouble is with people. Most of the time they don't want to understand."

1. According to what you now know about communication, wherein do you agree and wherein do you disagree with Mr. Akers and his assistant in their views of effective communication?

2. What additional considerations should personnel in this school system take into account in the future with reference to:

    a. Mr. Akers' behavior and staff members' perceptions of his behavior?

    b. The problem of word meanings in whatever message is conveyed by Mr. Akers to his staff?

    c. The special difficulties that communicatees face, at their end of the communication range, in receiving, interpreting, and responding to the messages sent to them by Mr. Akers?

COMMUNICATION THROUGH LITERARY AND AUDIO-VISUAL MEDIA

In American schools and school systems, communication of facts, ideas, values, feelings, and attitudes occurs by two principal means: the use of literary and audio-visual media, and face-to-face contact by staff members. The first of these means is the concern of the present section of this chapter; the second is the concern of the section beginning on page 244.

In the early days of organized curriculum improvement programs, the chief method of formal communication was the writing and "installation" of courses of study, which were conceived as detailed and prescriptive guides to the activities of teachers and pupils in classrooms and, occasionally, in other sites in and about the school.[9] The customary procedure was "to have a committee of representative teachers . . . meet with one or more of the assistant superintendents and with the director of the subject, if there [was] a director. The course thus prepared [was] submitted to the board of superintendents for approval and this [went] to the school committee (board of education) for authority to print as a school document."[10] The course of study was then "installed" by transmitting to school staffs a mandate from a highly-placed school official, and sometimes by conducting meetings to emphasize the importance of the document.

The real problem with courses of study has been that they have too often found their way into the bottom drawers of teachers' desks rather than into the nervous systems and thus into the ongoing activities of teachers and pupils. Despite this fact, prescriptive courses of study continue to be produced in a sizable number of American school systems, both large and small. Theoretically, however, curriculum workers have come to the view that it is as foolish to try legislating educational experiences for a large group of children simultaneously as it is to prescribe physical treatment aimlessly for numbers of children who are suffering from malnutrition. They recognize that courses of study tend to be repetitious of other courses of study, or even of the tables of contents of leading textbooks. Scissors and pots of paste are too often the chief tools by which unthinking, uncreative "curriculum builders" borrow ideas formulated by other people. Rigid courses of study are being perpetuated partly because administrators find them useful in achieving uniformity, or alleged uniformity, in educational experiences; in facilitating the orientation of new teachers; and in pacifying critical lay groups who want to be certain about "what our children are learning." The wise administrator knows that, after limited instruction-taking, the teacher is likely to do what she wants to do when her classroom door is closed. There is no such thing as idea-tight, uniform administration of the curriculum.

The last-mentioned fact has led in part to the development of less prescriptive and more generally helpful documents called curriculum guides, which enunciate principles and guidelines for teachers, and which contain helpful suggestions and aids, including lists of audio-visual materials, books, brochures, and articles. Baltimore, Maryland, for example, has prepared

---

[9] See W. W. Charters, *Curriculum Construction*. New York: The Macmillan Co., 1923; and Henry Harap, *The Technique of Curriculum Making*. New York: The Macmillan Co., 1928.

[10] National Society for the Study of Education, *The Foundations and Technique of Curriculum Construction*—Part II: "The Foundations of Curriculum Making." Bloomington, Ill.: Public School Publishing Company, 1926, p. 121.

several helpful, interesting, and well-illustrated guides, including its general "Guide to Elementary Education." Students of curriculum improvement should examine carefully several guides and several courses of study so that they may see the distinction between the two kinds of documents. Harap and Merritt compared curriculum guides issued in 1949 and 1950 with those issued between 1951 and 1953. They reported that the word "guide" appeared in 52 per cent of curriculum bulletins issued from 1951 to 1953, but that many publications were "still crude, shoddy, and hard to read." They considered the production of guides and courses of study a hit-and-run operation, usually unconnected with a sequential program of curriculum improvement and seldom based on research findings.[11] In some subject-matter fields, guides are being developed with considerable frequency—*e.g.*, in special education, foreign languages in the elementary school, guidance, business education, and kindergarten education. A redeeming feature in the development of guides is that reasonably large numbers of teachers are being involved in idea production and tryout.

In a study of curriculum guides, Nault has given helpful suggestions for making guides effective. He reports that guides should:

Be part of a total ongoing program of curriculum improvement;
Bring about modification of values, understandings, and skills;
Begin with teachers where they are;
Serve the primary purpose of the guide as expressed by teachers;
Contain appropriate content for grade levels;
Suggest available and usable source materials;
Contain sufficiently concrete and specific material;
Contain practical and realistic content;
Contain material adaptable to needs and interests of children;
Provide an ongoing program for implementing the guide;
Permit teachers to receive "on-call" assistance in implementing the guide;
Involve teachers in the implementation process;
Provide for "self-implementation" of the guide through built-in ideas and
    directions;
Provide for evaluation of the guide;
Involve building principals in development of the guide;
Involve teachers directly or indirectly at various times and places;
Develop in teachers good feeling toward the guide;
Expect consultant help in developing and communicating the guide to con-
    tribute to the guide's plan and purpose as seen by the staff.[12]

[11] Henry Harap and Eleanor Merritt, "Trends in the Production of Curriculum Guides," *Educational Leadership*, Vol. 13, No. 1, October, 1955, pp. 35–39.
[12] William H. Nault, "Can Curriculum Guides Be Effective?" *Educational Leadership*, Vol. 12, No. 7, April, 1955, pp. 410–414.

The keynote of these findings is *involvement*. Nault's suggestions remind one of the difficulty of communicating to others either the substance or the spirit of an experience which the recipients have not had. When curriculum materials are produced by a few persons only, these few persons can be expected to appreciate and use them with greatest satisfaction. However, staff members who have had no part in producing the materials may appreciate and use them relatively little. A major goal in the production of curriculum materials, then, is to involve personnel at different levels of operation and in different ways as ideas are being conceived and communicated. The schools need much inventiveness in creating ways of maintaining copious, vital involvement of staff members. School staffs should be helped to suggest new ideas, try ideas, write statements, participate in meetings, evaluate the guide, and feed back suggestions for improving the guide. Most curriculum documents should probably contain blank pages on which teachers can write reactions and suggestions to be communicated from time to time to the persons mainly responsible for the documents.

In the preceding discussion, the curriculum guide has been highlighted because it is the curriculum document most commonly prepared in American schools. Other materials include: statements of philosophy and objectives, policy statements, resource units, research reports, lists of teaching materials, and booklets and brochures on a variety of subjects. Each of these materials deserves a brief description.

STATEMENTS OF PHILOSOPHY AND OBJECTIVES

Beliefs about the role and purpose of a school or school system appear in statements of philosophy and objectives. These beliefs should be restated occasionally in revised form to help prevent the school or school system from stumbling along without direction. Minneapolis, Minnesota, has stated its objectives cleverly and attractively in a bulletin titled "Achieving the Objectives of Education—a Guide for Curriculum Development." Aberdeen, South Dakota, has tested the reality of its philosophy and objectives by requesting teachers to see what the Aberdeen statement could mean for good, everyday practice.

POLICY STATEMENTS

The policy handbook or policy guide has become fairly common in school systems. Policy statements are frequently enunciated by committees or task forces that compile instructional and other policies from school system records. Today, an abbreviated kind of policy statement, a summary of important committee decisions, is being produced. Wilmington, Delaware, has prepared a statement about selection and use of instructional materials to encourage use of a wide variety of materials and to urge impartial teaching about controversial issues. Minneapolis has written a guide to common practices in the classroom and a four-page manual of policies and procedures for curriculum development. The music department of the Fairfield, Connecticut, schools has issued a procedural statement governing the music program.

RESOURCE UNITS

These materials consist of "master" units written as resources to which teachers may refer in devising and tailoring units for use in their classrooms. Individual teachers and groups of teachers write resource units which contain sections like these: the nature of the unit problem; purposes of the unit in developing understandings, skills, and attitudes; sequence of the subject-matter content; nature of pupil experiences within the unit; methods of teaching the unit; resources, written and other, for learning; and ways of evaluating the learning experiences. State departments of education and the education departments of industries prepare resource units which form valuable starting points in developing more precise and usable teaching units. Dade County, Florida, has created numerous resource units in the language arts, the social studies, and basic education. With community agency cooperation, a committee of Washington, D.C., teachers has prepared resource units on community services.

RESEARCH REPORTS

Reports of research activities assume varied forms: articles in journals, mimeographed statements for staff distribution, and survey reports, to mention a few. In recent years, grants from foundations and the federal government have spurred issuance of printed reports like those concerning team teaching and educational television.

LISTS OF TEACHING MATERIALS

These lists are often formulated in a materials center in a school or school system for use throughout the organization. Books, magazines, films, filmstrips, still pictures, tape recordings, and other aids to learning are presented to teachers on annotated master lists. Among local school systems, the Montclair, New Jersey, lists have long been representative. Nationally, the Association for Supervision and Curriculum Development periodically distributes lists of the newer teaching and learning materials of interest to curriculum specialists.

BOOKLETS AND BROCHURES

Materials of this nature serve numerous purposes, from orientation of new teachers to lay understanding of instructional programs. Booklets and brochures are costly and time-consuming to prepare, and they should therefore be written only when their existence can be justified. Reasonably typical of booklets and brochures are the guides to educational trips which have been issued by the public schools in Grosse Pointe, Michigan, and Schenectady, New York.

In a culture in which there is already so much printed material that men are overwhelmed by it, printed materials of all sorts should be developed more selectively in American school systems. Principals' brief, daily bulletins are not always read. Surely, then, many inch-thick documents probably will be consigned to the same fate—the wastebasket. William Cotton suggests several guidelines for the production of written curriculum materials of all sorts. The most important of these guidelines, within four categories, are as follows:

1. Production of materials:
   should be done cooperatively;
   should be done in consideration of readers' experiences, needs, and interests;
   should be accomplished in consideration of timing and "saturation";
   should be accomplished with ample equipment, facilities, and time.
2. Design of materials:
   should provide for content that helps solve readers' problems;
   should display style that gains and holds readers' attention;
   should be physically attractive;
   should be applicable to educational levels.
3. The introduction process:
   should be achieved by face-to-face association;
   should involve follow-up activities;
   should help to make the materials welcome to the reader;
   should be accomplished by methods that are appropriate to the materials being introduced.
4. General guidelines:
   Materials should be geared to the local situation.
   Materials should become an integral part of the in-service program.
   Materials should lead to a variety of experiences in their use.
   Materials should provide for an interchange of ideas.[13]

[13] William Cotton, *A Study of Locally-Developed Written Professional Curriculum Materials* (doctoral dissertation). New York: Teachers College, Columbia University, 1952, pp. 107 and 108.

It is possible to develop and use materials wisely by planning carefully-selected activities within carefully-allocated blocks of time. Grand Rapids, Michigan, utilized a period of time for the following activities: involving nearly 1,000 teachers in area meetings to prepare a statement of philosophy; developing a series of handbooks for parent education; writing Grand Rapids' own textbooks for elementary-school children, with the ideas coming from the city's elementary-school teachers; publishing a local songbook; and producing a film.[14]

A glance at the Grand Rapids activities reveals one in five of them to be of an audio-visual rather than a literary sort. Audio-visual means of communication have been designed so seldom in school systems that the proportion of one in five is unusual. Curriculum workers have scarcely begun to explore the possibilities in presenting teaching demonstrations on film and in live telecasts, in reporting summaries of research findings by means of filmstrips, and in enunciating policies on the radio and on tape recordings. Media like films and filmstrips can cause the viewer to identify closely with the scene being presented, especially when the scene is both realistic and dramatic.[15] A few preliminary investigations have shown that in-service experiences for teachers which are provided audio-visually can create much greater learning effect than can the same experiences provided in literary form.[16] For example, Hunter College, of the City University of New York, has been conducting interesting experiments in the use of live television and kinescopes in the preparation of student teachers and in the in-service development of college professors.

SITUATION 10-2—HOW CAN THEY PRESENT IT MOST EFFECTIVELY?

The kindergarten-through-twelfth-grade Language Arts Committee of the Eberville Consolidated Schools has been conducting experiments in the teaching of linguistics. Individual members of the committee have found that pupils in the fifth, eighth, and tenth grades—the grades in which experiments have been tried—are making unusual progress in understanding and interpreting the structure of English. On a Tuesday afternoon in January, they meet in

[14] Marcillene Barnes, "Curriculum Materials in the Making," *Educational Leadership*, Vol. 11, No. 8, May, 1954, pp. 471–475.

[15] Catherine M. Broderick, "Research in the Use and Purposes of Instructional Materials," *Educational Leadership*, Vol. 13, No. 7, April, 1956, pp. 425–429.

[16] Elizabeth Burger, *The Use of Television for In-service Teacher Training* (doctoral dissertation). Charlottesville: The University of Virginia, 1960.

Mr. James's (the language coordinator's) office to plan means of attracting the interest and enthusiasm of other teachers on the Eberville staff.

"We can't possibly describe what we've done," says a tenth-grade teacher.

"No, we can't," replies an eighth-grade teacher. "The method we've used is strange enough to make analysis of English look like analysis of a strange language. Just the vocabulary we use presents a problem: *determiners, verb signals, patterns of writing,* and so on. Maybe we should buy copies of the books by Paul Roberts, Henry Lee Smith, and Charles Fries, and ask the teachers to read them so they'll understand what we're talking about. I'm convinced that the linguistic approach to teaching the structure of English is just what we need, but I've almost given up trying to convince other people who are entirely new to it."

After some discussion, Mr. James suggests that the committee think about its communication problem between now and the next week. "Concentrate on written and pictorial ways of communicating with our teachers," Mr. James suggests as the meeting concludes.

1. What is the first step you would take in helping people who had long used a formal grammatical approach become acquainted with a new method of language analysis?

2. What written or pictorial material would you hope to see prepared to give opportunity for careful study of the new method?

3. What additional, long-term learning opportunities would you need to provide?

COMMUNICATION VIA PERSONAL CONTACT

Much evidence has accumulated that, where geography, time, and facilities will permit, the most effective communication occurs through personal contact. Says a social scientist, "The oldest form of communication—word of mouth—shows no sign of being displaced by the newer media."[17] The mass media are helpful in reinforcing communication by word of mouth, and vice versa. But many persons believe that nothing should be put in writing, except in very tentative form, until it has been discussed, analyzed, and, if possible,

[17] Davison, *op. cit.,* p. 43.

experimented with. Discussion, with feedback to further discussion, greatly facilitates communication. Phenix refers to communication as a "personal transaction." Thus, "the real barriers to communication are not technical, but personal."[18]

Personal decision-making is influenced most by what the members of one's intimate group are saying and doing.[19] People communicate most readily with individuals they like and trust.[20] Each person tends to find within his own group one or more friends with whom he can communicate easily. Also, people who share common interests often communicate effectively about matters affecting their interests. They feel an "emotional kinship" with, and are usually geographically close to, the persons with whom they communicate. All of this would seem to make eminently good sense. Besides, it is supported by findings in sociology and social psychology.

The depths of communication through personal contact have, of course, been too little explored. More than a decade ago, Carl Rogers presented a paper which has remained a classic in the field of interpersonal communication. Rogers argued that the basic difficulty with human communication is our tendency to judge and evaluate, promptly and recklessly, the comments made by other people. The result is that people "miss each other in psychological space," failing to understand each other because each person is busy evaluating what the other person has said. Rogers suggested that real communication occurs only when people pause to listen to each other with an attempt at understanding. To achieve ability to listen, he suggested the following experiment:

> The next time you get into an argument with your wife, or your friend, or with a small group of friends, just stop the discussion for a moment, and for an experiment, institute this rule. "Each person can speak up for himself only *after* he has first restated the ideas and feelings of the previous speaker accurately, and to that speaker's satisfaction." You see what this would mean. It would simply mean that before presenting your own point of view, it would be necessary for you to really achieve the other speaker's frame of reference—to understand his thoughts and feelings so well that you could summarize them for him. Sounds simple, doesn't it? But if you try it, you will discover it one of the most difficult things you have ever tried to do. However, once you have been able to see the other's point of view, your own

[18] Philip H. Phenix, "Barriers to Academic Communication," *Teachers College Record*, Vol. 59, No. 2, November, 1957, p. 88.

[19] Elmo Roper, in Elihu Katz and Paul F. Lazarsfeld, *Personal Influence*. New York: Free Press of Glencoe, Inc., 1955, p. xv.

[20] George C. Homans, *The Human Group*. New York: Harcourt, Brace & World, Inc., 1950.

comments will have to be drastically revised. You will also find the emotion going out of the discussion, the differences being reduced, and those differences which remain being of a rational and understandable sort.[21]

Culbertson points to the need, in skillful listening, for a sensitive ear and careful observation. The listener should concentrate not only on the meanings of words but also on the meanings of *behaviors*. What does body posture tell? "What are the hands of the conferee saying, if anything? What emotional tone does the voice quality communicate? Are there silent symbols in eye contacts, pauses, or hesitations? Does the behavior of the conferee suggest that he is relaxed, tense, or threatened? What would he say if he sincerely expressed what he is feeling and thinking? Are there clues about sub-conscious motivations?"[22]

In individual conferences, group meetings, and informal settings, the curriculum worker needs to avoid the six bad habits of listening which are described in a leading book on the subject: 1) faking attention, or pretending to listen; 2) listening for facts without considering broader meanings; 3) over-concentrating on physical appearance and delivery at the expense of attending to verbal content; 4) yielding to distractions; 5) dismissing content as uninteresting; and 6) ceasing to listen because the content is hard to comprehend.[23] During conversations in the teachers' rooms of school buildings, as well as in formally-organized meetings for reporting progress, effective listening can contribute greatly to in-service growth.

Role-playing is an important means by which communication on a person-to-person basis can be facilitated. There is often a real advantage in reversing the roles to which two individuals are respectively accustomed, so that the participants may begin to perceive a conflicted situation from each other's viewpoint. For instance, a teacher who has participated in and supported an experimental project may defend it blindly, while a non-participant who has had absolutely no contact with the project may attack it bitterly. If the two agree to reverse their roles in a discussion of the project, each may be led to modify his extreme point of view, and the parties to the dispute may then be able to talk together more cogently.[24]

Sharp points to the importance of good communication between the

[21] Carl R. Rogers, "Communication—its Blocking and its Facilitation," a paper presented to the Centennial Conference on Communications, Northwestern University, October 11, 1951 (unpublished).

[22] Culbertson, *op. cit.*, p. 4.

[23] Ralph Nichols and Leonard Stevens, *Are You Listening?* New York: McGraw-Hill Book Co., Inc., 1957.

[24] For further development of this idea, see Kenneth D. Benne and Bozidar Muntyan, *Human Relations in Curriculum Change.* New York: The Dryden Press, 1951, pp. 272–282.

teacher and the "teacher educator," who is usually a supervisor or an administrator.[25] The principal of a school is in a unique position to help create a climate in which people can communicate, as well as to take a personal interest in problems that have group-wide interest. In his position as the first communication contact in an administrative hierarchy, he should make himself readily, even suddenly, available for conferences.[26] The subtleties of communication within the individual school remain, in part, a mystery. The story is told of the principal who thought he was on the best of terms with his staff, and who said "Good morning" to a teacher, only to overhear her asking a co-worker, "Now what did he mean by that?"

Face-to-face communication with persons who are elevated in the hierarchy or shifted in assignment becomes even more difficult because distance increases psychological static. Teachers often imagine strange things about other teachers and administrators whom they seldom see. A common, if secret, question is, "I wonder how I stand with my fellows and my bosses?" Social science research has shown that communication is improved by knowing how one is viewed by others, especially by persons in authority.[27] It is improved also by knowing which actions are permissible and which are taboo. One of life's most frustrating experiences is to find, belatedly, that a decision which an individual or a group has laboriously reached is beyond the authority and responsibility of that individual or group.

In a world in which people were created to mingle freely with each other, face-to-face communication will remain without equal as a medium for transmitting subtle cognitive and emotional content. The quality of face-to-face communication must, however, be improved radically in these times, when ideas and values are undergoing such rapid change. The following section of the chapter suggests means by which organizational arrangements can be made for face-to-face contact among teachers and other curriculum workers.

SITUATION 10-3—THE STORMS AT STONEHAM CENTER

The April faculty meeting at Stoneham Center Elementary School was about to get under way. At least, the clock said it should. But Ed Ringo, the new, young principal, had not yet arrived.

[25] George Sharp, *Curriculum Development as Re-education of the Teacher.* New York: Bureau of Publications, Teachers College, Columbia University, 1951.

[26] Marcella R. Lawler, *Curriculum Consultants at Work.* New York: Bureau of Publications, Teachers College, Columbia University, 1958, pp. 105–107.

[27] J. A. C. Brown, *The Social Psychology of Industry.* Baltimore: Penguin Books, Inc., 1954, p. 212.

"He must have had a flat tire again," remarked Elsie Kingsland, the oldest member of the group.

"Always excusing Mr. Ringo's actions, aren't you?" retorted Miss Kermit tartly.

Miss Kermit's remark proved to be the gun that opened another battle. When Ed Ringo arrived breathlessly 35 minutes later, he found a donnybrook in progress. Ed had already learned that there were two or three troublemakers in the faculty of 24, and Miss Kermit was one of them. Originally, he had hoped to team the teachers in groups of three or four so that they could exchange ideas, engage in some simple experimentation, and ease the problem of continuity among grade levels. Abstractly, the idea was excellent, but it apparently couldn't work at Stoneham Center. Not now, anyway. Next, Ed thought of organizing informal grade-level meetings simply to share ideas about good teaching. Miss Perry, who seemed to be a ringleader for evil causes, had sabotaged that idea by remarking at the February faculty meeting, "I wouldn't be caught giving my best ideas to anyone. Let other people learn for themselves. I always erase my blackboard as promptly as I can so no one else will have a chance to borrow what I do."

"Face-to-face communication!" thought Ed. "Only 24 teachers, and I can't get most of them to have anything to do with each other. What can I do?"

1. Discuss the Stoneham Center problem as you see it.

2. Ed asked the question, "What can I do?" How should he behave just to keep the situation from growing worse?

3. What other question or questions might Ed have asked?

4. If you were in Ed's place, what long-range plans would you make for improving interpersonal communication among the 24 teachers and the principal?

ORGANIZING FOR BETTER COMMUNICATION

Let us now turn our attention to marshaling and integrating forces for communication to improve the curriculum in schools and school systems. Most communication activities today are hit-or-miss, without being part of a comprehensive plan. Occasionally, however, a school system organizes a committee on communication that plans and coordinates a series of communication activities. In general, the planning should take into account criteria like these:

1. *Balance should be achieved in choosing media of communication concerning curriculum projects, according to special purposes to be served.* Brief written reports may be used for one purpose; tape recordings for another; individual contacts with staff members for another; news bulletins for another; and visitation of meetings for still another. As Forsdale has said, "Appropriate communication behavior in one situation, with one audience, for one kind of purpose, is not necessarily appropriate in another setting with another audience for another purpose."[28]

2. *Communication units should be kept small.* This criterion applies in both large and small school organizations. Large groups, approaching a membership of 40 or 50 persons, tend to impede communication. Seven to 10 persons may constitute a group of optimum size. However, some differences in viewpoint and talent should be sought in forming groups, because these differences enrich feedback, which in turn produces further improvement in communication.

3. *Messages should usually be brief, direct, and pointed.* There is no sense in compounding numbers of words unnecessarily. Several brief messages are often more effective than a single comprehensive one.

4. *Ample time for communication is decidedly necessary.* Face-to-face contacts, the preparation of written messages, and use of electronic devices all require time.

5. *Both formal and informal communication channels should be employed.* An example of the former is the pre-arranged faculty meeting for sharing understandings and insights; an example of the latter is permitting teachers to assemble where they wish, in groups of differing sizes and constituent personnel, to discuss curriculum problems that concern them.

6. *Lines of communication should be kept short.* This criterion applies especially to vertical communication, which is aided by decreasing the number of hierarchical levels through which the message must go from bottom to top and from top to bottom in the organization. For example, what happens in a faculty meeting in School X could easily be reported to the Curriculum Steering Committee without being told and retold to numerous intermediaries.

7. *Some person or group should watch over communication activities in the school or school system.* Without supervision and perspective, planning and coordination are likely to go awry. Perhaps the best answer is formation of a central committee on communication. However, much care should be

[28] Louis Forsdale, "Helping Students Observe Processes of Communication," *Teachers College Record*, Vol. 57, No. 2, November, 1955, p. 128.

exercised to see that the members of such a committee are not merely unwilling representatives of faculties or departments.

8. *Emergent communicators should be sought among members of the staff.* Experience indicates that certain personnel do very well as communicators. They need only an invitation to serve an ongoing organization whose purpose is improved communication.

9. *Invention is needed in developing new communication practices.* Consider the following suggestions:

> Within each communication group, an official communicator should be designated by his peers. He should possess some skill in communication and should be one of the best accepted members of his group. He should receive communications from other portions of the school and school system, as well as from the outside educational world, and should assume leadership in transmitting ideas and urging examination of them. In addition, he should organize dyads of the most compatible persons for informal conversation about these ideas. When he has gathered the reactions of his group to a given set of ideas, he should transmit these reactions to a traveling communicator (a "wandering minstrel") who can inform the idea originators about the reactions. Each official communicator should hold his position as long as his group wishes him to retain it. If the official communicator is not the chairman of his group, he should assist the chairman in planning the development of new ideas and the modification of old ones, and he should then communicate the indigenous thinking of his group to other communication units in the school system. Continuous feedback of ideas and reactions to ideas is important.[29]

In the West Orange, New Jersey, curriculum improvement program of the early 1950's, a committee on communication reported that the following methods of communication were in use:

> Brief written reports are issued at intervals to persons who request them. Frequently these are summaries of the recent work of action groups.
>
> Teacher members of the Central Curriculum Committee confer with teachers and principals in the schools they represent. Often the conferences are in the nature of informal conversations held wherever people meet. Sometimes there are small groups meeting in lunchrooms. At other times, they are more formally organized portions of faculty meetings. One of the advantages of conferences in the local school is that they capitalize on face-to-face, two-way communication.
>
> Members of the CCC are instrumental in maintaining curriculum bulletin boards in local schools and in displaying curriculum materials on office counters, in school libraries, and in teachers' restrooms.

[29] Ronald C. Doll, "Communicating Educational Ideas," *Educational Leadership,* Vol. 18, No. 2, November, 1960, pp. 109–113.

Leaders and other key persons in action groups are sometimes invited to attend meetings of the Central Curriculum Committee to report for their groups and to receive advice and promises of assistance. Hearing the reports and the discussions of reports of action group members is helpful to communication between groups, between groups and the CCC, and between CCC members and the staffs of local schools.

Other agents of communication include status persons who discuss curriculum projects in meetings and in less formal situations. The supervisor of elementary education, for example, attends many action group meetings and subsequently, in supervisory meetings which she herself calls, encourages participants in curriculum activities to share information and insights with non-participants.

Action group recorders have been given limited training. Reports of meetings prepared by recorders are sent to the central curriculum office where they are duplicated and forwarded to CCC members, Institute [Horace Mann-Lincoln Institute of School Experimentation] personnel, and action group members who are directly concerned with the matter being reported.

Tape recordings are sometimes made of summaries of group decisions, curriculum proposals, or teacher-made units. Recordings which might be of interest to large groups of staff members are then transferred to discs for playback in local schools. An example is a disc reporting the development of a social studies unit.

An informal news bulletin is issued irregularly to all staff members. This bulletin would have more attention if communication committee members felt that written materials had a great deal of value for communication purposes, but the tendency has been to distrust the written word as a communication medium.

One work conference has been tried, partly as a communication device. The evaluation of the work conference on reading held in February, 1951, showed that it was valuable enough to be worth repeating. Similar conferences, and even more elaborate ones, are tentatively scheduled for the future.[30]

The methods described above were obviously suitable in the West Orange situation, but they merely suggest variations in communication procedures that can be used in other school systems. Recent research has revealed several additional ideas which may affect organization for communication:

Theoretical communication structures are not necessarily the actual ones. Considerable study is needed to determine just how communication is occurring.[31]

[30] Ronald C. Doll, A. Harry Passow, and Stephen M. Corey, *Organizing for Curriculum Improvement*. New York: Bureau of Publications, Teachers College, Columbia University, 1953, pp. 63 and 64.

[31] George E. Ross, *A Study of Informal Communication Patterns in Two Elementary Schools* (doctoral dissertation). Urbana, Ill.: University of Illinois, 1960.

Big schools and school systems do not necessarily suffer from mal-communication because of their size. In a study of school administration, "communication problems were reported somewhat less frequently in the larger schools than in the smaller schools."[32] Additional evidence needs to be accumulated concerning this matter.

Curriculum planners should become acquainted with the teaching situations of the members of planning groups so that they may know the experiential backgrounds which influence the members' words and actions.[33]

Status affects communication. Information and ideas initiated by top-level administrators move into channels of communication more readily than information and ideas initiated by teachers.[34]

Of the means of communication, individual school faculty meetings are primary.[35]

Teachers with two to six years of experience *may* be best at understanding and accepting communicated messages.[36]

Much time should probably be spent in analyzing teachers' free responses to materials they have tried. "Despite its faults the free response analyzed qualitatively and quantitatively seems to be the best means we have at present of gaining specific information about what is actually communicated. . . ."[37]

The film *A Communications Primer*, which is based on research and experience, suggests four ways of "getting messages through:" 1) make deliberate use of repetition; 2) strengthen the power of the signal; 3) beam the signal more specifically to the audience; and 4) reinforce the signal with other media.[38]

Finally, experience in curriculum improvement suggests the following guidelines in organizing for better communication:

1. Develop good human relations.
2. Provide for interchange of ideas.
3. Communicate at levels of interest and understanding.
4. Secure common understanding of what is communicated.

[32] F. H. Knower and P. H. Wagner, *Communication in Educational Administration.* Columbus, Ohio: Center for Educational Administration, Ohio State University, 1959.

[33] Lawler, *op. cit.*, p. 107.

[34] Ralph M. Peters, *The Effectiveness of Internal Communication in Selected School Systems in East Tennessee* (doctoral dissertation). Nashville: University of Tennessee, 1960.

[35] *Idem.*

[36] *Idem.*

[37] Ruth Strang, "What Is Communicated," *Educational Forum*, Vol. 18, No. 1, November, 1953, p. 19.

[38] Forsdale, *op. cit.*, p. 128.

5. Use a variety of media.
6. Maintain a cooperative spirit in the process of communication.
7. Distribute curriculum materials with discretion.
8. Provide needed facilities, materials, and services.
9. Provide time for communication.
10. Insist on attractive publications, and on pictorial and graphic materials of high technical quality.[39]

The following situation emphasizes the significance of master planning for improved communication:

SITUATION 10-4—A PLAN FOR BANKSDALE

Banksdale Central School District had two high schools, five junior high schools, 16 elementary schools, and a pupil population of about 15,750. Under the guidance of an assistant superintendent in charge of curriculum and instruction, 13 recognized curriculum projects were under way. "Recognition" of the projects was the responsibility of a central curriculum committee, the members of which knew that, in addition to the 13 acknowledged projects, there were numerous other, more informal ones, chiefly at the individual school level. Like many central steering committees, the Banksdale committee discovered that not only were the committee members ignorant of such curriculum improvement activity in their school system, but few school faculties were even acquainted with faculty members of other schools in the district.

We are now listening to some of the discussion in a central committee meeting:

Member A: How is it I'm just hearing of the work the teachers in Pleasant Valley School are doing in science? Science is my own field.

Member B: The bigger the system becomes, the worse off we'll be. Imagine trying to keep track of all the things that are happening in the different schools. I guess we'll just sit here and talk to ourselves without knowing what's going on.

Member C: Stewartsville has solved the whole problem. They have a staff publication that tells what's happening. I recommend that we get someone to serve as editor of a publication of our own. Each of us could be a news representative.

[39] Paul Witt, "Effective Communication in Curriculum Development," *Teachers College Record*, Vol. 51, No. 5, February, 1950, pp. 286–295.

Member A: I have a better idea. People don't want to read. Let's tape record reports of what's going on, and mail the recordings each month to every school for playback in faculty meetings.

Member D: But the teachers in our schools don't even know each other! Hadn't we better begin by introducing ourselves to each other?

1. Indicate which of the comments made by the committee members seem to you to make sense.

2. What other random ideas can you think of? Simply list them without any effort to organize them in a communication complex.

3. In a school system of the size of Banksdale, what steps do you consider absolutely essential in organizing a program to improve communication about instructional matters? If your proposals can be expressed in chart form, make a chart of your organization for communication.

SUMMARY

Communication of curriculum matters is complex chiefly because human beings and their interactions are so complex. Curriculum workers show a desire to communicate symbolically through literary media such as curriculum guides, statements, reports, and brochures, but they have done less to explore the possibilities in communicating through audio-visual materials. Even though face-to-face communication is the most natural and apparently the most effective means of communication, curriculum personnel have done little to develop it into a lively, useful art. Communication seems to proceed best when it is carefully planned according to tested principles which curriculum workers can use.

SELECTED BIBLIOGRAPHY

Cotton, William, *A Study of Locally-Developed Written Professional Curriculum Materials,* unpublished doctoral dissertation (New York: Teachers College, Columbia University, 1952).

Culbertson, Jack, "Recognizing Roadblocks in Communication Channels," *Administrator's Notebook*, Midwest Administration Center, The University of Chicago, Vol. 7, No. 7, March, 1959.

Doll, Ronald C., "Communicating Educational Ideas," *Educational Leadership*, Vol. 18, No. 2, November, 1960.

Johnson, Roy I., Marie Schalkamp, and Lloyd A. Garrison, *Communication: Handling Ideas Effectively* (New York: McGraw-Hill Book Co., Inc., 1956).

Katz, Elihu, and Paul F. Lazarsfeld, *Personal Influence* (New York: Free Press of Glencoe, Inc., 1955).

Knower, F. H., and P. H. Wagner, *Communication in Educational Administration* (Columbus: Center for Educational Administration, Ohio State University, 1959).

McCloskey, Gordon, "Principles of Communication for Principals," *Bulletin of the National Association of Secondary School Principals*, Vol. 44, No. 257, September, 1960.

Nichols, Ralph, and Leonard Stevens, *Are You Listening?* (New York: McGraw-Hill Book Co., Inc., 1957).

Schramm, Wilbur, "Educators and Communication Research," *Educational Leadership*, Vol. 13, No. 8, May, 1956.

————, *The Process and Effects of Mass Communication* (Urbana, Ill.: University of Illinois Press, 1954).

chapter eleven

Plans for initiating programs, assigning roles to participants, and achieving communication among personnel must be made to fit
within major strategies for improving the curriculum. When efforts at improving the curriculum are categorized into larger wholes, they form six
major strategies which are commonly used in American school systems today.
They are:

1. Improving the curriculum through master planning for the entire school
   system;
2. Improving the curriculum at its heart, *i.e.*, in the classroom and the individual school;
3. Improving the curriculum through in-service education of professional
   personnel;
4. Improving the curriculum through supervising the work of these personnel;
5. Improving the curriculum by re-organizing pupil experiences, and by reorganizing the school itself;
6. Improving the curriculum through the use of evaluation, research, and
   experimentation.

Each of these strategies is described in the present chapter.

Promising
Strategies
for Improving
the Curriculum

If one were to visit any American school system where a wide-awake program of curriculum improvement was under way, he would find perhaps one, two, or three of the strategies prominently in use. However, if he were to return to the same school system ten years thereafter, he might find somewhat different strategies being employed in differing degrees of emphasis. Time and circumstances alter cases.

In deciding which strategy or strategies they will use at a given time, school personnel often try to determine what is in greatest need of attention. For example, a school system which has recently employed large numbers of new teachers may become a center for the in-service education of these teachers. Meanwhile, another school system which has long been inclined toward planning by central office supervisors may develop freedom and initiative among the teachers in individual schools who wish to experiment with new educational practices. Of course, any two or more strategies may be used simultaneously in the same school system. Obviously, too, it is impossible to tell which of the six strategies is "best." Differing needs and situations make each of them valuable, but their probable relative usefulness needs careful assessing before any one of them is adopted.

IMPROVING THE CURRICULUM THROUGH
MASTER PLANNING

Master planning involves establishing purposes, policies, and criteria which are to guide curriculum improvement throughout an entire school system. This action is accomplished by individuals and groups based either temporarily or permanently in places of central authority. We have seen in earlier chapters that most of the work in curriculum improvement which was done during the 1920's and the 1930's, in the earliest days of formal curriculum planning, was done in central offices of school systems. Though the site of planning has moved increasingly to the individual school, the central office has retained its functions of initiating, leading, and guiding major actions for curriculum change. Several arguments have been advanced for giving the central office a maximum of authority. One argument is that a systemwide approach brings the schools close to the community as a whole, with the result that citizens appreciate where the entire teaching staff stands on important educational issues. Another argument is that "across-the-board activity" is administratively neater and easier to manage. A third is that communication is improved because there are fewer conflicting actions and procedures. Other arguments are these:

> Time is saved by avoiding detailed analysis of the needs and problems of individual schools.
> There is maximum assurance that a given project or product has received the blessing of the powerful central office.
> Coordination and comprehensiveness can be made keynotes of systemwide activity; hence, things can run smoothly and handsomely on a large scale.
> A major result of systemwide activity is continuity—the presence of a common thread in the curriculum.

Obviously, not all of these arguments are equally valid. However, for reasons of coordination, desirable uniformity, and economy of time, school systems will continue to perform master planning activities which will consist of conducting large staff meetings, issuing directives, preparing policy statements, organizing major projects for study and research, developing certain course guides and unit plans, announcing purposes and objectives, writing reports, collating lists of materials, and publishing booklets, pamphlets, and brochures on a variety of subjects.

Most of the activities of a master planning nature which have just been mentioned are completely familiar to anyone who has worked in school systems employing 100 or more teachers. Meetings of the whole school system staff are commonplace in smaller systems. Some systems conduct these meetings once a month, and though the meetings are of doubtful worth for making policy, they do tend to assure common understanding of systemwide procedures, and they bring personnel together who might otherwise seldom see each other.

Directives concerning matters about which there is no need for discussion may also be issued by central authority. Rules for the safety of pupils and teachers which are to be enforced and taught in classrooms would be one example of this. Other appropriate subjects would be board of education decisions and the conclusions of central curriculum committees.

Policy statements frequently result from lengthy deliberation, and are themselves often lengthy. Policy handbooks, which guide the operation of entire school systems, are now being prepared in many communities. Limited statements of policy are being issued concerning selection and use of teaching materials, instruction about controversial issues, the assigning of homework, and procedures for reporting to parents. For instance, Wilmington, Delaware, has prepared a statement to encourage the use of a wide variety of teaching materials and to urge impartial teaching about controversial issues. The curriculum steering committee in Minneapolis has produced a guidebook regarding common practices in school work and a four-page manual of policies and procedures for curriculum development. The music department of the Fairfield, Connecticut, schools has issued a procedural statement about the music program.

Additional written materials sometimes seem to come in floods from central offices. These materials include course guides, most of which require the finesse in production that elaborate documents need; announcements of purposes and objectives for all the schools; numerous lists and schedules; reports on many subjects; and sophisticated-looking booklets, pamphlets, and brochures. Much more important than the written materials themselves is the master planning which precedes their production. In addition to developing policies, master planners for school systems concern themselves with philosophies, purposes and objectives, and also with major projects in instruction and inquiry which affect all the schools.

The superintendent and his aides are much involved in master planning in Baltimore and in numerous other cities. Baltimore does a great deal to coordinate planning: *e.g.*, the *Guide to Elementary Education* published by the schools in that city reflects months of systemwide planning. Whenever a large project in curriculum development or research is approved by a board of education, it is likely to receive its impetus and direction from the central office of the school system. Boards of education, superintendents, and their assistants make contracts with universities, foundations, and individual consultants for curriculum services. Committees representing the school system at large still decide many details of the instructional program, and central office supervisors and other specialists guide program development in both general and specialized curriculum fields. In some school systems, public relations personnel work in central offices with teachers on ways of interpreting the schools to the public, and research divisions continue their activity in the central offices of at least the larger school systems.

Centralized planning works best when it accomplishes those things which do not rightfully belong to the individual school. Some actions should be undertaken by an individual, e.g., by a superintendent or an assistant superintendent in charge of instruction, or by a small group of people on behalf of all personnel in the system. These actions should be accomplished chiefly for three reasons: coordination, desirable uniformity, and economy of time and effort. The case for coordination needs no pleading. The expression "desirable uniformity" suggests that some uniformity in school systems is *not* desirable. Therefore those who would encourage uniformity should determine whether it is really needed. "Economy of time and effort" refers to the importance of having certain tasks performed by one agency, without unnecessary duplication by several other agencies. Duplication of effort is one of the great ills of organizations, and it needs to be rooted out of school systems which have existed for years without analysis of roles or even the most elementary time study.

With these cautions in mind, one must acknowledge that centralized activity will and should continue in school systems. The best leadership and facilities are likely to be found in central offices. Power in master planning can be had by several means, including 1) designating someone to have the responsibility and authority for systemwide activity, 2) organizing a central steering committee to guide this activity, 3) working closely with lay advisory committees or other groups of citizens, and 4) forming special-interest committees or task forces to assume the responsibility for particular systemwide assignments. There are, of course, certain dangers in master planning. One of these is failure to involve enough professional personnel and laymen in the decision-making process. Another is the well-known tendency of central offices to overemphasize paper work. A third is quickness in making systemwide, and unfortunate, comparisons of teachers and children. A fourth is the compulsion to issue military-like directives. These dangers are theoretically reduced by bringing the planners and the planned-for together in individual schools. Curriculum activity in classrooms and schools, which is actually subject to the same hazards but in lesser degree, is the subject of the next section of the chapter.

ACTIVITY 11-1—FINDING EVIDENCES OF MASTER PLANNING IN A SCHOOL SYSTEM

Identify a school system or a district of a large city system in which you will be permitted to inquire about the curriculum planning that is conducted centrally. Keep in mind the examples of master planning which have been given above, but do not limit your inquiry to these. Ask one or more responsible persons in the central offices what phases of the curriculum are determined centrally. Inquire about the ways in which decisions about the curriculum are communicated to the schools, and ask to see documents which are used in the communication process. If you compare your findings with those of another inquirer, you will both learn much about master planning.

IMPROVING THE CURRICULUM IN THE CLASSROOM AND THE INDIVIDUAL SCHOOL

When the teacher closes his classroom door, much of the *real* curriculum of the school goes into operation. Most of the best curriculum improvement that occurs anywhere is accomplished where the teacher and his pupils are. In the classroom of the individual school, teacher and pupils live together five or six hours each school day. Here the differences among children are revealed. Here the teacher, no matter how stringent the supervisory authority of the school, is free to try some of his own ideas and ways of working, and to put into practice what he has learned elsewhere. Here is the "cutting edge," the real frontier of education.

In the individual school, teachers of similar children, teachers with like professional problems, can meet most readily. In faculty meetings or in small, informal groups, they can discuss their problems, share information about possible methods of solving them, and design investigations in an attempt to find new solutions. Unless a domineering principal, an equally domineering central office, or the community itself proposes numerous matters for study which are foreign to the concerns of the faculty, the problems selected for consideration are likely to be the real and immediate ones of the faculty itself.

The real problems may be, for instance, what to do with certain troublesome discipline cases, how to talk with parents during parent-teacher conferences, and what supplementary books to order with the dollars allocated for this purpose. Some of the real problems of teachers, such as the fatigue of children who watch television too late at night, originate in the community and require that teachers cooperate with parents and other school patrons. Other problems, such as those connected with methods of teaching spelling to intermediate-grade children, require attention by teachers only.

One of the advantages of the individual school as a curriculum planning unit lies in the smallness of many faculty groups. Small faculties make for much face-to-face contact and ease in getting together. In large high schools, teachers often meet in departmental groups, with occasional meetings occurring interdepartmentally. In large elementary schools, teachers assemble according to grade level and according to proximity to other teachers' classrooms.

More than just the problems of the local school need to be discussed by faculties. The complexity of school-community relations and of entire school systems causes many problems of the community and of the whole system to concern the faculties of individual schools. Examples of these problems are collection of money for welfare drives and the selection of members of system-wide curriculum committees. The individual school cannot afford to remain aloof from educational and social influences elsewhere. Caswell has described the role of the individual school as follows:

> In brief, the "grass-roots" approach which views the individual school as the operational and planning unit does not mean that each school in a system should go its own way without regard for the others. It means, rather, that problems which are dealt with on a systemwide or partial-system basis should arise out of the work done by individual school staffs and feed back into use through these staffs. The channel is from the individual school to the system and back to the individual school rather than from the top down, as under the traditional systemwide approach.[1]

Curriculum improvement in classrooms and schools begins with teachers, who conduct two major kinds of planning, that which they do privately and that which they do with children. On another level, of course, teachers engage in cooperative planning with other professional personnel. But day-to-day planning by the practitioner begins either in the privacy of one's own place of study or in the process of interacting with children in the classroom.

---

[1] Hollis L. Caswell, *Curriculum Improvement in Public School Systems.* New York: Bureau of Publications, Teachers College, Columbia University, 1950, p. 78.

Teacher-pupil planning is discussed in many professional books for teachers. The present book, designed as it is primarily for present and potential leaders of teachers, will here treat very briefly planning done by individual teachers and by organized groups of teachers in individual schools. Throughout the years, much planning by teachers has centered upon development of the unit, that plan for organizing pupil experiences which contributes, during several days or weeks, to achievement of one or more definite objectives, and which is believed to have within it unity for both learners and teacher. Note the following review of the unit's characteristics, which bring it into contrast with the daily lesson and the subject-matter topic:

The unit is generally planned more carefully.

It usually lasts longer.

It has more definite and consistent direction because it contributes to the achievement of acknowledged purposes.

It consists of a better unified body of subject-matter. Its unity must be perceived by learners as well as by the teacher. Mature pupils can find unity in blocks of subject-matter which are not related obviously and concretely to their needs. Thus a high-school senior may detect unity in subject-matter organized by a textbook author who knows the whole sweep of his subject and writes about it from the standpoint of a specialist. Most pupils in elementary and secondary schools thrive best, however, on units which most closely represent their current concerns and needs.[2]

Classroom teachers should be helped to prepare units of three sorts: resource units, unit plans, and functional units. The first of these, *resource units*, are master units written as resources on which teachers may draw in subsequently tailoring units for use in their own classrooms. In workshop situations, teachers often help to write resource units which contain sections like these: the nature of the unit problem; purposes of the unit in developing understandings, skills, and attitudes; sequence of the subject-matter content; nature of pupil experiences within the unit; methods of teaching the unit; resources, written and other, for learning; and methods of evaluating the experience. Minneapolis has printed an interesting "resource guide" containing three resource units on living in Minneapolis. The Dade County, Florida, schools have prepared numerous resource units in the language arts, the social studies, and basic education.

Many teachers develop *unit plans*, which are written with particular groups of pupils in mind. Thus, one or more teachers may devise a unit plan

[2] William H. Burton, *The Guidance of Learning Activities*. New York: Appleton-Century-Crofts, Inc., 1952, pp. 393–403.

for teaching a portion of subject-matter. The plan may be based on a previously-prepared resource unit, or it may be created *de novo*. The authors concern themselves with purposes, content, pupil activities, teaching procedures, human and material resources, and evaluation methods. The Section on Secondary Education of the Pittsburgh Public Schools demonstrates to teachers the need to incorporate in unit plans sufficient opportunities for pupils to do the following:

> To analyze problems into areas;
> To discover sources of information;
> To use and organize tabular, graphic, and statistically arranged facts;
> To recognize differences between facts and opinions;
> To refrain from drawing conclusions based on inadequate data;
> To use resource persons and direct experiences from community life;
> To improve relationships with fellow-students through the committee approach;
> To test the accuracy of various democratic principles and values.

When teachers prepare unit plans, they do so with their pupils in mind but without direct and immediate contact with them. Thus many unit plans are made during vacation periods in preparation for coming days of teaching.

Teachers become really specific in their planning when they create *functional units* with their pupils. These are units that propose precise learning experiences which pupils help to plan. Miel describes the steps in planning a unit on transportation: discussing ways of approaching the unit and ways of securing information; deciding to write letters and do other searching for information; establishing reasons for studying transportation; deciding upon a method of study, which proved to be taking an imaginary trip; and engaging in the imaginary trip.[3] Despite the imperfections and general fumbling one can find in instances of teacher-pupil planning, the dividends which cooperative planning in classrooms pays in pupil interest and achievement are bringing about its acceptance as a valid instructional procedure.

In the individual school as a whole, four procedures have been found especially helpful in encouraging curriculum planning. The first of these is to designate a principal who is an able educational leader. Today many school systems expect central office coordinators, supervisors, and consultants to serve less and less as "bosses." The real authority for the instructional program of the school rests increasingly with the principal. Central office personnel who come into the school building are actually advisers to the princi-

---

[3] Alice Miel and Associates, *Cooperative Procedures in Learning.* New York: Bureau of Publications, Teachers College, Columbia University, 1952, pp. 84 and 85.

pal. In the language of the army and of industry, they are staff officers, while the principal is a line officer responsible only to the superintendent or to one or more assistant superintendents. If the principal is to be an adequate director of instructional programs, he must have full qualifications for educational leadership—superior preparation, high mental ability, patience, broad understanding, a sense of humor, and other characteristics required for his role. Often, curriculum improvement receives its first impetus in the principal's office. All too often, however, it dies there. The executive of the individual school has correctly been called a gatekeeper of desirable change. He can either open the gate wide or close it abruptly, as many an enterprising teacher has learned.

Another procedure for making the individual school a strong unit for curriculum planning is to conduct meetings according to the best principles of group process. The past ten or fifteen years have seen large gains in our knowledge of what makes meetings "click." In some communities, teachers and administrators have had an opportunity to experiment with techniques for solving the problems of managing meetings, e.g., how to begin a meeting efficiently, how to deal with the overtalkative participant, and how to use the contributions of the cynical member.[4] Faculty meetings and other professional meetings have long been unpopular with teachers, partly because of the poor meeting process which has prevailed. School administrators and prominent faculty members have held the floor excessively, and the meetings themselves have too often been used merely for making administrative announcements.

Under thoughtful leadership, meetings of several kinds may be used in the individual school for curriculum planning. Teachers may meet as a whole faculty, by grade levels, by departments, as building task forces, and as members of steering committees. When it seems appropriate and desirable, laymen may attend some of the meetings. Depending upon who attends, meetings may be called to consider policy for the whole school, details of subject-matter by grade level or age grouping, the program of a teacher's own department as it relates to the programs of other departments, the advisability of using certain business-sponsored teaching aids in the school, and numerous other matters. In large schools, the principal sometimes organizes a cabinet or steering committee which represents the faculty and acts for it with respect to issues that need not or cannot immediately claim the attention of the whole staff.

For all staff meetings in the individual school, there are certain common ground rules which teachers and principals should know and observe:

[4] Stephen M. Corey, Paul M. Halverson, and Elizabeth Lowe, *Teachers Prepare for Discussion Group Leadership.* New York: Bureau of Publications, Teachers College, Columbia University, 1953, *passim.*

1. Call meetings when teachers are alert.

2. Arrange for social contacts and refreshments before or after meetings.

3. Devote meetings on a continuing basis to one or more important topics, rather than staging "one-shot performances" in single meetings.

4. Encourage faculty participation in planning the meetings.

5. Seek out subject-matter which is of real concern to the persons who participate.

6. Keep the meetings "on the beam."

7. Use what man has learned about effective group procedures, *e.g.*, arrange for clarification of the problem or situation under discussion, encourage requests for information, urge a search for facts rather than mere opinion, plan frequent summaries of progress made during the meeting.

8. Evaluate meetings by means of discussion or prepared evaluation forms; then use the data in planning subsequent meetings.

A third way of stimulating curriculum planning in the individual school is to provide ample opportunity for teacher counseling. Good as meetings may be for helping people change their behavior, person-to-person contacts can often be even more effective.[5] These contacts must, of course, be of a wholesome and constructive sort. When the principal confers with a teacher in an effort to help her improve her teaching, he should try to forget that he is the wielder of authority in the school, and should behave instead as her helpful co-worker and gentle adviser. As the term is being used here, counseling differs greatly from telling or bossing. Helpful counseling tests the knowledge and skill of the educational leader. Though the leader is often a principal or another person with status, he may well be another teacher who has developed special skill and understanding which the counselee needs. In this way, the "big brother" or the "big sister" of the new and inexperienced teacher is an emergent leader who needs all the counseling know-how he or she can master. If the leader-counselor performs well, his influence will be felt not only by the counselee but also by other teachers who will almost inevitably hear of his success. Contacts on a one-to-one basis can build lasting understanding that is both personal and professional. Sometimes the leader himself needs counseling by other staff members; therefore he should be prepared both to request it and to receive it. Though helpful counseling can be had in the central offices of the school system and through outside organizations, agencies, and independent practitioners, the ideal locale for counseling is the individual

---

[5] For a description of methodology in individual counseling, see Dugald S. Arbuckle, *Teacher Counseling*. Reading, Mass.: Addison-Wesley Publishing Company, Inc., 1950.

school, where proximity produces contact and familiarity breeds confidence.

A fourth method for effecting curriculum improvement in the individual school involves introducing new teaching-learning materials and facilities and the changed methods which are necessarily associated with them. The technological revolution has brought with it promising instructional equipment, the full impact of which has not yet been felt: audio-visual devices like overhead projectors, kinescopes, tape recorders, and video tape; teaching machines of a variety of kinds, as well as programmed materials without benefit of machines; educational television; and numerous other resources. Some of the newer resources, *e.g.*, video tape and educational television, seem to be made for telling and showing, listening and seeing. Other resources, *e.g.*, teaching machines, encourage private skill-development and fact-acquisition. Teachers' functions and methodology must change as new materials and facilities are introduced more widely. Teachers who are "master tellers" will be given opportunities to practice their art with the help of overhead projectors, kinescopes, video tapes, and closed-circuit television. Other teachers, or some of the same teachers, will help pupils learn skills and acquire facts in sequence, perhaps in "skills laboratories" which house teaching machines and a wealth of materials. The functions of teachers which may remain least associated with new materials and equipment include guiding problem-solving through teacher-learner interaction and helping learners find meaning in the wealth of knowledge to which they are exposed. In any event, new resources, including paperback editions of books, are now finding their way into schools and classrooms at a rapid rate, and they will naturally be put to use chiefly within individual schools.

One may wonder whether the emphasis which has been placed on the importance of the individual school in curriculum planning implies that every school should develop its own exclusive and different curriculum. To expect the individual school to stand completely alone in curriculum planning would be foolhardy. There are at least two important reasons for this: 1) Similarities as well as differences exist among schools in the same system; these similarities should be capitalized upon through central or systemwide planning. 2) Improving the curriculum from the ground up in each building unit would prove wasteful of time and funds. Whatever can be done legitimately in a central place should be done there. The remainder will be sufficient to keep the staffs of individual schools more than amply occupied.

School people and parents often worry about differences among the curricula of schools within the same system. What happens, they wonder, when a fifth-grade child moves from School D to School A and finds that fifth-graders in his new school are learning something quite different in the social studies? Worries of this kind have doubtless been exaggerated. The pace and content of learning in Schools D and A may correctly vary, as they may indeed among several fifth-grade classrooms within a large individual building. Furthermore, a given experience in the social studies, or in any other subject, may, within limits, be as valuable as another experience. The most important question is whether the diverse experiences contribute directly to goals of education which have been set for the system and for the individual school. The question, then, is *what experiences best serve definite purposes.*

Much of the hope of improving the curriculum in classrooms and individual schools depends upon our ability to upgrade the quality of teachers. This fact focuses attention on a third strategy of improvement, in-service education, which is discussed on the following pages.

ACTIVITY 11-2—SOME PRACTICAL PROBLEMS IN PLANNING

In planning educational experiences, there are several alternatives to developing units of instruction. One alternative is to follow a topically- or chronologically-organized textbook. Another is to use a "grasshopper approach," hopping from topic to topic without any long-range plan. Can you think of other, more constructive alternatives? Are there situations in which unit planning should not be used? If so, describe such a situation.

Now think how you would proceed to help a teacher who exhibited the following symptoms of poor planning:

A tendency to skip from subject-matter item to subject-matter item without regard to sequence.

A failure to identify and follow cues from pupils which indicate that the pupils are confused by the subject-matter and are becoming disinterested in it.

ACTIVITY 11-3—PLANNING EFFECTIVE MEETINGS

Many a school faculty feels that the number of meetings called in its school impedes rather than facilitates curriculum improvement. Independently or in conjunction with others, prepare answers to the following questions:

1. Why should meetings in individual schools be held at all?
2. Who should plan the meetings?

3. **When should the meetings be held?**
4. **Where should they be held?**
5. **In general, what content should be emphasized in the meetings?**

IMPROVING THE CURRICULUM THROUGH IN-SERVICE EDUCATION

Organized in-service education is a conscious attempt to help school personnel improve their experiences, with the expectation that they in turn will help to improve children's experiences. To say it another way, organized in-service education rests on the assumption that children's lives will not be changed very much unless the professional and personal lives of their teachers are made ever richer with fruitful experience. The term *teacher* is meant to include any professional person—principal, supervisor, curriculum coordinator, guidance counselor, superintendent—who directly or remotely influences the lives of pupils educationally.

The basic argument for organized in-service education has been stated by the Austin, Texas, Board of Education:

> It is axiomatic in the professional, business and industrial fields that those persons who are involved continue to study and to grow. The doctor who does not continue to study soon becomes antiquated in his field. The man who was an expert mechanic on the Model T Ford can do little with a modern automobile unless he has continued to study the new developments. The bankers hold regular courses for in-service education so as to be able to meet the new demands and follow the new laws. Likewise with teachers.

> Whether a teacher is new to the school system or is a veteran educator, whether he has no experience or many years of experience, he needs the benefit of an effective in-service program. The school that does not have such a program soon lags behind. A teacher who lacks opportunities for some type of in-service education quite likely becomes antiquated. No school and no faculty is static. Staff members either are striving to improve the program of their school or an increasingly poorer job of teaching is being done and the youth that the school is set up to serve are thereby being penalized.[6]

The goal of all curriculum improvement activity is improved experiences for teachers, and therefore for pupils. When a practicing member of

[6] School Board of Austin, Texas, "Why In-Service Education?" *Educational Leadership*, Vol. 9, No. 1, October, 1951, pp. 9 and 10.

our profession works on a course guide which is to be issued from the central offices of his school system, or when he serves on a school faculty committee to improve utilization of audio-visual aids, he gains experience which will presumably make him a better teacher or administrator. He is receiving in-service education as he seeks to improve the curriculum. If one were to ask him his purpose, he would probably say that he had a special task to perform for his school system or individual school. He would tend to think of his own learning as being incidental to the task at hand. Thus, while he is learning under these circumstances, he is learning less consciously than he might.

As has been said, planned or organized in-service education makes manifest the goal of increased and improved learning on the job. School systems which have organized fairly comprehensive programs of in-service education include Arlington County, Virginia, and Racine, Wisconsin. Arlington has, in recent years, conducted five or more workshops during each school year, arranging staff meetings on released time and scheduling teacher intervisitations. Racine has developed a three-way approach involving courses, citywide workshops, and both workshops and study programs in individual schools.

MEDIA OF IN-SERVICE EDUCATION

The best in-service programs are developed to achieve balance among activities. Each school system and each school should consider for itself the quantity and quality of in-service activities it will support.

Among the media which are used commonly in in-service programs are these:

1. Meetings and institutes
2. Conferences and work conferences
3. Courses
4. Study groups
5. Intervisitations
6. Workshops
7. Clinics, consultant services, and other media

1. *Meetings and institutes*——These two media are time-honored and traditional. Throughout the years, the term "meeting" has come to mean a single session of several minutes or hours during which the talking is done chiefly by a few of the participants. Recently, meeting process has been studied from the standpoints of productivity, effective communication, and good human relationships.[7]

---

[7] See Matthew B. Miles, *Learning to Work in Groups*. New York: Bureau of Publications, Teachers College, Columbia University, 1959.

Teachers' institutes have generally consisted of series of meetings during which scheduled speakers have presented their points of view about the same or different subjects. Typically, institutes give teachers who attend them little opportunity to react to what has been said. Recently, however, the austerity of the old-fashioned institute has been mollified by introducing conference techniques which provide for increased interaction.

2. *Conferences and work conferences*——These two media of in-service education give teachers opportunities to confer, to compare notes, and to interact. Both conferences and work conferences often include speakers on their programs, and they permit small-group discussion of varied topics which may relate to a single theme. The theme could be, for instance, "How May We Evaluate Our Schools?" Sub-topics could then deal with matters like evaluation in specific subject-fields, evaluation of guidance services, and evaluation of parent-teacher relationships.

The most important difference between the conference and the work conference lies in their relative duration. Work conferences are the longer of the two, frequently lasting several days and involving a variety of work activities. Because they are longer, work conferences often have more complex programs of general meetings, special-interest sessions, and discussion groups. Both conferences and work conferences are widely used for in-service education by state, county, and local groups.

3. *Courses*——Perhaps the commonest of all in-service activities is the course. Teachers feel pressure from at least two sources to take courses: a) self-imposed pressure to improve in service, and b) pressure for certification, salary advancement, or promotion, externally imposed by boards of education and state certification agencies. Courses, unlike most other in-service media, are measurable in credits offered, time allotted, and marks received. Though teachers take most of their in-service courses on college and university campuses, the "campus" of the school system itself is becoming a site for course offerings. An authority on a given subject, perhaps a college professor, is invited to appear at intervals at a school site to conduct a course for which credit on the salary guide may be offered by the local board of education. Sometimes the board finances the whole venture; in other instances, it finances only the efforts of those teachers who do not desire or cannot afford to pay tuition and thus receive credit at the instructor's college or university. Very often, courses conducted on the home grounds of the local school system do more to meet the needs of enrollees than courses meeting on university campuses and enrolling students from numerous school systems. New York City and Toronto, Canada, have long been noted for the number of in-service courses they offer within their own school systems. When courses become

numerous, they need to be guarded against duplication and lowered quality.

4. *Study groups*——Formal or informal study groups are sometimes organized in school systems to improve the participants' understanding of selected problems or situations. Groups of several people, including teachers and laymen, meet at intervals to study, for example, new findings in child development. Some time ago, Minneapolis organized study groups to consider desirable pupil behavior patterns, children's mental health, the needs of cerebral palsied children, and effective reading readiness programs. Study groups in Elgin, Illinois, have included numbers of laymen.

Study groups are organized by instructional leaders in school systems, by curriculum committees, by local teachers' associations, and by outside professional organizations like state branches of the Association for Supervision and Curriculum Development. Hollis L. Caswell and others organized study groups throughout the State of Virginia many years ago. Virginia and a few other states retain their interest in study groups today.

5. *Intervisitation*——The loosely-planned visiting days which were formerly on the calendars of school systems have partially given place to more carefully planned intervisitations. "Directed visiting" focuses the visitors' attention on specific things to be seen. These include situations similar to the visitors' own, as well as situations different with respect to grade level, subject-matter, and nature of pupils being taught. Planned intervisitation is proving especially helpful to new, inexperienced teachers, though it can also benefit a school system's experienced personnel. Long Beach, California, has planned its intervisitations carefully, releasing teachers from their regular duties to see demonstrations they specifically need to see.

6. *Workshops*——The term workshop recalls the Negro spiritual containing the words, "Everybody who talks about heaven ain't goin' there." Not everyone who thinks he is conducting or attending a workshop is doing so, because all sorts of educational meetings have been called workshops. The workshop has been defined by Kelley as differing from meetings, gatherings, and classes by including planning sessions, work sessions, and sessions for summarizing and evaluating.[8] This definition implies that the workshop is a democratically-organized and rather lengthy medium of in-service education. It permits varied activities which may include listening to consultants, discussing common problems, reading professional literature, assembling materials, watching film presentations, playing roles, filling evaluation forms, and picnicking. Not the least important of the workshop's features are the

[8] Earl C. Kelley, *The Workshop Way of Learning.* New York: Harper & Row, Publishers, 1951, p. 137.

social proximity and the good feeling that can be developed among participants. Another important feature is the devotion to solving problems that seem most significant to the participants.

Workshop sessions may be held on consecutive days for several weeks, as during the summer months. Sometimes sessions are conducted at intervals ranging from a few days to a week. In any event, time is scheduled so that programs like the following can operate:

> *First hour:* General Session (singing, whole-group planning, listening to consultants, viewing films, etc.)
> *One-and-a-half hours:* Special-Interest Groups (discussion by each group of a subject of special interest to it)
> *One-half hour:* Informal Conferences (with staff and other workshoppers)
> *One hour or more:* Study and Planning Period (study, research, planning, trips and tours)
> *One hour or more:* Activities (social events and sports)

A program of this kind may constitute a full day's work, or it may be condensed to occupy a shorter period. Workshop participants should be given full responsibility for helping to plan their own programs.

Among the school systems which have done much to develop effective workshops are Corpus Christi, Texas, and Arlington County, Virginia. These systems have sponsored workshops during both summers and the regular school year. Baltimore has issued an interesting bulletin titled "Information for Workshop Leaders." When the roll of in-service media has been called, well-conducted workshops will rank among the highest in profit and enjoyment.

7. *Clinics, consultant services, and other media*——Arriving prominently on the horizon of in-service activities is the short-term educational clinic. Akin to the brief clinic sessions conducted by business management groups, the educational clinic serves persons who band together to discuss pressing school problems. A given problem is presented and explored quickly. Resources for its solution are then described: research data, helpful practices, places to visit, persons to consult. "Brainstorming" for fruitful ideas may become the chief activity during a clinic session. This activity consists of suggesting ideas quickly and without evaluation. Later, the ideas are explored for feasibility, often with the discovery that certain ideas which were initially considered ridiculous can be amended and used.

Consultants to school systems sometimes aid greatly in the process of in-service growth. Within a few months, the public schools of Montclair, New Jersey, employed consultants in the teaching of science, programs for gifted children, secondary-school articulation, personnel procedures, and administrators' use of professional time. The ways in which consultants should behave on the job has become a subject for special study.[9] Investigators of this subject have concluded that consultants should guard against excessive speech-making, the giving of ready-made answers, failure to show concern for the problems of the employing group, and the feeling that everything consultants say should be accepted. A well-oriented, skillful consultant can offer the lift that raises teachers' insights and interest level, and therefore helps to move projects along.

Other, miscellaneous in-service media tie closely to supervisory procedures which will be discussed in the next section of the chapter. They include:

Observation of demonstration teaching;
Directed reading and study;
Travel;
Summer session and extension teaching;
Professional writing (articles, textbooks, etc.) ;
Sociological studies of the community;
Attendance at conventions, conferences, and
    meetings outside the school system.

In a previous section of this chapter, the close relationship between in-service education and curriculum improvement has been mentioned. Organized programs of in-service education may be said to serve as one of the two or three major, direct stimuli to curriculum improvement. By organizing in-service programs, teachers and administrators consciously set aside time for activities that promote curriculum change. The blocks of time they reserve pay off in great or slight progress, depending largely on two factors: the concern staff members feel for the idea or subject being dealt with, and the cooperativeness and good feeling engendered by the program. The twin spark-plugs of concern and cooperativeness can fire the whole curriculum program in a school system. Cooperative study helps to reveal hidden problems, and organizers of the best in-service programs encourage staff members to work on those problems which, after due consideration, prove to be most significant to the members' own thinking. Then they watch ways of working together to see that these ways encourage good human relationships. In-service programs based on the viewpoint mentioned above supply an excellent take-off site for further curriculum study and planning.[10]

[9] See Marcella R. Lawler, *Curriculum Consultants at Work.* New York: Bureau of Publications, Teachers College, Columbia University. 1958.

[10] For a detailed report of cases in in-service education, see Harold Spears, *Curriculum Planning Through In-Service Programs.* Englewood Cliffs, N.J.: Prentice-Hall, Inc., 1957.

ACTIVITY 11-4—THEMES AND PROCEDURES FOR PLANNING IN-SERVICE PROJECTS

In-service projects organized in various school systems within recent years include the following:

In Baltimore, Maryland, the theme: "How can we develop leadership among our staff members?"

In Aberdeen, South Dakota, the theme: "Let's find out what our goals should be, and then make them visible through concrete action."

In Nyack, New York, the theme: "We need wide involvement of the people who should become fully aware of our more pressing problems."

In Van Dyke, Michigan, the theme: "We must plan a variety of helpful, coordinated activities designed to meet teachers' needs."

Who should determine the theme of a project or a program? What should be the deciding factors in determining the theme?

When the theme has been determined, how would you help decide which in-service media (institutes, workshops, etc.) to use?

IMPROVING THE CURRICULUM THROUGH SUPERVISION

At one time, school personnel seemed to think of supervision as being distinct and different from curriculum improvement. Supervisors were originally employed to inspect teaching and to build programs of instruction which teachers would closely follow. With the advent of curriculum specialists, supervisors were assigned to "supervise," and curriculum coordinators were designated to direct curriculum planning. Experience has shown, however, that the duties of supervisors and curriculum coordinators inevitably overlap, and that people who carry these titles should constitute a service team for better teaching and learning.

Traditionally, teachers have disliked what some of them call "snoopervision." Old-style supervision has emphasized inspection and rating of the teacher's work. According to the perceptions of the supervised, inadequate effort has been expended in helping teachers with the problems that concern them. The day the supervisor comes to visit the classroom is still regarded in some schools as a black day of fear and distrust. Adverse feelings about supervision have caused teachers to perpetrate all sorts of artful dodges, like changing suddenly to a specially-prepared lesson or "passing the red book" to announce to other teachers the supervisor's arrival in the building. Fortunately, the role of the supervisor is shifting, in many school systems, to that of a helping teacher or consultant. Teachers and supervisors should work cooperatively to improve the quality of pupils' experiences.

School systems that can afford them often develop unusually strong supervisory programs. These programs depend significantly for their success on quantity and quality of the supervisors and on functions they serve. Great Neck, New York, has employed large numbers of well-qualified consultants who help classroom teachers with the subjects they teach and with problems of child guidance and teaching materials. School districts with less financial ability usually have available a full-time or a part-time principal for each school building, together with one or more central office supervisors. One may check the supervisory staffing of the school district he knows best against the following list of supervisors and consultants who can be found in certain communities of 30,000 to 40,000 population:

Consultant(s) in art

Consultant(s) in music

Consultant(s) in health and physical education

Consultant(s) in reading

Consultant(s) in speech and hearing therapy

Consultant(s) in science, mathematics, the social studies, and/or the language arts

Consultant(s) in home economics

Consultant(s) in the industrial arts

Psychologist(s)

School social worker(s)

Supervisor(s) of elementary education

Supervisor(s) of secondary education

Coordinator of instructional materials (or audio-visual specialist)

Public information or public relations officer

Director of curriculum or instruction (assistant superintendent in charge of instruction)

This is not, of course, an exhaustive list of titles, but it suggests several of the more common interests of those school systems that wish to increase their services to pupils and teachers.

Within recent years, school systems have employed more "generalists" —persons who know the general professional problems which teachers encounter. Thus a generalist who does not recognize an acceptable Spanish accent may nevertheless supervise Spanish teachers. If a teacher's accent is considered questionable, a temporary consultant who knows Spanish thoroughly may be employed to determine, within a very few minutes or hours, whether the teacher's accent needs improving. Generalists help teachers with the most significant, pervasive aspects of their total task, such as classroom management and climate, methods, and materials. Public scares sometimes increase temporarily the number of subject-matter specialists on supervisory staffs. Throughout the years, however, certain school systems, such as those in Ann Arbor, Michigan, and Brookline, Massachusetts, have employed subject-matter specialists whose responsibility has extended from kindergarten through the twelfth grade.

Perhaps the most natural and productive situations calling for the teamwork of supervisors and teachers grow out of ongoing curriculum study. For example, development of a course guide in the social studies may require classroom experimentation with content, methods, and materials. Two or three central office supervisors, several principals, and a score of teachers may involve themselves in the project, working in classrooms, meetings, and conferences, and planning both the experimentation and the guide. In situations of this kind, the fear and the artificiality that have often characterized supervision tend to disappear.

SUPERVISORY TASKS

A good program of supervision serves many functions, all of which relate to the educational welfare of children. Teachers may expect to find their supervisors engaging in activities like these:

Holding meetings and group conferences;
Conferring with individual teachers;
Visiting classrooms;
Working on curriculum committees;
Organizing and conducting in-service programs;
Helping teachers select textbooks, audio-visual aids, and other materials;
Working with teachers on plans and units;
Helping select and use standardized tests;
Speaking to parents and other groups of laymen;
Maintaining relationships with teacher education institutions and the state department of education;
Orienting new teachers to their jobs;
Writing policy statements and other curriculum materials;
Arranging intervisitation;
Conducting workshops, institutes, and conferences;
Attending meetings of professional organizations;
Helping teachers develop tests and instructional materials;
Planning demonstration teaching;
Interviewing candidates for teaching positions.

Alert supervisors recognize that they must work differently in different situations: *e.g.*, with seasoned, experienced teachers; with first-year teachers; with parent groups; with fellow supervisors and administrators; with varied groups of teachers in a kaleidoscope of settings. Supervisors are involved regularly in curriculum improvement activities so diversified as to challenge their utmost adaptability and ingenuity. In general, however, supervisors are concerned with three giant tasks: 1) helping to determine purposes of education and helping to see that these purposes are adhered to in daily practice; 2) giving democratic instructional leadership; and 3) keeping channels of communication in school organizations open. If they are not careful, supervisors fall into the habit of manipulating teachers to achieve the ends that the supervisors themselves consider desirable. Patience, longsuffering, and willingness to see the other person's point of view are among the fundamental qualities that supervisors should possess. Four leadership roles of supervisors have been classified by the Webster Groves, Missouri, Public Schools as leadership to meet individual differences among pupils, leadership for faculty growth, leadership for coordination of programs and services, and leadership in integrating school and community life.

Of the numerous procedures which supervisors have developed, a few have become very popular. These include classroom observation, supervisor-teacher conferences, group work, and demonstration teaching. Each of them will be described briefly.

Classroom observation——Most time-honored among supervisory procedures is observation of classroom teaching. Competent supervisors ask themselves questions like the following as they begin to observe a teacher's classroom work:

> What is this teacher trying to do?
> How do the activities now in progress relate to our educational purposes and to the ways in which children develop and learn?
> What use is being made of materials and equipment?
> How do the organization and management of the classroom help with accomplishment of the work at hand?

As supervisors stay longer in classrooms, they ask themselves questions of a different order:

> What sort of motivation is occurring here?
> How appropriate and varied are the teaching procedures?
> How are pupils being given opportunities to develop responsibility, initiative, and other self-directive behaviors?
> How appropriate is the subject-matter to the apparent abilities and needs of these pupils?

How are work-study skills being developed?
How are individual differences being recognized and cared for?

By visiting a large number of classrooms, supervisors within a given school system are able to identify specific needs for curriculum improvement.

Supervisor-teacher conferences——A second, common procedure of supervision is the supervisor-teacher conference. In the best sense, conferences are mutual counseling sessions. When a conference is part of a team enterprise between supervisor and teacher, it goes somewhat like this:

We plan for our conference by considering its purpose and some of the items to be discussed.

We try to make the conference genuinely informal by holding it in an informal setting and by behaving informally.

We show respect for each other's point of view and give each other opportunities to save face.

We set goals for ourselves in identifying, analyzing, and prosecuting one or more problems.

We come to tentative conclusions and suggest next steps.

We recognize that our common efforts help *us* grow.

We try to be constructive and also specific.

We keep records of the conference.

Conferences that have the marks of constructiveness and informality often yield ideas and encouragement which can greatly facilitate curriculum improvement.

Group work——Supervisors have conducted meetings ever since supervisory positions were first established. In the past, meetings, group conferences, and institutes have often been dominated by supervisors who have had their own special ideas and programs to sell to teachers. However, if one operates on the assumption that *all* participants in a meeting have ideas of their own, then the meeting becomes a sharing session which is centered around problems that require solution. Many problems of curriculum and teaching are proposed and then moved toward solution in meetings in which the supervisor is willing to listen to others. Hence, the effectiveness of a supervisor can be gauged largely by the degree to which he helps groups of teachers release their potential for creativeness.

Demonstration teaching——The procedure called demonstration teaching consists of showing teachers, or having them shown, one or more facets of instruction which they presumably need to see. The demonstrator may be either the supervisor himself or an especially competent classroom teacher. Purposes of demonstration teaching include: orienting new or inexperienced teachers to their work; focusing the attention of experienced teachers on specific teaching behaviors; and permitting teachers to observe individual children or groups of children.

The following steps in planning and staging demonstrations have proved to be productive:

> The supervisor plans the demonstration with the observer so that the demonstration may meet the observer's needs.
>
> The supervisor arranges the demonstration carefully with the demonstrator, being sure that the demonstrator can provide the kind of experience the observer needs.
>
> The supervisor is certain to effect the release of the observer from regular classroom duties during the period of the observation.
>
> The supervisor keeps the number of observers in any one classroom at an absolute minimum.
>
> After the observation, the supervisor gives the demonstrator an opportunity to say what he attempted to do during the demonstration.
>
> The supervisor invites the observer to state what he saw during the observation.

Other supervisory procedures, some of which are similar or akin to procedures used in organized in-service education, are intervisitation, directed reading (in which professional reading is planned for and with teachers), preparation of written bulletins, exhibits and bulletin displays, courses, professional conventions, and selection and development of teaching materials.

Teachers seem to consider supervision effective when it supplies stimulation, encouragement, ideas, materials, and skill in trouble-shooting. As a strategy of curriculum improvement, supervision has the advantage of dealing with down-to-earth situations, building consciousness of highly specific needs for improvement, and keeping close to the feelings of teachers. Muriel Crosby has pointed to some of the potential contributions of supervisors to curriculum planning. She asks the following evaluative questions about programs of supervision:

> Has rapport between participants deepened?
>
> Have teachers developed a greater freedom in expressing opinions and sharing ideas?
>
> Does leadership move more freely and frequently from person to person?
>
> Is there greater teacher initiative?
>
> Are teachers better able to identify their own problems?
>
> Do they seek help more frequently?
>
> Are teachers better able to identify the needs of boys and girls and meet them in more satisfying ways?[11]

[11] Muriel Crosby, *Supervision as Cooperative Action*. New York: Appleton-Century-Crofts, Inc., 1957, p. 117.

ACTIVITY 11-5—SURVEYING TEACHERS' NEEDS
FOR SUPERVISORY HELP

J. Minor Gwynn, an authority in the field of supervision, surveyed teachers along the Atlantic coast to learn ways in which they believed their supervisors could help them best. The top five needs for help which these teachers identified were associated with: 1) planning, 2) finding teaching materials, 3) evaluating pupil progress, 4) establishing discipline or control, and 5) solving professional, community, and social problems.

Conduct a similar survey of your own, even though your sample of teachers will necessarily be smaller. Combine your findings with those of your fellow-students.

How do your combined findings compare with those of Dr. Gwynn? What implications do your findings have for the organization and nature of supervisory programs?

IMPROVING THE CURRICULUM BY REORGANIZING PUPIL EXPERIENCES AND BY REORGANIZING THE SCHOOL

An important action for curriculum change is the action involved in moving items of subject-content and major blocks of experience from one part of the school program to another, adding new subjects and new subject-matter, and, on rare occasions, dropping subjects. Here are some well-known instances of action to reorganize pupil experiences:

> The trivium, consisting of three basic subjects, gave place to the quadrivium, with its four basic subjects.
> The kindergarten has now assumed certain of the earlier functions of the first grade.
> A state legislature has mandated two years of American history in high school to replace the former one-year requirement.
> Driver education has come into vogue in high-school programs.
> A reasonably large number of elementary schools now teach modern foreign languages.

Major curriculum reorganization of the kinds just mentioned becomes obvious to the public.

> Curriculum reorganization proceeds on the assumption that rearranging

and altering pupils' experiences can improve the quality of learning. Placing subject-matter content in different sequence, substituting new experiences for old (or old for new), and combining subjects to achieve greater psychological unity can, we know, sometimes facilitate learning.[12] Much more evidence is needed, however, concerning many changes in curriculum organization which have been made in the name of improvement.

As we have seen, the organization of the curriculum has both vertical and horizontal dimensions. Vertically, the child progresses from level to level on the ladder of learning experiences. Thus he moves from third to fourth to fifth grade arithmetic in vertical sequence and with the assurance that a thread of continuity runs through his three years of arithmetic experience. Viewed horizontally, the curriculum has breadth or scope. That is, ideally it provides sufficiently varied experiences to comprehend the child's life needs, now and, to a degree, in the future. Because all of one's life needs cannot be prepared for in a single year of schooling, specific needs are presumably attended to year by year according to the child's current intellectual, physical, and social development. The horizontal dimension assumes an integration of educational experiences. Integration consists of relating experiences to each other in a sensible way, so that the curriculum does not consist merely of a mosaic of little pieces. Thus, elements of English and history may be integrated in a child's program. While the child must achieve his own integration of subject-matter, it has been believed that he can be aided in the process by placing similar and related areas of subject-matter together, as in the social studies or in the language arts.[13]

As has been indicated in Chapter 5, questions of scope, sequence, continuity, and balance, and other matters of concern to the "curriculum engineer" remain unsettled. In order to provide better-organized experiences for pupils, however, several major thrusts into curriculum reorganization have been made. In most of these, the center of attention has been upon the experiences of pupils. Recently, attention has shifted to reorganizing the school so that, somehow, pupils' experiences will be improved. To improve learners' experiences directly, effort has been expended, and continues to be expended, in adding and subtracting courses, combining school subjects into broad fields of knowledge, organizing core-type programs, and applying an experienced point of view. Recent experiments in reorganizing the school as an in-

---

[12] Ralph W. Tyler, *Basic Principles of Curriculum and Instruction.* Chicago: University of Chicago Press, 1950, pp. 41–53.

[13] National Society for the Study of Education, *The Integration of Educational Experiences,* 57th Yearbook of the Society, Part III. Bloomington, Ill.: National Society for the Study of Education, 1958, Chapter 6.

stitution have included shifts toward departmentalization of elementary schools, regrouping of pupils for instruction, formation of teacher teams, the use of teacher aides, and introduction of instructional innovations. These two separate approaches to improvement, with their sub-parts, will be treated briefly.

REORGANIZING LEARNING EXPERIENCES DIRECTLY

This approach may be implemented by adding and subtracting courses or portions of courses. In many school systems, the additive process has resulted in a crazy quilt patchwork of offerings. Teachers find it easy to organize each new course logically, without much reference to the needs of learners or the structure of the subject-matter. Later, they let relevance of course-content to real-life situations diminish further as the course becomes crystallized and institutionalized. Pessimistic as these comments may sound, much benefit to the curriculum has, of course, come from adding subjects and courses. Subtraction, badly as it is often needed, has occurred with much greater infrequency and trepidation. Surely the additive method of curriculum development needs to be used much more judiciously than it has been in the past.

Another method of reorganizing learning experiences directly is combining school subjects into broad fields of knowledge. Studies of the content of certain subjects has shown their interrelationships with similar subjects. Thus, spelling relates closely to written composition and reading; history ties logically to geography, economics, and sociology. Though university professors are able to continue teaching their compartmentalized specialties to advanced students, elementary- and secondary-school teachers are faced with pupils' practical questions about our world which demand answers that often cut across subject-matter lines. Today the broad field of the English language arts includes writing, speaking, reading, spelling, and listening. Similarly, broad fields have been developed under the titles "social studies" and "general science."

The modern elementary school has discarded ten- and fifteen-minute periods for the teaching of 12 or 15 separate subjects each school day. Instead, the school tends toward the scheduling of longer periods in the language arts, the social studies, the general arts (music, drawing, handicraft), arithmetic and science, and health education. Similarly, but less markedly, the program of studies of the up-to-date secondary school contains broad-field offerings like general mathematics, dramatic arts, family living, general language, and problems of democracy. Much of the movement toward the broad-fields approach to curriculum organization seems incidental or accidental rather than well planned. As a consequence, some broad-field offerings have proved to be as far removed from reality for pupils as the original, fragmented subjects. Nevertheless, when they are carefully designed, offerings in broad fields of knowledge can take the deadliness from logically-organized subject-matter by substituting an interesting, meaningful organization of material.

A third way of reorganizing learning experiences directly is developing *core-type or general education programs*. During recent years, secondary schools have experimented with core, general education, common learnings, and block-of-time programs. The experimentation has been so widespread and varied that the meanings of these terms have become greatly confused. Perhaps no one can define "core" to the complete satisfaction of all users of the term. However, in general, the core has these characteristics:

It cuts across subjects or subject-fields, interrelating two or more subjects.
It is scheduled for at least a "double period" during the school day.
It emphasizes the guidance and development of pupils by having them with one teacher for a rather lengthy period of time during the school day.

The best core programs are, as a rule, centered in the interests, needs, and concerns of pupils. They emphasize cooperative planning by pupils and teachers, and they use wide varieties of teaching materials.

One suspects that terms like "common learnings," "general education," and "block-of-time" have evolved partly from human inventiveness and partly from guilt feelings about calling a given curriculum organization a core program. Many so-called core programs have perpetuated the teaching of isolated, logically-organized subjects but have made them the responsibility of one teacher or a team of teachers working in a longer block of time. Core-type programs, whatever their name, often combine the language arts and the social studies for two or more periods a day under the direction of a "core teacher" whose chief qualification is interest in children and in a changed organization of the curriculum. As examples of core-type programs, Glencoe, Illinois, has had its two-period block of time combining English and the social studies; Arlington County, Virginia, has had a junior-high-school general education program interrelating literature, grammar, composition, spelling, geography, civics, and history; and Dade County, Florida, has been teaching "basic education," the units of which include "Better Foods at Lower Cost," "Man's Basic Needs," "Our American Heritage," and "How Can I Improve My Personality?"

Advocates of core-type programs disagree among themselves regarding the best organizing center for the core. Some of them maintain that man's life activities should constitute the central learnings. These life activities consist, for example, of earning a living, using our technological resources, maintaining our health, and forming desirable group memberships. A core program based on life activities could be centered about "persistent life situations" as identified by Stratemeyer and others.[14] Other advocates of core-type programs consider the generalized needs, concerns, and interests of youth to be an appropriate organizing center. They rely heavily on the research of Havighurst, Remmers, Gesell, and others for data about these generalized needs, concerns, and interests.[15] Still other enthusiasts for the core believe that only the needs, concerns, and interests of the pupils with whom the teacher is currently working should constitute the organizing center for their learning experiences. According to this point of view, the content of a core cannot be predicted in advance. Rather, it emerges through teacher-pupil planning, out of the life experiences of particular groups of pupils.

Core-type programs have attracted much curiosity among teachers and administrators. For a time, the largest discussion groups at national educational conventions were those which dealt with the core. However, curiosity has not necessarily led to action. Core-type programs have been organized in numbers of junior high schools but in relatively few senior high schools.[16] A school which desires to install a core-type program is often beset with the problems of poorly-oriented teachers, inadequate or unsuitable teaching materials, and misinterpretations by parents and other citizens. Secondary-school pupils appear to need the core-type experience which the more fortunate elementary-school children have had under the direction of guidance-minded teachers with whom they spend time each day working on challenging problems that cut across subject-lines. However, it is unwise to create the mere form of the core without implanting its spirit and true substance. Much of the spirit and substance are associated with the interests of individual pupils, the use of problem-solving procedures, and conversion of classroom, school, and community into learning laboratories.

A fourth way of reorganizing learning experiences has been tried by several curriculum planners. Using what may be termed a *life functions ap-*

---

[14] Florence B. Stratemeyer and Associates, *Developing a Curriculum for Modern Living*, Second Edition. New York: Bureau of Publications, Teachers College, Columbia University, 1957.

[15] See Robert Havighurst's writings regarding developmental tasks; the results of H. H. Remmers' study of 15,000 adolescents; and Arnold Gesell's findings about the characteristic behaviors of adolescents and younger children.

[16] Grace S. Wright has prepared a number of United States Office of Education releases concerning the progress of core programs in American schools.

proach, these planners have tried to determine what activities pervade most learners' lives from early childhood through adulthood. The activities fall into categories such as physical and mental health, living constructively with other persons, and enjoying beneficial leisure-time activities. Stratemeyer and her associates have made a categorization of activities under the general designation "persistent life situations." The Stratemeyer categorization is a careful one, combining elements of the social scene with understandings of human growth and development.[17] However, the life functions approach has been criticized for failing to permit adequate recognition of the emerging needs of learners, and for failing to provide a sufficient bridge to the classroom experiences which must implement the design. It has the advantage of taking into account social and cultural realities, meanwhile combining items and blocks of subject-matter according to prescribed purposes, and recognizing many of the general interests and needs of learners.

Finally, in seeking to reorganize learning experiences directly, curriculum workers have, in a few instances, applied the so-called *experience point of view.* Educational theorists have sometimes held that pupils' programs of learning should be organized as exclusively as possible around the current experiences of the pupils themselves. The experience curriculum, which is most extreme in point of view, proceeds from the following bases: tangible and concrete goals which pupils clearly accept; current problems of pupils which the pupils themselves have full opportunity to state and to help solve; and sequence and scope of learning which is determined by pupils' maturational levels, growth processes, and personality integration. In communities which have been deprived of cultural and technological advantages, such as Holtville, Alabama, and the Pine Mountain Settlement in Harlan County, Kentucky, pupils have been given opportunities to help adults solve unusually significant personal and community problems. In helping to solve these problems, the pupils have learned much traditional subject-matter in nontraditional ways. Taken to the ultimate, the experience point of view would provide for the individual pupil total satisfaction of his educational needs and, in addition, opportunities for exceptional personality integration. School systems do not pretend to attain these goals for the thousands of different pupils whom they serve. Problems of financing, scheduling, and staffing present only a few of the many barriers. Nevertheless, the experience point of view has influenced practice to a limited extent as schools have sought to deal more effectively with individuals. Examples of this influence may be seen in broadened guidance programs and school activities programs, as well as in

17 Statemeyer and Associates, *op. cit.*

work experience which adolescents enjoy under joint auspices of schools and employers.

Obviously, the ideal answers to problems of curriculum organization have not been found. Several alternatives to the subject curriculum have been proposed, but none of them fully satisfies the need of schools to make appropriate contact between learners and subject-matter. No doubt a major reason for failures to date is that there exists no adequate theory on which to base decisions about curriculum design.

REORGANIZING THE SCHOOL AS A PRIMARY OBJECTIVE

It is possible to affect pupils' experiences by giving major attention to the organization of the school in which they learn. The focus of discussion in the preceding section was on the nature of pupils' experiences. In this section, the focus is on altering the school as an institution, with the hope and expectation that pupils' experiences will consequently be improved. What will happen, ask certain educational planners, if pupils' and teachers' time is used differently, if teachers have altered responsibilities and novel kinds of help, and if scientific technology is put to work in the schools? Reorganization of the school requires changing such factors as the duration of time teachers spend with given groups of pupils, what the sizes of instructional groups are to be, whether or not teachers are to work alone or in teams, how teachers can cooperate and thus interrelate their teaching activities, whether teachers should be aided by paraprofessionals or neophytes, and whether pupils are to be closely graded or permitted to proceed at their own pace in a nongraded school. Some of the media which have been employed recently to create varied effects through reorganization are teacher aides, team teaching, large- and small-group instruction, the nongraded elementary school, and the departmentalized elementary school.

Either paraprofessionals or inexperienced laymen, or both, have served as aides to teachers in, for instance, Bay City, Michigan, the Catskill Area of New York State, and the New York City Public Schools. These personnel are assuming functions which range from reading pupils' compositions and assisting with classroom procedures to monitoring hallways and patrolling lavatories. Team teaching, meanwhile, has assumed several variations which have as their common element cooperation between or among teachers who constitute either a permanent, year-long team or a temporary one. Members of teams plan cooperatively, appear together before large pupil groups, and subdivide large groups for more intimate, independent instruction.

Very much involved with the concept of team teaching is, therefore, the practice of varying group size according to major purposes for teaching: large groups for information-giving and small groups for problem-solving, general discussion, and teacher-pupil interaction. Lloyd Trump has exploited this plan for providing variety in group sizes, adding a third category of pupil activity which consists of individual study and inquiry. Thus the *Trump Plan* calls for use of large groups, small groups, and individual initiative.[18]

Most of the plans for reorganizing schools which have been described so far have had greatest effect on the secondary schools. Elementary schools have had their own brand of team teaching and teacher assistance for a long time, in the form of subject supervisors and helping teachers who have functioned with "regular" teachers in self-contained classrooms. At this level of schooling, the concept of the nongraded school and revived proposals for departmentalization have caused most discussion. Suggestions have been made for eliminating the assignment of pupils to grades, allotting instead a block of several years' time for pupils to complete the work they are able to accomplish within an administrative unit of the school system. A retreat from the self-contained classroom, in which one teacher has almost complete responsibility for her pupils throughout the school day, has been proposed under several plans for departmentalizing the elementary school.

One of the most controversial of the plans has been a system of "dual progress" developed by George D. Stoddard at New York University. Stoddard has expressed the view that the core of an elementary-school child's program should be a guidance-language arts-social studies complex which can be managed by a homeroom or core teacher, and that the remaining subjects ought to be distributed among specialist teachers whose expectations of pupil achievement accord with the pupils' presumed abilities. Students of elementary education have observed that both the current proposals for creating nongraded schools and those for achieving departmentalization have had long histories. The novelty in current proposals often consists of certain additions to and alterations of older concepts.

Plans for reorganizing schools have been accepted more readily than many persons originally predicted they would be. During the school year 1960–1961, 15 per cent of elementary schools and 12 per cent of secondary schools were using some form of team teaching, and only 55 per cent of elementary schools had retained the policy under which they formerly operated self-contained classrooms. The Project on the Instructional Program of the Public Schools, which is sponsored by the National Education Association

---

[18] See J. Lloyd Trump and Dorsey Baynham, *Guide to Better Schools, Focus on Change.* Skokie, Ill.: Rand McNally & Co., 1961.

and which is responsible for the figures in the preceding sentence, predicted in 1962 that several present trends toward reorganization of schools would continue for at least another five years.[19]

Prospects for improving pupils' experiences within reorganized schools seem to depend on a significant condition: if teachers are given more time away from their routine duties, or away from duties in which they lack competence, they should be expected to spend this time productively in performing professional tasks. These tasks might include becoming better acquainted with individual learners, working closely with alienated or disadvantaged learners, and helping learners improve the quality of their thinking and the clarity of their values. A great danger in focusing on reorganization of schools is that it may become equated with curriculum improvement. The two may or may not be the same.

ACTIVITY 11-6—AN INVESTIGATION OF LOCAL TRENDS AND TENDENCIES IN REORGANIZATION

Note the numerous ways of reorganizing pupils' experiences and of reorganizing schools which have been mentioned above. Learn what is being done, under the heading of reorganization, in a school or school system you know well. What advantages and what deficiencies do you see in the plans for reorganization which are now in operation and which are projected? Compare your findings with those of other investigators.

SITUATION 11-1—IMPROVING CURRICULUM DESIGN, OR CHANGING THE ORGANIZATION OF THE SCHOOL?

The superintendent and the principals of the Bellevue Public Schools had spent nearly a year in studying plans for altering the allocation and use of pupils' and teachers' time. In the process, they had considered core-type programs, plans for team teaching, the employment of teacher aides, and part-time use of programmed learning. It was time now to decide what should be done both to improve the curriculum and to impress the community. Sometimes

<hr>

[19] National Education Association, *The Principals Look at the Schools.* Washington, D.C.: The Association, 1962, Chapter 2.

the latter objective seemed to take precedence over the former. At a crucial meeting on April 23, Principal Elbert James said: "We can talk about improving the organization of the curriculum, or about improving the organization of the school, but the two actions are not necessarily the same. Manipulating external things is often popular and sometimes easy; improving the experiences of children may be difficult and even unpopular. I hope we're concerned about experiences, and that we'll ignore gadgetry and moving people around."

To what extent do you agree with Principal James's point of view? Suppose you made organizational changes in the school itself. How could you tell whether these changes had improved the quality of children's learning experiences? Be specific as to the change or changes you have in mind, and as to methods of determining their effect.

IMPROVING THE CURRICULUM THROUGH EVALUATION, RESEARCH, AND EXPERIMENTATION

Curriculum improvement may be undertaken by raising the question, "How good are certain aspects of the schooling we provide?" When an answer has been found by means of evaluation, research, or experimentation, constructive action may then be taken.

Evaluation is a broad and continuous effort to inquire into the effects of utilizing educational content and process according to clearly-defined goals. A teacher may evaluate her pupils' progress in reading, or a team of evaluators may assess the quality of several areas in the life and service of a school.

Before, during, or after evaluation, one may conduct systematic inquiry for the purpose of solving one or more instructional problems. This careful inquiry is called research. Briefly stated, it consists of conjecturing intelligently about possible steps in solving the problem, taking one or more actions in line with the conjecture, and then observing whether the actions have brought the results which were anticipated or predicted in the conjecture.

A third means of getting evidence, experimentation, is said to move education out on the frontier. Experimentation is a means of trying new content and procedures, and of testing ideas in action. It does not, like research, usually provide definitive data on which one can rely, but it does offer many cues to improved practice.

EVALUATION, RESEARCH, AND EXPERIMENTATION IN
THE CLASSROOM

The classroom may become the site of important data-gathering which leads to curriculum improvement. Within the classroom, curriculum leaders can help teachers interpret data derived from administering standardized evaluation instruments. These instruments fall generally within the following categories:

Tests of mental ability (intelligence)	Interview schedules
Achievement tests	Observation schedules
Anecdotal records	Personality inventories
Appreciation tests	Projective techniques
Aptitude tests	Rating scales
Attitude inventories	Sociometric devices
Checklists for purposes of observation	Vocational interest inventories
Diagnostic tests	

Teachers who are unfamiliar with standardized instruments in any of the categories above should consult a good general reference concerning evaluation.[20]

Teachers evaluate informally every day on the basis of their own tests or their own subjective judgment. In its informal sense, evaluation is simply a part of living. Research, on the other hand, comes less naturally. So little research has been conducted in American classrooms that data about even the most important facets of education—the learning process, the learners, and methods of teaching—are fragmentary. Occasionally, teachers are involved cooperatively in broad-scale research in the teaching of reading, spelling, and other school subjects. In the past, this research has been sponsored by university groups and by individual professors, or else by research bureaus in school systems. Actually, the quantity of well-directed, carefully-sponsored research involving classroom teachers has been small.[21]

Though few teachers have had opportunities to engage in formal research, they do experiment informally. At a low level of experimentation, they often move pupils from seat to seat to quell disruptive behavior. The teacher who wishes to be more certain of what is happening when he creates change uses procedures of operational research, or "action research," as it is some-

---

[20] For example, the latest available edition of H. H. Remmers and N. L. Gage, *Educational Measurement and Evaluation.* New York: Harper & Row, Publishers.

[21] See John B. Barnes, *Educational Research for Classroom Teachers.* New York: G. P. Putnam's Sons, 1960.

times called. Action research has been defined by Corey and others as research conducted "in the heat of combat." It has been called by others controlled experimentation by means of which practitioners study their problems
to guide and correct their decisions and actions. The elements of the over-all
action-research design are:

> Identification of a problem area about which an individual or a group feels
> enough concern to take action.
> Selection of a specific problem and formulation of an "educated guess"
> (hypothesis or prediction) that states a goal and a way of reaching it.
> Careful taking of action, recording of action, and collection of evidence to
> determine the degree to which the goal has been reached.
> Drawing conclusions or making generalizations from the evidence as to the
> worth of the actions in reaching the desired goal.
> Continuous retesting of the generalizations in practical school situations.[22]

Consider an example of the use of this process:

A teacher became disturbed about the disinterest and poor performance
of her eighth-grade pupils in written composition. She made the hypothesis
that if writing were more closely related to the real life experiences of children, both the children's interest in writing and the quality of their writing
would improve. She learned from her pupils by interview, by a specially-
prepared inventory form, and by observation what they thought of their
present composition projects. She also analyzed, from the viewpoints of
fluency of expression and technical quality, two or three samples of her
pupils' written work. She then arranged a series of excursions to an airport,
to a construction project, and to the United Nations center in New York. Subsequently, she encouraged the children to write about one or more of these
excursions, inquired by the methods indicated above about their interest in
describing the excursions, and analyzed the new compositions for fluency and
technique. The evidence showed some improvement in both interest and performance, with interest showing more improvement than performance. The
teacher generalized that a writing project originating in real life experience
resulted, at least for her group of pupils, in improved interest and performance
in writing. She realized that this was a tentative conclusion that merited additional testing in her own and other classroom situations.

The procedures in research or experimentation of this kind have been
attacked as lacking the tightness and neatness of more careful research. However, they may be defended as providing the classroom teacher with some evi-

[22] See Stephen M. Corey, *Action Research to Improve School Practices.* New
York: Bureau of Publications, Teachers College, Columbia University, 1953, pp. 40 and 41.

dence on which to base his decisions. Perhaps the greatest handicap to performing action research is lack of understanding and skill which is required by researchers, who need also an experimental outlook, understanding of the research process, and skill in formulating testable hypotheses. In his immediate environment, the researcher should have a supportive administrative staff, favorable community climate, adequate resources, and open lines of communication. The classroom researcher should become familiar with at least the better-known references concerning research; the *Encyclopedia of Educational Research*; the *Review of Educational Research*, which is published periodically by the American Educational Research Association; the *Journal of Educational Research*, another periodical; *Education Index*, which does for education what the *Reader's Guide to Periodical Literature* does for general literature; the *Bibliography of Research Studies in Education*; and compilations of research studies by Phi Delta Kappa, a men's fraternity in education.

The problems which research and experimentation help to solve usually come to the teacher's attention from one or more of the following sources: the teacher's own feeling of need, criticisms by laymen of the program of the school, and evidence of shortcomings revealed by evaluation. The teacher who feels dissatisfaction with conditions as they are is ready, psychologically at least, to undertake reasoned inquiry.[23]

EVALUATION, RESEARCH, AND EXPERIMENTATION IN WHOLE SCHOOLS AND SCHOOL SYSTEMS

Entire schools and school systems may be involved in evaluation, research, and experimentation in the form of surveys, opinion polls, follow-up studies of graduates and early school-leavers, use of standard evaluation instruments, and large, cooperative research projects. These procedures are discussed here as a prelude to commentary in the next chapter about the evaluation of programs of curriculum improvement, which must be studied differently from the ways in which the curriculum itself is evaluated.

Surveys——Comprehensive studies of schools and school systems, resulting in recommendations for their improvement, are called surveys. Teams of university staff members and the personnel of survey firms have customarily conducted surveys "from the outside looking in." After a series of visits, conferences, and interviews, the surveyors have usually prepared printed or mimeographed reports to communicate their findings and recommendations.

[23] Concerning procedures in experimentation, see A. W. Foshay and J. A. Hall, "Experimentation Moves Into the Classroom," *Teachers College Record*, Vol. 51, March, 1950, pp. 353–359.

Within recent years, external surveys have been partially replaced by self-surveys and cooperative surveys.

In self-surveys, staff members of school systems organize to study their own curriculums and facilities. Often, they use as criteria the objectives of teaching and learning which they have previously developed, or which they have borrowed from educational literature or other school systems.

Cooperative surveys represent a compromise between external surveys and self-surveys. They call for the joint efforts of school system personnel and specially-employed external surveyors. Cooperative surveys are said to avoid some of the disadvantages of both external surveys and self-surveys. For instance, external surveyors sometimes know so little about the institution being surveyed that their reports contain inaccuracies. On the other hand, self-surveys show incompleteness and improper balance because local personnel frequently lack the necessary experience and vision for the survey task. Cooperative surveys tend to bring together the understandings and skills which are required.

Opinion polls——A second procedure for studying curricula of schools and school systems is relatively quick and informal. It consists of asking people within and outside the schools what they think of various aspects of schooling. Opinion polls have been used comprehensively by Harold C. Hand and associates, of the University of Illinois, in cooperation with the Illinois State Department of Public Instruction.[24] The purpose of opinion polls is usually to discover agreement regarding strengths and weaknesses of school curricula. Polls have certain public relations values, and they may set the stage for curriculum improvement. Teachers and administrators often use opinion polls to identify points along the educational front at which gains can be made with maximum public support.

Follow-up studies——Both graduates and early school-leavers are the subjects of follow-up studies of educational, occupational, and personal accomplishments. These studies help to answer questions like the following:

> What kinds of experiences do graduates and early school-leavers believe the schools should offer their pupils?
> To what extent have the schools in question offered these experiences?
> How well has subject-matter content within the range of these experiences been taught?
> How successful have graduates and early school-leavers been in applying to life situations what the schools have taught them?
> What modifications in the school program should be made for similar groups and individuals in the future?

[24] See Harold C. Hand, *What People Think About Their Schools*. New York: Harcourt, Brace & World, Inc., 1948.

One of the classic studies of early school-leaving was made by Dillon, who found "symptoms of vulnerability" to school-leaving which suggest a creaking curriculum and poor interpersonal relationships between teachers and pupils:

> A general regression in scholarship as one moves up the educational ladder.
> A tendency to fail grades in the elementary school.
> Similarly, frequent grade- and subject-failures in the secondary school.
> Greater infrequency of attendance as one advances from elementary to secondary school.
> Frequent transfers from school to school.
> A feeling of insecurity or lack of belonging in the school.
> An obvious lack of interest in school work.[25]

High-school guidance personnel sometimes make statistical follow-up studies of college students and business employees who are graduates of their schools. These studies are often so superficial that one wishes more studies could be made in depth. Deeper studies could begin by assembling individual alumni and small groups of alumni for interviews, conferences, and meetings to reveal genuine feelings and to develop creative ideas about appropriate schooling for children and youth of varied backgrounds.

Use of standard evaluation instruments——Evaluation of several areas of the curriculum may be accomplished by using standard evaluation instruments. Perhaps the most widely used of these is a document called the *Evaluative Criteria*, which was prepared by the Cooperative Study of Secondary School Standards, assisted by the American Council on Education, the National Association of Secondary School Principals, the National Education Association, and the United States Office of Education. It is applied by a half-dozen regional accrediting associations, such as the Western Association of Colleges and Secondary Schools and the comparable New England Association. The evaluators who use it review each school's curriculum organization or design, its pupil activities, its plant, its administration, its guidance and library services, and its faculty personnel. Standard questions, arranged within categories, are asked about every school in which the *Criteria* is made the evaluation document.

The West Virginia Association of Secondary School Principals has prepared a set of curriculum evaluation procedures for West Virginia's schools. These procedures, which have been adopted by the State Department of Education, are arranged in three categories: "Facts About Our School and Community," "What Are the Present Educational Offerings in Our Community?"

---

[25] Harold J. Dillon, *Early School Leavers—A Major Educational Problem.* New York: National Child Labor Committee, 1949, p. 82.

and "This We Propose."[26] Other state departments of education and a few additional organizations have originated or adopted published evaluation instruments:

Elementary Classroom Teachers' Association and Elementary School Principals' Association, "Self-Evaluation in the Elementary School," Elementary School Bulletin No. 11 (Trenton: State of New Jersey, Department of Education, 1946).

Illinois Association of School Boards, "Characteristics of a Good School" (Springfield, Ill.: Illinois Association of School Boards, February, 1947).

Elementary Education Division, Virginia State Department of Education, "Looking at Our Elementary Schools" (Richmond: State Department of Education, July, 1949).

South-wide Workshop on Elementary Evaluation, *Elementary Evaluative Criteria* (Nashville: Executive Committee of the Southern Association's Cooperative Study in Elementary Evaluation, 1949).

These are but a few of the instruments which have formed bases for more recent developments. A study group in New England has now prepared a comprehensive instrument for evaluating elementary schools, and another group at the University of Texas has developed criteria for evaluating junior high schools. Standard evaluation instruments, which are meant to be generally applicable to numerous schools, are obviously not tailored to the evaluation needs of any one particular school. Whenever possible, they should be supplemented with items of response which relate to situations in the particular school which is being evaluated.

Large, cooperative projects——School systems occasionally have opportunities to participate in projects in research and experimentation which are of national, regional, or statewide scope. The federal government, universities, foundations, educational associations, and private business concerns are among the agencies now sponsoring large-scale projects. Government funds, foundation grants, and private capital have been moving increasingly into what is nominally research activity. Developing spelling lists, experimenting with educational television, and trying out materials to be published by major instructional projects are three of the activities which have been under way in numbers of school systems at the same time.

---

[26] West Virginia Association of Secondary School Principals, *Curriculum Evaluation Procedures for West Virginia Schools*. Charleston, W. Va.: State Department of Education, June, 1954.

During the past 30 years, several large projects have been developed in elementary and secondary schools. In 1933, 30 schools engaged in a study of the relationship between high school and college known as the *Eight Year Study*.[27] The Stanford Social Education Investigation, regional in scope, was carried on by Stanford University with a grant from the General Education Board to encourage experimentation in social studies teaching and to stimulate cooperation between school systems and the university in curriculum improvement.[28] Other long-term projects have been sponsored by the Horace Mann–Lincoln Institute of School Experimentation, Teachers College, Columbia University, and by several regional professional groups. A great need exists in the large instructional projects of the present day for honest research and experimentation.

Evaluation, research, and experimentation can open the door to curriculum improvement. They are useful largely to the extent to which the evidence they turn up is used to advance improvement. Much depends, then, upon the willingness of school personnel to employ data for functional purposes in the improvement process.

SITUATION 11-2—A GUIDE TO RESEARCH BY CLASSROOM TEACHERS

John B. Barnes, writing in *Educational Research for Classroom Teachers* (p. 211), suggests nine questions to be asked by school leaders before they encourage teachers to undertake projects in research and experimentation:

1. **Does the school problem which you have in mind definitely limit the operation of your school or decrease the value of your educational program?**
2. **Can your educational program be improved by concerted study, reflection, and research on this problem?**
3. **Are the various school publics—students, teachers, school board members, parents, and general public—aware of this educational problem?**
4. **Have teachers and parents discussed the problem under consideration and failed to solve it?**

[27] Wilford M. Aiken, *The Story of the Eight Year Study*. New York: Harper & Row, Publishers, 1942.

[28] I. James Quillen and Lavone A. Hanna, *Education for Social Competence*. Chicago: Scott, Foresman & Company, 1948.

5. Has the school board discussed this problem at a regular board meeting?
6. Is this educational problem one that seems perennially to cause concern?
7. Have you carefully identified, described, and analyzed the problem?
8. Do you see its parts, its ramifications, its possible causes?
9. Can you list on paper the effect which this school problem has on the educational program?

Which of these questions seem most important in guiding projects in evaluation, research, and experimentation which you have in mind?

What are these projects? Make a written plan for conducting the evaluation, research, or experimentation in one of the projects.

SUMMARY

This lengthy chapter has discussed six major strategies for improving the curricula of elementary and secondary schools. Each of these strategies is in use today in numerous school systems, yet none may be said to have value or worth in excess of the others. Ideally, the strategies are employed in combination, according to the needs of the schools and school systems in which they are in use. Master planning for the entire school system is needed, but the real impact of curriculum improvement occurs most potently in individual schools and especially in the classrooms of these schools. It has become axiomatic that the experiences of learners are unlikely to improve unless the experiences of their teachers improve. To achieve teacher improvement, the strategies of in-service education and supervision have been devised.

In direct attacks on problems of curriculum organization, planners have tried to find alternatives to the inadequate subject curriculum, yet the broad-fields curriculum, the core curriculum and its adaptations, the life functions curriculum, and the experience curriculum have all fallen short of fond expectations. A final strategy described in this chapter involves inquiry about the curriculum conducted according to the methods of evaluation, research, and experimentation. A clear distinction is made here between inquiry about the effectiveness and worth of a curriculum and inquiry about the effectiveness and worth of programs for improving the curriculum. The latter consideration forms the content of the next and concluding chapter of the book.

SELECTED BIBLIOGRAPHY

1. Improvement through Master Planning

American Association of School Administrators, *American School Curriculum*, 31st Yearbook (Washington, D.C.: The Association, 1953).

———, *The Superintendent as Instructional Leader*, 35th Yearbook (Washington, D.C.: The Association, 1957).

Anderson, Vernon E., *Principles and Procedures of Curriculum Improvement* (New York: The Ronald Press Company, 1956).

Caswell, Hollis L., *Curriculum Improvement in Public School Systems* (New York: Bureau of Publications, Teachers College, Columbia University, 1950).

McNally, Harold J., and A. Harry Passow, *Improving the Quality of Public School Programs* (New York: Bureau of Publications, Teachers College, Columbia University, 1960).

Saylor, J. Galen, and William M. Alexander, *Curriculum Planning for Better Teaching and Learning* (New York: Holt, Rinehart & Winston, Inc., 1954).

2. Improvement in Classroom and Individual School

Arbuckle, Dugald S., *Teacher Counseling* (Cambridge, Mass.: Addison-Wesley Publishing Company, Inc., 1950).

Burton, William H., *The Guidance of Learning Activities* (New York: Appleton-Century-Crofts, Inc., 1962).

Miel, Alice, and Associates, *Cooperative Procedures in Learning* (New York: Bureau of Publications, Teachers College, Columbia University, 1952).

Wiles, Kimball, *Teaching for Better Schools*, Second Edition (Englewood Cliffs, N.J.: Prentice-Hall, Inc., 1959).

3. Improvement through In-service Education

Kelley, Earl C., *The Workshop Way of Learning* (New York: Harper & Row, Publishers, 1951).

Lawler, Marcella T., *Curriculum Consultants at Work* (New York: Bureau of Publications, Teachers College, Columbia University, 1958).

Miles, Matthew B., *Learning to Work in Groups* (New York: Bureau of Publications, Teachers College, Columbia University, 1959).

National Society for the Study of Education, *In-service Education*, 56th Yearbook, Part I (Chicago: University of Chicago Press, 1957).

Spears, Harold, *Curriculum Planning Through In-service Programs* (Englewood Cliffs, N.J.: Prentice-Hall, Inc., 1957).

4. Improvement through Supervision

Burton, William H., and Leo J. Brueckner, *Supervision: a Social Process* (New York: Appleton-Century-Crofts, Inc., 1955).

Crosby, Muriel, *Supervision as Cooperative Action* (New York: Appleton-Century-Crofts, Inc., 1957).

Franseth, Jane, *Supervision as Leadership* (New York: Harper & Row, Publishers, 1961).

Swearingen, Mildred E., *Supervision of Instruction: Foundations and Dimensions* (Boston: Allyn and Bacon, Inc., 1962).

5. Improvement by Reorganizing Pupil Experiences and Schools

Alberty, Harold, *Reorganizing the High School Curriculum* (New York: The Macmillan Co., 1953).

Chase, Francis S., and Harold A. Anderson, eds., *The High School in a New Era* (Chicago: University of Chicago Press, 1958).

Conant, James B., *The American High School Today* (New York: McGraw-Hill Book Co., Inc., 1959).

Goodlad, John, and Robert Anderson, *The Nongraded Elementary School* (New York: Harcourt, Brace & World, Inc., 1959).

Hopkins, L. Thomas, *Interaction: the Democratic Process* (Boston: D. C. Heath & Company, 1941).

National Education Association, *The Principals Look at the Schools* (Washington, D.C.: The Association, 1962).

Wright, Grace S., *Block-Time Classes and the Core Program in the Junior High School* (Washington, D.C.: United States Office of Education, Bulletin 1958, No. 6).

6. Improvement through Evaluation, Research, and Experimentation

Barnes, John B., *Educational Research for Classroom Teachers* (New York: G. P. Putnam's Sons, 1960).

Corey, Stephen M., *Action Research to Improve School Practices* (New York: Bureau of Publications, Teachers College, Columbia University, 1953).

Good, Carter V., *Introduction to Educational Research* (New York: Appleton-Century-Crofts, Inc., 1959).

Remmers, H. H., and N. L. Gage, *Educational Measurement and Evaluation* (New York: Harper & Row, Publishers, 1957).

part three

Program
Evaluation

chapter twelve

PROFESSIONAL LITERATURE ABOUT EVALUATION as a general theme exists in profusion, but little has been written about evaluating programs of curriculum improvement. As a consequence, ways of evaluating programs have seldom been devised with care, and no one really knows whether most programs are causing significant improvement in the schools. Extraneous considerations, such as the prestige of the author of a proposal for curriculum change, are often permitted to replace evidence of the proposal's real effectiveness.

Two reasons are commonly advanced for evaluating curriculum improvement programs. One is the significance to program participants of knowing what they have accomplished. This knowledge tends to improve their morale and to supply guideposts by which they may plot further action. The other common reason is the need to justify expenditures of time, talent, and money —expenditures about which curriculum leaders are likely to be questioned at any time.

Certain basic principles of evaluation need to be reviewed at the beginning of the present discussion. *Evaluation* may be defined as a broad and continuous effort to inquire into the effects of utilizing educational content

Evaluation of Curriculum Improvement Programs

and process according to clearly-defined goals. In terms of this definition, evaluation may be expected to go beyond simple measurement, and also beyond simple application of the evaluator's values and beliefs. If evaluation is to be a broad and continuous effort, it must rely upon a variety of instruments which are used according to carefully-ascribed purposes.

SOME BASIC PRINCIPLES OF EVALUATION

Evaluation, as it is now conducted in schools, ranges from the highly informal to the highly formal. At a basic level of informality, it consists of judging, estimating, or giving opinions about the extent to which certain changes in school improvement programs have occurred. At the more formal level, it involves carefully collecting and treating data about progress toward prescribed goals. In all circumstances, it has as an important characteristic the collection of evidence of some sort. This evidence may indicate merely that movement has occurred from the beginning to the end of an allotted period of time, or it may indicate the presence of carefully-directed, goal-oriented movement. The difference between the two is usually a difference between aimlessness and careful aim.

The nature of evidence varies, then, with respect to an informality-formality continuum. For instance, an evaluator may judge informally that people's attitudes have changed in a given direction by observing one or two behavioral cues, or he may undertake a formal evaluation of attitude change by conducting interviews and observations and by administering attitude inventories, with all instruments having been chosen or developed to suit his purposes. In this way, formality implies scholarly care.

One of the characteristics of evaluation is an *acknowledged presence of values and valuing.* The act of valuing, which is a conscious recognition and expression of the values which an evaluator holds dear, is a necessary initial step in the evaluation process. For instance, the Council on Basic Education values intellectual experience in the three R's for elementary-school children at the expense of certain social and emotional experiences in the school program. Accordingly, the Council encourages inquiry which discovers the virtues of intellectual rigor. Whenever an evaluation project is initiated by any group, it expresses beliefs which the evaluator holds about what is worth evaluating. At the conclusion of the evaluation episode, the investigator makes value judgments regarding the effects of the episode. These value judgments help to determine what he will investigate on the next and subsequent occasions.

A related characteristic of evaluation is its *orientation to goals.* Without setting a goal, one cannot tell much about the nature and direction of his progress or achievement. A thorough program of education subscribes to many goals: *e.g.,* goals of information-getting, understanding, skill-development, feeling and perceiving, critical thinking, and attitude change. When goals have been adopted, ways of evaluating their achievement should be thought of immediately. Achievement of goals is accomplished by designing experiences that fit or accord with the goals, and the effects of experiences can be evaluated with reference to the goals. Consistency of both evaluation devices and learning experiences with an established list of goals is a necessity of good educational planning which is too often ignored.

Another characteristic of effective evaluation is its *comprehensiveness.* Evaluation must, as we have seen, be as broad as the goals to which it relates. Making it broad is not easy, a fact which is indicated, for example, by the difficulties with which we evaluate changes in attitudes and appreciations. To be comprehensive, evaluation must make use of numerous and varied media, some of which are yet to be invented.

Still another characteristic of thoroughgoing evaluation is *continuity.* Most chapters on evaluation in education textbooks, including this one, appear at the ends of the books. The consequent implication might erroneously be that evaluation comes last in an educational enterprise. Actually, it should be made frequent and recurrent, continual if not continuous. It is needed at almost every stage of every enterprise, and it should be accomplished with imagination, skill, and appropriateness.

Appropriateness of evaluation suggests a need for two additional, related characteristics: *diagnostic worth* and *validity*. Instruments of evaluation should have worth in diagnosing specific aspects of educational situations. In this sense, they should achieve "diagnostic fit." The instruments to be used should also be valid, *i.e.*, they should have the utmost ability to describe what they purport to describe. Needless to say, many instruments in use today lack validity and also reliability, which, as applied to the curriculum, consists of ability to measure the effects of an educational experience accurately on repeated occasions.

Finally, evaluation should serve to integrate findings about educational phenomena. The ultimate object of evaluating is *not* to leave data in a diverse and unintegrated state, but to combine significant findings so that their real meaning is evident. Organization and interpretation of data thus become important tasks in evaluation which create that desirable characteristic called *integration*.

Inasmuch as evaluation is concerned with progress toward goals, it is important to know whether, when, and in what directions progress is occurring. To this end, criteria of progress like the following need to be established:

1. Are we really moving toward our goals? (*Theme:* perceptibility of movement)
2. How much movement is present? (*Theme:* time and space)
3. How fast is movement occurring? (*Theme:* rate)
4. What, precisely, can be said about direction(s) of movement? (*Theme:* aberrant motion)
5. How does the general movement we have discovered relate to other movements toward change or improvement? (*Theme:* relevance within the whole complex of improvement)

These criteria have implications for the nature and the evaluation of curriculum improvement programs. They imply that such programs should "get somewhere," and that they should move as far within their allotted life-spans as possible. In the United States, we expect movement to be rapid. However, movement may not always occur in a straight line: variations in movement may create significant side effects which supply new outlets for study and growth. For instance, a recent inquiry into the uses of closed-circuit television in preparing student teachers at Hunter College has resulted in favorable find-

ings about the intrinsic worth of student teaching in the preparation of classroom teachers. Fundamental movement, with its variations, almost inevitably
relates to other movements, and effects of the whole complex of movements
should be seen in perspective.

DIMENSIONS OF PROGRAM EVALUATION

Based on the nature of evaluation as described above, two major dimensions of the evaluation of curriculum improvement programs are identifiable.
One dimension is that of *quantity:* how much of the program is to be evaluated? The other dimension is that of *quality:* what goals are being highlighted in this evaluation, and how does achievement of these goals assure
quality?

THE DIMENSION OF QUANTITY

1. *Evaluating the whole program*——The amount or portion of a program to evaluate is a matter for careful decision. It is possible to evaluate programs comprehensively, generally, and as a whole. Such evaluation is of a
survey sort and is necessarily superficial. Nevertheless, the survey helps participants in curriculum improvement see "the whole forest" in which they work.
When the goals of a program have been determined, criteria under general
headings like those proposed by the Association for Supervision and Curriculum Development should be prepared with direct reference to the goals. Under
several general headings—"Educational Objectives," "Role Perception," "Organizational Structure," "Group Action and Morale," "Experimentation,"
"Communication," "Resources," and "Evaluation"—the Association has
listed specific criteria of effective leadership for program improvement. Criteria noted under the heading "Group Action and Morale" are typical of the
specific criteria which appear under the general headings:

Group Action and Morale

1. Administrative officials encourage cooperative planning and deliberation
   by school staff and other groups.
2. Groups evidence movement toward mutually held goals, productivity in
   achieving these goals, and maintenance of group solidarity.
3. Individuals and subgroups evidence high morale as they work together.
4. Human relations skills are in evidence in all aspects of the school's functioning.

5. The staff acts rationally in resolving issues and in seeking solutions to problems.

6. Qualities that enhance interaction of persons in the group may be described in terms such as initiative, originality, communication, empathy, cooperation, understanding, cohesiveness, morale, productivity.

7. Decisions regarding program changes are cooperatively made on the basis of the most objective data obtainable.

8. The total staff is encouraged toward realizing its potential.

9. Teachers encountering teaching or other difficulties feel free to seek assistance.[1]

Criteria may be made more general than these. For example, only five general criteria were stated, and were justified by reference to educational literature, in evaluating effects of the International Paper Company Foundation's assistance to secondary education in six school districts:

Criterion I: In the total context of the teaching-learning situation there should be provided, through varied subject-matter, materials, and methods, opportunities for individual pupils to acquire habits, skills, information, and attitudes which will aid them to become contributing citizens in a democracy.

Criterion II: The organizational, administrative, and supervisory pattern, through cooperative planning, implementation, and evaluative procedures, promotes the continuous improvement of the school program and the competence of the professional staff.

Criterion III: The members of the professional staff display a unity of purpose, a sense of worth, and an appreciation of their efforts, and those of others, in the improvement of the school program.

Criterion IV: Student personnel services should result in a continuous process of pupils, parents, teachers, counselors, and other specialists working together to assist each pupil in achieving greater self-understanding, self-direction, and self-realization in a democratic society.

Criterion V: The school, through community study, interpretation of the school program, use of community resources, and working closely with lay citizens, strives to become an integral part of community life.[2]

[1] Association for Supervision and Curriculum Development, *Leadership for Improving Instruction*, 1960 Yearbook. Washington, D.C.: The Association, 1960, pp. 166 and 167.

[2] Ben Wallace and John P. Gower, *An Evaluation of the Effects of Participation by Six School Districts in the International Paper Company Foundation's Program of Assistance to Secondary Education* (unpublished doctoral dissertation). New York: Teachers College, Columbia University, 1960, *passim.*

When criteria are too numerous, their use in evaluation becomes an unduly protracted affair. When they are too few, the evaluator may have to search out their meanings before he can use them concretely in evaluation. McNally and Passow have provided an extensive but excellent list of criteria for survey evaluation of programs. Specific criteria appear under headings designated by roman numerals:

I. Scope and Objectives of the Program

1. The program is comprehensive in scope, dealing with all aspects of the educational needs of the community served by the school system.
2. The program improvement objectives—both short-range and long-term—are clarified to guide organization and activities.
3. The concept which guides program improvement is that the curriculum consists of the experiences children have under the direction and guidance of the school; improving the quality of the program means improving the quality of those experiences.
4. The curriculum improvement program is based on the premise that educational quality will change only as the perceptions, attitudes, values, understandings, and skills of staff members change.
5. There is common direction and purpose to the separate components of the curriculum improvement program.

II. Initiating Program Improvement Activities

1. Channels are provided for communicating curriculum problems to a central planning and coordinating group.
2. Materials are sent to individuals and groups to keep them abreast of new developments.
3. Regular opportunities are provided for individuals and groups to have contact with new ideas and practices through conferences, professional meetings, and school visits.
4. Periodic evaluation of learning and teaching are analyzed for leads to improving program quality.
5. Classroom and school conditions—e.g., climate for learning, personnel and material resources, teaching methodology—are appraised regularly.

III. Administration of the Curriculum Improvement Program

1. Trained leadership is provided for curriculum work.
2. General responsibility for all services related to curriculum and teaching is assigned to a single administrative officer or department.
3. The central office staff provides resource specialists to assist in developing the programs of the various schools in the system.
4. Supervision functions as a means of instructional improvement, part of the broader plan of the curriculum program.
5. The individual school is the operational and planning unit for curriculum improvement.
6. The central office functions to encourage and aid the staff of individual

schools to develop a unified curriculum adapted to the particular neighborhood and pupils served.

7. There is a central professional committee for the development of general policies and for the coordination of activities.
8. Time and facilities are provided for committees and individuals to engage in program improvement activities.
9. Funds are budgeted for program improvement activities.

IV. Organization for Curriculum Planning

1. The organization reflects the goals and purposes of the school, helping to create conditions for program planning similar to those at which the school is aiming in instruction.
2. Individuals and groups at each planning level are supported and encouraged so that they can contribute effectively to the improvement of the total program.
3. Responsibilities of individuals in the organization are clearly specified.
4. The organization facilitates coordination of diverse activities of planning and action groups.
5. Communication among the various individuals and groups working at program development is facilitated.
6. Assignments of committees are clearly stated, and the committees are discharged when their work is completed.
7. The activities of individuals and groups preparing curriculum plans and materials are organized to facilitate adaptation and use by the other personnel.
8. The organization is effectively related to local conditions.

V. Participation in Curriculum Planning

1. Provision is made for those who will be affected by the policy or action decisions which may emerge from the work of the group to participate at some level of planning.
2. Those individuals whose classroom practice is expected to change as a consequence of the improvement program are encouraged to participate.
3. The emergence of leadership at all levels of planning is facilitated.
4. Lay persons, including parents and students, are involved in the processes of curriculum development wherever they can contribute their special competencies.

VI. Procedures and Techniques Used in Curriculum Improvement

1. A variety of activities are provided in order that each member of the instructional staff may participate in the program in a way recognized by him as being of value.
2. Professional staff growth is considered the primary avenue of curriculum improvement.
3. Provisions are made for the development of skills necessary for undertaking curriculum improvement activities.
4. Separate strands of curriculum work are interrelated to build a consistent, comprehensive educational program.

5. Effective communication among individuals and groups involved in planning, as well as others who are concerned, is maintained.
6. Ways for translating plans into practice are constantly considered.
7. Products, other than changed behavior of individuals, are developed on a tentative basis to be tested.

VII. Evaluation of Curriculum Improvement Programs

1. Continuous evaluation of the procedures in the improvement program and of the changes which result is made an integral part of the curriculum program.
2. Techniques of evaluation employed are consistent with the principles accepted for curriculum development.
3. Provision is made for the practical testing on a limited basis of ideas for curriculum improvement and for the dissemination of results.
4. Systematic gathering and appraisal of evidence serves as a basis for determining need for changes in curriculum planning and improvement activities, and for consequent modifications.
5. Evidence is sought of the effectiveness of curriculum planning in changing the quality of instruction.
6. The objectives of the program, both short-range and long-range, are specified in terms of a) the changes sought in the educational program, and b) the changes sought in staff perception and operation.[3]

These criteria are directed heavily toward process. Many school personnel prefer to place their emphasis upon what their programs do to change the substance or content of the curriculum. Because of the difference in criteria which evaluators are willing to accept, each evaluation team should develop its own criteria to suit its own particular purposes and situation. Criteria may, of course, be stated in either declarative or interrogative form: *e.g.*, "New ideas are continually being brought into the school system for analysis and trial" or "Are new ideas being brought into the school system continually for analysis and trial?" Criteria worded in these ways suggest the use of a checklist indicating simply presence or absence of facts in the situation which cause the situation to meet or fail to meet the criteria. With additional effort, the situation may be rated as to the extent to which it meets the criteria: *e.g.*, to very great extent, to great extent, to some extent, to little extent, to very little extent.

Most persons who use rating scales have a strong urge to quantify the results. Actually, quantification often proves fruitless because the worth of a program is scarcely the simple sum of its ratings, whatever the criteria used. Users of rating scales need to recognize that some criteria carry heavier value

[3] Harold J. McNally and A. Harry Passow, *Improving the Quality of Public School Programs*. New York: Bureau of Publications, Teachers College, Columbia University, 1960, pp. 311–320.

or weight than other criteria. Therefore, relative weighting of the criteria should be established prior to the act of rating. Following the rating, item analysis may yield greatest understanding of the program's strengths and weaknesses. Some criteria, under their appropriate headings, should be used to reflect substantive progress, *i.e.*, progress in developing the content of the curriculum; other criteria, progress in using process of improvement. Evaluation of an entire program would not be complete unless reasonably balanced attention were given to both products of the program and processes employed in operating it. Valid evaluation of substantive progress usually requires such careful inquiry that evaluators achieve it as they investigate a portion or segment of the program. This fact suggests that consideration should now be given to evaluating component elements of programs.

2. *Evaluating component elements of the program*——Obviously, each curriculum improvement program contains component elements or parts which may be evaluated in depth. Evaluating a portion of a program may, of course, provide a slanted view of the program as a whole, but it does permit study in depth which lends confidence concerning the findings. An example of a program element which has received evaluation in depth is the core experience provided in the seventh and eighth grades of the Fallsington, Pennsylvania, Public Schools. Some time after Fallsington had moved from a traditional to a core program for some of its seventh- and eighth-grade classes, an effort was made to determine how well pupils were achieving academically and how they were performing in several other ways. Pupils who had been in core and in traditional classes were grouped together, having been equated with respect to age, sex, intelligence quotient, and several other factors. All pupils in the experimental and the control groups were given standardized achievement tests, and the quality of their marks, their traits as seen by teachers, the quantity of school activities in which they participated, and their attitudes toward various aspects of school life were noted. The data revealed that pupils who had come from core classes were ahead of pupils from traditional classes in achievement test scores, marks, teachers' ratings of traits, and quantity of activities. No difference between the two groups was found with regard to attitudes concerning aspects of school life.[4]

Practitioners often object to engaging in investigation of this kind because it is so time-consuming. However, for those who want to be as sure as possible that their undertakings are worth the effort, careful evaluation provides the answer. An obvious basic need in educational evaluation is the cre-

---

[4] Bernard Schwartz, "An Investigation of the Effects of a Seventh and Eighth Grade Core Program," *Journal of Educational Research*, Vol. 53, December, 1959, pp. 149–152.

ation of evaluation designs that fit educational problems more exactly than the stock designs that have been borrowed from the physical sciences.

Emphasis in the preceding example was placed on the way in which organization of school time and arrangements affects pupils' learning. Inquiry more directly substantive in nature may be used in answering the question, "If easier—or more difficult—learning content is provided, what are the over-all effects on learning?" To date, few specific answers to this question have been sought. Inquiry which has been conducted by nationally-known subject-matter projects has consisted mainly of informal experimentation in introducing more difficult content into the elementary and secondary schools. The experimenters report that children *seem* to learn the newly-placed content with success, or with difficulty, without comprehending its true meaning, or in some other generally describable way. In many instances, what is being evaluated is perhaps not so much the difficulty of given educational experiences as the effect of communicating subject-matter content in more understandable form. Evaluation data appear also to be subject to the "Hawthorne effect," an aura of favorable feeling and even excitement which surrounds participants who are receiving satisfying attention through their participation in the program.[5]

Where skill development can be observed directly, as in pupils' ability to type or to drive automobiles, complex evaluative systems need not be used to determine when the desired skills have been developed. However, even in these cases, one may neglect important data about the functioning of the human organism. For instance, undue nervousness may accompany skill development and go largely unnoticed in the evaluator's preoccupation with development of the skill. To make evaluation appropriately comprehensive, one must view the effects of educational experience broadly, taking into account the wholeness and complexity of the learner.

The scarcity of evidence about suitable placement of subject-matter is indicated by the following example. Several midwestern high schools have been delaying the teaching of formal grammar until the eleventh and twelfth grades. Meanwhile, Winnetka, Illinois, reports: ". . . formal grammar study, once postponed until Grade 8, is now spread, at least in part, to the intermediate and lower grades, giving the children a longer exposure for the assimilation of grammar concepts and freeing the curriculum in eighth grade for more work in literature, composition, and creative writing."[6] Discrepan-

[5] For information concerning one group of projects, see John R. Mayor and John A. Brown, "New Mathematics in the Elementary School," *School Review*, Vol. 70, No. 1, Spring, 1962, pp. 102–111.

[6] Mildred Whitcomb, "How to Make 'Progressive' Education Work," *Nation's Schools*, Vol. 70, No. 4, October, 1962, p. 60.

cies of this kind would be less likely to exist if more evidence were at hand regarding desirable placement of content.

Many other facets of substantive change in the curriculum need assessing. What, for instance, are the effects of providing different kinds of materials for program enrichment? Of attempting individualization? Of meeting differences in cultural background and socio-economic status? Answers to these and other questions concerning curriculum content are only beginning to be found.

Additional component elements of curriculum improvement programs are of a process rather than a substantive nature. How a program is initiated, how it is organized and administered, and what procedures and techniques are used in keeping it operating are three of the general process categories which should be subjected to inquiry. Each category may be divided into smaller parts or elements. For example, an element of administration of programs is administration of communication systems, one question about which is, "How freely and efficiently are messages about events in the program under evaluation being disseminated to and from interested, concerned personnel?"

Some of the important issues about the process of curriculum improvement center in the selection of activities in which program participants are to engage. Broderick, Levin, and Mason raised the question, "What characteristics of curriculum development activities do teachers themselves identify as important in terms of improving their work with children and youth?" They asked 244 elementary- and secondary-school teachers in three school systems in the New York metropolitan area to react to a list of 20 activities by identifying the most helpful and the least helpful activities with regard to providing better learning experiences in their classrooms. The investigators also asked the teachers to select from 60 characteristics of curriculum improvement activities those characteristics which caused them to choose particular activities as being most helpful and least helpful. Elementary-school teachers considered grade-level meetings to be most helpful, while secondary-school teachers favored department meetings. Both elementary- and secondary-school teachers chose general staff meetings as being least helpful.

> Activities in which teachers participated in groups were designated by more teachers as most helpful than were activities in which teachers participated as individuals, such as conferences with principal or supervisor, or studying written communications.

The following three characteristics were most often mentioned as reasons for considering activities helpful: 1) "We examined our classroom practices." 2) "We participated in discussions." 3) "The problem was important to me."

On the other hand, the following characteristics limited or inhibited the helpfulness of activities: 1) "I was required to be part of the activity." 2) "Only teachers were in this activity." 3) "A small number carried responsibility."[7]

Additional studies of ways of working for curriculum improvement are badly needed. Experience seems to indicate that the ways personnel organize and operate in doing their work, and especially the ways they interact with each other, are at least as important to long-term improvement as the precise actions they take.

DIMENSIONS OF QUALITY

The preceding discussion of how much of a program to evaluate has inevitably turned from time to time to illustrations of discovery of quality. Four qualitative questions seem especially pertinent in evaluating curriculum improvement programs:

1. How has pupils' learning improved as a consequence of initiating and continuing this program?
2. How has the behavior or the performance of classroom teachers improved?
3. How have the attitudes of teachers toward learners, learning, and teaching improved?
4. How have the procedures which have been used in changing the curriculum proved effective in creating desirable change?

In evaluating programs, perhaps only one or two of these questions can feasibly be answered at a given time. One or more demonstrations of attempts to answer each of the four questions are given below.

1. *Effects of programs on pupils' learning*——The time and effort spent in attempting to improve the curriculum should lead to favorable and measurable effects on pupils' learning. Many persons regard these direct effects on learning as being greatest among the potential effects of program improvement. However, spectacular improvements in learning speed, efficiency, and durability are rare. Zimmerman reports the modest sort of improvement which may generally be expected. In comparing the effects of departmental and unified seventh-grade programs, he found that pupils' achievement in English and the social studies, as well as their adjustment, improved about equally in the two types of program. The variability of achievement test scores in English and the social studies did increase for unified program pupils, but

---

[7] Catherine M. Broderick and Barbara T. Mason, "What Questions Need We Ask About Staff Participation?" *Educational Leadership*, Vol. 15, No. 6, March, 1958, pp. 343–346.

they did not increase for departmental program pupils.[8] Occasionally, of course, improvements in learning may be more marked than those which Zimmerman found.

On the other hand, program changes may not eventuate in any demonstrable improvement in learning. One of the most interesting, promising projects in elementary- and secondary-school mathematics is that of the School Mathematics Study Group. Two doctoral studies have recently been completed concerning the effects of SMSG materials on pupil achievement. Williams found little difference in mean achievement in grade nine between pupils in SMSG mathematics and pupils in traditional mathematics, the slight difference favoring the traditional program. In grade ten, he found no significant difference in the achievement of two matched groups of pupils. He concluded that traditional algebra textbooks were at least as effective as the SMSG materials in developing mathematical competence in grade nine.[9] Similarly, Shuff's study at seventh- and eighth-grade levels led him to question the superiority of SMSG text-materials in improving the achievement of pupils in these grades.[10]

These two sources of evidence are obviously insufficient to condemn the content and materials advocated by the School Mathematics Study Group, but they do invite further inquiry about the contributions of the newer instructional projects and about the effects of traditional content and practices as well. While innovations may have on their side improved ways of communicating subject-matter and the presence of the "Hawthorne effect," traditionalism has in its favor the emotional set which accompanies satisfaction with what one has always done. In the long run, the chief contribution of the newer projects in instruction may lie in the insights about content and method which teachers develop or receive as they adopt and try eclectically small segments of total programs. Perhaps, then, whole projects or programs may not make the contribution that small segments may make, often in an incidental way.

[8] William A. Zimmerman, *Departmental and Unified Seventh Grade Programs in English and Social Studies: a Study of Changes in Subject Matter Achievement and Personal Adjustment* (unpublished doctoral dissertation). Syracuse, N.Y.: Syracuse University, 1962.

[9] Emmet D. Williams, *Comparative Study of School Mathematics Study Group and Traditional Mathematics* (unpublished doctoral dissertation). Minneapolis: University of Minnesota, 1962.

[10] Robert V. Shuff, *A Comparative Study of Achievement in Mathematics at the Seventh and Eighth Grade Levels Under Two Approaches, School Mathematics Study Group and Traditional* (unpublished doctoral dissertation). Minneapolis: University of Minnesota, 1962.

Whatever the means by which revised programs contribute to improved learning, there is evidence that continuous curriculum development has beneficial effects. For instance, Godbey, in his study of school systems in Wayne County, Michigan, found that those systems with continuous programs of several years' duration reported the highest pupil achievement. Outstandingly favorable changes in achievement were not immediate, but constant curriculum study resulted in gradually-improving achievement test scores.[11] It must be remembered that teachers are the chief persons who engage in curriculum study. Therefore, the development which teachers acquire through curriculum study *should* affect pupils' learning. This is the thesis upon which evaluators study the effects of programs on teacher behavior or performance.

2. *Effects of programs on teacher performance*——While the education of children may actually proceed more informally, *i.e.*, outside and beyond the direction of teachers, than was once assumed, one of the important objectives of curriculum improvement programs continues to be an upgrading of teachers so that they may behave more and more helpfully in working with learners. What do curriculum improvement programs really accomplish in the upgrading or re-education process? Fragmentary evidence shows that the in-service aspects of programs affect teachers' performance favorably. In addition, much informal data supplied by supervisors and participant teachers themselves reveal that classroom teachers behave more insightfully and effectively as a consequence of their experiences in curriculum improvement activities.

In 1953–1954, the Minneapolis Public Schools conducted "A Qualitative Study of the School Day." At Minnehaha Elementary School, the study focused on the teaching of arithmetic. Teachers who engaged in group study and experimentation were found to behave differently as a result of their in-service experience. Specifically, they grew in comprehension of arithmetic and in their ability to teach it, in their attitudes toward each other, and in their understanding of children.[12]

A major contribution to change in teacher behavior has been made by Daniel Prescott and his staff of child-development specialists at the University of Maryland. Each teacher who works with the Prescott group is asked to observe a child over a lengthy period of time, and to keep an anecdotal record of the child's behavior. The teacher learns to observe physical and biological

---

[11] James L. Godbey, *Evaluation of Curriculum Development Practices in Selected School Systems of Wayne County, Michigan* (unpublished doctoral dissertation). Detroit: Wayne State University, 1960.

[12] National Society for the Study of Education, *In-service Education*, 56th Yearbook, Part I. Chicago: University of Chicago Press, 1957, pp. 138–140.

development, growth in self-concept, peer-group relationships, intellectual development, cultural and social influences, and adjustment mechanisms. As a result of their practical study of children during periods as long as six years, some teachers, at least, behave more understandingly toward pupils in their classrooms.[13]

Lulu Way found that teachers' knowledge of principles of child growth and development affected their classroom performance, particularly in the social studies. Interestingly, she concluded that if one wanted to choose a good teacher of reading, arithmetic, the social studies, and natural science in the elementary school, he need only know how the teacher teaches arithmetic to see how he follows child-growth principles in other subjects.[14]

3. *Effects of programs on teacher attitudes*——Teachers' attitudes are closely related to their behaviors. In fact, because an evaluator cannot see or gauge attitudes directly, he must infer them from behaviors. He knows, meanwhile, that favorable attitudes are very important to the success of any worthwhile project.

Attitudes of participants and non-participants toward the West Orange, New Jersey, improvement program were assessed on two separate occasions. Following are some of the findings in the first assessment:

1. The attitudes of West Orange teachers at the beginning of the study were only partially formed.
2. The attitudes of active participants in the program toward the importance of curriculum improvement became slightly more favorable. The attitudes of non-participants became somewhat less favorable.
3. The attitudes of participants toward the ways of working which were used became decidedly more favorable. The attitudes of non-participants seem to have become more favorable also, though to a lesser degree.
4. Both participants and non-participants seem to have found most value in the teacher problem-centered and voluntary approach on which the program was established and on which it sought to operate. They agreed that the concerns of teachers make a natural starting place for curriculum change; that the security of all teachers should be protected; and that volunteering should be a keynote of the program. They were especially cognizant of teacher welfare, and they apparently felt that their own securities were being built rather than threatened.

[13] Jewell P. Haddock, *A Study of Teachers' Sensitivity to Human Growth and Development Principles Before, During, and After Participation in a Three Year Program of Child Study*, as reported, with similar studies, in Richard M. Brandt and Hugh V. Perkins, *Research Evaluating a Child Study Program*, Vol. 21, Serial No. 62, No. 1. Lafayette, Ind.: Society for Research in Child Development, 1956, pp. 74–76.

[14] Lulu R. Way, *A Study of the Relationships Between Knowledge of Child Growth Principles and Their Applications in Multiple-Grade Teaching in Certain Counties in Nebraska, South Dakota, and Michigan* (unpublished doctoral dissertation). Lansing: Michigan State University, 1957.

5. Active participants showed improved attitudes toward the methods of action research (*e.g.*, hypothesis-making, evidence-seeking, experimentation in the classroom) and specifically toward the importance of good group work.

6. Most evidence of negative attitudes appeared among non-participants. Expenditures of time and money loomed large in their thinking. They were impressed with the amount of time needed to effect what they considered to be curriculum improvement, and they suspected that money allocated to the curriculum program was being partially wasted.[15]

The second assessment, in which many of the same instruments of evaluation were used, revealed similar differences in attitude between participants and non-participants. However, as the experiences of participants in an improvement program seem satisfactory or gratifying over a period of time, non-participants apparently hear favorable reports of the program, and their own attitudes then become more favorable.[16]

Evaluations of teachers' and administrators' attitudes toward phases of programs and toward particular program activities will be needed increasingly as programs become more complex and varied.

4. *The effectiveness of procedures*——Certain procedures or ways of working function very well at given times and places. The ways of working which were described in Chapter 11 were reported under six general strategies or major procedures for promoting desirable change. One of the unknowns in most situations is just which of the ways of working under the six strategies succeed best in effecting curriculum improvement. Offhand judgment by teachers often indicates that workshops and personal conferences with friendly, knowledgeable supervisors yield greatest returns in improving their own practices. Other evidence points to the effectiveness of cooperative action research, organized study groups, and blocks of time during which pupils work with the same teacher. Most of the evaluation of procedures which has been done to date has consisted of asking teachers and supervisors what procedures have been most helpful in improving teachers' practices. Several studies have been made of the effect which re-organized learning experiences have on pupil achievement. Surely much more thorough and diversified evaluation of procedures and ways of working is needed.

[15] Ronald C. Doll, *Teachers' Attitudes Toward the Initial Steps in a Curriculum Improvement Program* (unpublished doctoral dissertation). New York: Teachers College, Columbia University, 1951, pp. 180–182.

[16] Stanley Dropkin, *Attitudes of West Orange Teachers by Types of Participation* (unpublished doctoral dissertation). New York: Teachers College, Columbia University, 1954.

A few briefly-stated examples of evaluations of procedures and ways of working appear below.

Participants in workshops are sometimes asked questions like these: How has the workshop experience changed your attitudes toward teaching practices and methods? What changes in your practices and methods do you attribute directly to the workshop? What practices and methods have you learned which you expect to try within the next three months? Describe briefly a practice you have learned in the workshop which seems to you to be much better than a practice you are now using.

Landry had supervisors keep records of their day-to-day activities. According to his method, time logs and anecdotal records may be evaluated in consideration of the supervisor's views of his own accomplishments, evidence from research studies, and opinions of authorities in supervision. These criteria assist in determining which supervisory procedures are productive, and which are not.[17]

Flanagan devised a critical-incident technique which solicits from respondents those incidents which they believe to have had the greatest effect in changing them from previous to present viewpoints, or which reveal effective behaviors of the persons who work with them. Several doctoral studies have depended heavily upon this technique for identification of effective procedures.[18]

A study of the effects of the in-service program in a Nebraska community showed that teachers had gained in providing for individual differences among children, in their ability to plan and work together, in their use of instructional materials, and in their employment of "more practical" classroom procedures.[19]

A few studies of the effects of re-organized time arrangements on pupil achievement have been pursued. The Fallsington study and the work by Zimmerman have already been noted in this chapter. One of the other studies of this type was conducted in the Evanston Township Public Schools, where the correlated or "combined-studies" classes were compared with conventional classes to determine relative achievement in English, history, and the social studies. Pupils in the combined-studies classes did as well as or better than

[17] Thomas R. Landry, *et al.*, "An Approach to Evaluation of Supervisory Practices," *Educational Leadership*, Vol. 16, May, 1959, pp. 485–488.

[18] John C. Flanagan, "The Critical-Incident Technique," *Psychological Bulletin*, Vol. 51, July, 1954, pp. 327 and 328.

[19] Glenn E. Pickrel, *A Study of the In-service Program in the Westside Community (Nebraska) Schools* (unpublished doctoral dissertation). Lincoln: University of Nebraska, 1960.

pupils in conventional classes in English, and markedly better in United States history and the social studies.[20]

The illustrations above relate to three of the six strategies for improving the curriculum which were reported in Chapter 11, specifically to in-service education, supervision, and reorganizing pupil experiences. Of the three, most has been written about evaluation of procedures and ways of working in supervision. The remaining three strategies in Chapter 11—improvement through master planning, improvement in the classroom and in the individual school, and improvement through evaluation, research, and experimentation —contain many areas for possible inquiry. As an example relative to both master planning and the individual school, much investigation needs to be conducted concerning the relative effectiveness of actions taken by superintendents and other central office personnel and those taken by principals and teachers in individual schools.

In the studies which have been conducted, evidence has mounted to show that teachers seek to reject poorly-planned or authoritatively-imposed activities, and that they want procedures which encourage relationships with other staff members and their own participation in administration. Thus, it appears that teachers desire real opportunities to exercise initiative in improving the schools.[21]

SOME COMMENTS ABOUT METHODOLOGY

The literature on evaluation points to several major means by which evaluations of programs may be achieved. These means include the usual questionnaires, interviews, standardized tests, and observations of behavior. The advantages, disadvantages, and uses of these and other media are discussed so extensively in books on evaluation that they need not be reviewed here. In general, however, all program evaluation may be said to rely on observation "as a means for obtaining the necessary data for valuing and for making comparisons between what is observed and the desired goals."[22]

[20] Leslee J. Bishop, *A Critical Study of the Evanston Township Combined Studies Program* (unpublished doctoral dissertation). Evanston, Ill.: Northwestern University, 1960.

[21] Mearl F. Gerheim, *Teacher Evaluation of the Nature and Effectiveness of In-service Teacher Education in Selected School Districts* (unpublished doctoral dissertation). Pittsburgh: University of Pittsburgh, 1959.

[22] Virgil E. Herrick, "The Evaluation of Change in Programs of In-service Education," in National Society for the Study of Education, *In-service Education* (56th Yearbook), Part I. Chicago: University of Chicago Press, 1957, p. 321.

Herrick, the author of this quotation, indicates several ways in which observation as a generic method may be improved:

1. *Observation should be sharply focused.* When one defines the objectives of his evaluative study, he helps focus his observations. What he observes must then relate to his objectives, and to achieve focus, one must eschew pursuit of extraneous objectives, "keeping his eyes from wandering."

2. *Observation should be repeated.* Extent of change can be determined by repeating observations. Before-and-after testing, the administration of achievement tests during the autumn and again during the spring, and repeated recording of anecdotes are examples of needed repetition.

3. *Observation should be broadened in its range.* The acknowledged complexity of educational phenomena should prevent observers from "putting on the blinders" so that they see the scope of their evaluation problem in too limited a way. While focus is badly needed, so, too, are willingness and ability to see concomitant effects. For example, experimentation which frees pupils to write creatively may weaken the technical quality of their writing, or may at least cause technical quality to be neglected. Evaluators should not laud one effect without being aware of the other and thereby being in a position to correct it.

4. *Observation should be conducted by more than one person or group.* Different individual observers and groups of observers tend to see things differently. Confidence in an observation is usually increased when the different persons and groups see the same things.

5. *Observation should be recorded with care.* The results of observation may be recorded in their raw, original state or in an interpreted form. Records of the first sort include pictures, sound recordings, stenographic transcriptions, and anecdotal data. Records in interpreted form appear as test and inventory data, interview reports, and responses to scales and checklists. The first, original sort of record needs analysis and interpretation so that the changes it suggests can be properly understood.[23]

The importance of methodological care in evaluating improvement programs is emphasized by a relook at the key questions posed on page 305: Are we really moving toward our goals? How much movement is present? How fast is movement occurring? What precisely can be said about direction(s) of movement? How does the general movement we have discovered relate to other movements toward change or improvement? These questions should be answered with diligence and discrimination by those who wish to know whether their programs and practices make a difference in improving

[23] *Ibid.*, pp. 321–324.

the schools. Furthermore, the instruments of evaluation which are used in answering the questions must be the best that can be adopted, adapted, or devised.

A MODEL FOR EVALUATION OF PROGRAMS

Recapitulation of the content of this chapter leads to the positing of a model for the evaluation of improvement programs. The following model is presented in the form of actions which should be taken as nearly in sequence as possible:

1. Decide how much of the total program is to be evaluated.

2. Depending upon whether the whole program or a part of the program is to be evaluated, state clearly the goals of the whole program or the part. An example of a goal is as follows: "The curriculum improvement program is to be well administered."

3. Clarify the goals by stating criteria which you are willing to accept in determining when the goals have been attained. You should state several criteria for each goal. By stating criteria, you consider what you will accept as evidence of goal attainment, and you begin to think about ways of gathering the evidence. One criterion which relates to the goal above is: "Trained leadership is provided for curriculum work."

4. List also the criteria of progress as an important step in thinking of ways in which progress may be evaluated: "Are we really moving toward our goals?" "How much movement is present?" and so on, as noted previously in this chapter.

5. Think of processes and instruments which you might use in satisfying the criteria in items 3 and 4. Given the goal, "The curriculum improvement program is to be well administered," and one of the criteria relative to it, "Trained leadership is provided for curriculum work," how are quantity and quality of trained leadership to be gauged? By examining the qualifications of our leaders with reference to the qualifications of leaders in corresponding job categories elsewhere, and also with reference to our own expectations? By observing the performance of our leaders in terms of accepted norms of leadership behavior and in terms of our own special expectations? Now what about progress? Are our leaders proving to be better trained? How much improvement in training is evident during what period of time, and at what rate has the improvement occurred? What is the nature of our leaders' move-

ment toward further training? Is it in a "straight vocational line," or is it varied, dealing with subject-matter and interests other than those in professional education? How does the further training of our leaders seem to relate to the whole pattern of improvement that is being sought in our schools?

6. Select and apply processes and instruments which will give you the breadth and depth of evidence you need. Expect that, in general, the processes and instruments will capitalize upon *observation*, which should be sharply focused, repeated, broadened in range, cooperatively conducted, and carefully recorded. In the instance being described, cumulative records of individual local leaders will need to be examined with care; these leaders will need to be observed in action; the qualifications of leaders elsewhere will need to be learned by questionnaire or other means; discussions will need to be held by local personnel to consider their own expectations of leaders and the training of leaders; and the findings will have to be recorded for subsequent analysis and interpretation.

7. Generalize concerning the whole complex of findings to draw conclusions which are necessarily tentative. To do this, you must compile the findings in conscious relationship to the several goals to which you have subscribed, and then interrelate the findings.

The complexity of evaluation like this must be immediately apparent, but so must its worth in knowing what a program or part of a program has accomplished, in supplying cues to future action, and in justifying expenditures of time, talent, and money. Evaluation of the many different effects of a program require development of many different evaluation designs. The number and ingenuity of these designs must increase during coming years so that evaluation may proceed more effectively.

A PLEA FOR CAREFUL EVALUATION OF OLD AND NEW IDEAS AND MOVEMENTS

Like nearly everything else in this fast-moving age, programs and practices in elementary and secondary education are changing rapidly. Team teaching, the nongraded elementary school, the Trump Plan, educational television, teacher aides and paraprofessionals, teaching machines and programmed learning—what will be next in the parade of innovations? The practices, devices, and arrangements which the innovations supplant and supplement have dominated the educational scene with little evaluation to gauge their worth. Now there is danger that the innovations themselves will go largely unevaluated, and this failure would be as tragic as the failures of the past.

Consider programmed learning. Here is an innovation which, five or ten years hence, may occupy the time and energy of curriculum leaders to a considerable extent, for programmed learning appears to hold great promise in achieving individualization. To have some notion of what programmed learning is accomplishing, curriculum leaders need to help assess the effects on pupil achievement of using programmed materials in discharging certain functions in teaching and learning. They need also to learn what happens to both pupils and teachers when a teaching staff relinquishes some of its responsibilities to a teaching device, and when the time of teachers must be utilized in other ways. Curriculum leaders cannot afford to be satisfied with demonstrations; they must secure the best evidence they can.

A curriculum leader reports that the thinking of a committee considering introduction of teaching machines into his school district has proceeded as follows:

> Many of the investigations of contributions by teaching machines to learning indicate that machines speed instruction in several school subjects. We realize, of course, that the machine is generally less important than the programming. One site in which machines with adequate programs are especially useful is the language laboratory. Here, machines can be adapted to a variety of purposes in aiding learning. Perhaps flexibility of use is proving to be a major factor in the success of language laboratories. Certainly evidence is accumulating in New York City and elsewhere that language laboratories facilitate the learning of languages. Assuming that reports about these laboratories will continue to be favorable, what can our school district do to establish an economical and efficient language laboratory? To know how efficient our own language laboratory is, and to prepare the way for possible expansion of machine teaching and programmed learning in our district, we shall want to devise a system of evaluation to fit our own purposes and activities in using our language laboratory. Expenditures of pupils' and teachers' time and of taxpayers' money should be based, whenever possible, on valid evidence. Having spoken in so facile a way about what we should do in the future, let us resolve now to answer two questions as concretely as possible: Who, exactly, has evaluated the effectiveness of language laboratories, and with what results? How can we learn our language teachers' views of the uses and possible usefulness of one or more language laboratories in our district? We want to know that what we buy is valuable, and we want to be reasonably sure that it will be put to good use. We are not seeking merely to be fashionable when we find that neighboring school districts have installed laboratories.

The sequel to this discussion, reports the curriculum leader, has been installation of two language laboratories, the worth of which are now being evaluated before additional laboratories are installed.

The object is not to resist innovation or to uphold tradition merely for the joy of doing so. The object is to validate programs and practices, old or new. While this action cannot be taken on nearly enough occasions, funds *should* be set aside and personnel *should* be made available for the purpose. Otherwise, curriculum improvement programs must proceed largely by caprice. From evaluation data, curriculum workers derive not only assurance concerning what they have done and are doing but also goals which guide their future action.

SUMMARY

This chapter forms a fitting capstone to the book by emphasizing the importance of evaluating both the content and the process of curriculum change. The chapter has reviewed some basic principles of evaluation, has suggested the desirability of deciding how much of a curriculum improvement program is to be evaluated, and has noted some dimensions of quality in programs. Following a few general comments on the methodology of evaluation, the reader has been presented a model for the evaluation of programs and then has been warned that both old and new practices and projects are in need of evaluation. The significance of much that has been said in previous parts of the book depends upon the actual improvements in content and process which evaluation of programs and their effects reveals.

SELECTED BIBLIOGRAPHY

Ahmann, J. Stanley, and Marvin D. Glock, *Evaluating Pupil Growth* (Boston: Allyn and Bacon, Inc., 1958).

Brandt, Richard M., and Hugh V. Perkins, *Research Evaluating a Child Study Program*, Vol. 21, Serial No. 62, No. 1 (Lafayette, Ind.: Society for Research in Child Development, 1956).

Festinger, Leon, and Daniel Katz, eds., *Research Methods in the Behavioral Sciences* (New York: Dryden Press, 1953).

Furst, Edward J., *Constructing Evaluation Instruments* (New York: Longmans, Green & Co., Inc., 1958).

Heyns, Roger W., and Ronald Lippitt, "Systematic Observational Techniques," in Gardner Lindzey, ed., *Handbook of Social Psychology* (Reading, Mass.: Addison-Wesley Publishing Company, Inc., 1954).

McNally, Harold J., and A. Harry Passow, *Improving the Quality of Public School Programs* (New York: Bureau of Publications, Teachers College, Columbia University, 1960).

National Society for the Study of Education, *In-service Education,* 56th Yearbook, Part I (Chicago: University of Chicago Press, 1957).

Payne, Stanley L., *The Art of Asking Questions* (Princeton, N.J.: Princeton University Press, 1951).

Thorndike, Robert L., and Elizabeth Hagen, *Measurement and Evaluation in Psychology and Education* (New York: John Wiley & Sons, Inc., 1955).

Wrightstone, J. Wayne, Joseph Justman, and Irving Robbins, *Evaluation in Modern Education* (New York: American Book Company, 1956).

Appendix

Conversations with selected practitioners of curriculum improvement led to the compilation of 26 specific concerns about progress in improvement. These concerns, substantially in the form in which they were originally stated, were then submitted to a jury of 160 other practitioners (curriculum coordinators, principals, and supervisors), each of whom was asked to select the three or four concerns of greatest import to him. The concerns are listed below, from the greatest frequency to the least frequency of selection.

Though members of the jury reside in all sections of the United States, the number of jurors is small, their selection did not proceed according to any particular rationale, and their judgments should be checked by using the same list of concerns with other populations. The list might prove worth administering to curriculum leaders in one's own school district, region, or county. Additional concerns might, of course, be added to the list.

FREQUENCIES WITH WHICH SPECIFIC CONCERNS WERE SELECTED BY 160 PRACTITIONERS

Rank	Statement of Concern	Number of Perso Selecting This Concern	Percentage of Total Selectors Which the Number Represents
1.	Providing better continuity or articulation between elementary schools and high schools, or between grade levels in a school	68	43.5
2.	Finding time for curriculum work	50	31.3
3.	Preparing curriculum materials that are really used	41	25.6
4.	Knowing just what to do to organize for curriculum improvement	38	23.9
5.	Working with people in groups in such a way that they are both productive and happy	36	22.5
6.	Providing enough leadership, with both time and ability to lead	34	21.3
7.	Finding ways of evaluating progress in curriculum improvement	31	19.4
7.	Having enough of the right kinds of materials and clerical assistance	31	19.4
8.	Causing personnel to work on problems of real concern to them, rather than on someone else's problems	28	17.5
8.	Determining how broad a range of subject-matter the schools should try to teach	28	17.5

FREQUENCIES WITH WHICH SPECIFIC CONCERNS WERE SELECTED
BY 160 PRACTITIONERS (*continued*)

Rank	Statement of Concern	Number of Persons Selecting This Concern	Percentage of Total Selectors Which the Number Represents
9.	Knowing enough about human development and learning to assure reasonably appropriate experiences for children	23	14.4
10.	Encouraging openmindedness and an experimental outlook	21	13.1
11.	Knowing learners' environments well enough to make realistic statements about the effect of the environments on the learners	18	11.3
11.	Finding ways of making curriculum decisions that involve more than exchanging opinions	18	11.3
12.	Concentrating on an appropriate number of projects a year, as opposed to spreading effort among too many projects	17	10.6
13.	Knowing how to select and balance activities in curriculum improvement	15	9.4
13.	Deciding when "curriculum revision" does not violate the best we know about children, learning, and the social order	15	9.4
14.	Finding out whether a given sequence of teaching and learning is desirable	12	7.5
15.	Involving pupils properly in curriculum improvement	11	6.9
15.	Keeping the program under way at a satisfying speed	11	6.9
16.	Selecting curriculum workers by letting them volunteer, by appointing them, or by some other means	10	6.3
17.	Changing educational philosophies and goals without using undue time in the process	9	5.6
18.	Taking into account what the community thinks, without misinterpreting or overestimating the importance of community thinking	8	5.0
19.	Finding improved ways of working with laymen in curriculum planning	6	3.8
20.	Knowing when we have dealt with a problem adequately, so that we need not return to it in the immediate future	4	2.5
21.	Finding curriculum materials which have been prepared by others, and which we can use in our own situation	3	1.9

Index